A NEW UPDATE OF SWINDON STEAM

by

L.A.SUMMERS

Great Western Society
2007

Published by the Great Western Society
Didcot Railway Centre, Didcot, Oxon, OX11 7NJ, England

www.didcotrailwaycentre.org.uk

ISBN 978-0-902956-13-1

L.A.Summers has asserted the right under the Designs and Patents Act 1988 to be regarded as the author of this book.

Copyright: L.A.Summers 2007

All Rights reserved. No part of this book may be reproduced, stored in a retrieval system or transmitted in any form or by any means, electronic, mechanical, photocopying, recording or otherwise without the prior written authority of the author and publisher being first obtained. Reproduction on websites of extracts, however small or paraphrased without written permission is breach of copyright.

Printed for the publisher by
AMPM Technical Services, Tackley, Kidlington, Oxon

Introduction

According to the RCTS *Railway Observer* it was sometime during August 1949 and according to family recollection, around August 30. My father having a rostered rest day from his occupation as a WR engine driver at Didcot decided that we would have a family day at Western Super Mare. We caught the 0530 Paddington at 0649 from Didcot to Bistol and changed there into a Trowbridge-Taunton local train to continue to our destination. However, it was somewhere west of Didcot possibly at Wantage Road or Challow where the platforms were served by loops off the main line that we passed a light engine going west. Being not quite six years old I was confused about the interest that my father and elder brother took in the engine and recalled that it was Swiss. Nonsense of course but easy to understand the error because this was the time when the Brown Boveri gas turbine was first at work. In any case I remember that it was a steam locomotive and in my mind's eye I can still see its smoke rising above the boiler. So what engine aroused this interest? It can only have been *Duke* class 4-4-0 9083, *Comet*, the first engine that my father drove when he became a driver in 1941 and which around that date was sent from Didcot to the stock shed at Swindon from which it sallied forth, only once for a few days in November 1950 before returning in January 1951 from Machynlleth and being withdrawn.

We all have memories like this. O.S.Nock recalled in vivid detail seeing a Dean 4-2-2 flash over the level crossing between Theale and Southcote Junction and Hamilton Ellis had a similar experience in 1920 only to discover that the last 4-2-2 had been withdrawn five years earlier! He was convinced that what he had seen was not a *Barnum class* 2-4-0 as was gently suggested to him and claimed some authority for his belief when he discovered that the last example was still to be seen in Swindon dump even then. These sightings were recalled in the first railway books that in later years I took out of the library. Both gentlemen were very readable, especially CHE who could craft a description of a locomotive or a railway scene as no one else before or since. Even then I demanded technical detail which probably I did not really understand though I could see that a 4-6-0 with 6'6" driving wheels and 250lbs boiler pressure was always superor to a 4-4-0 with 6'9" driving wheels and 200lbs pressure. If only!

Over 40 years of subsequent reading of engineering papers, original railway records, books and magazines have evoked reactions which would themselves fill a book but two at least have been the impetus behind my writing this volume. Already by the late 1950s the histories of our railways had become like clichés, set in the mind, accepted and unchallenged, repeated time and time again, often by the same writers, sometimes by new entrants to the *genre* who were just saying the same thing in a different way. Biographies of locomotive engineers tended to be an account of their design work with a bare minimum of personal data grafted on. An understanding of the importance of background and personality as contributing to actual design work seems not to have been very widely recognised. The reader has only to think of the LMS locomotive department under Hughes and particularly Fowler to see what happens when dominant external personalities are able to exert pressure against quieter but better - qualified officers. Different but no less cogent evidence is available in the personality of Edward Thompson, frustrated in his ambition and doomed to spend many years dealing with the achilles heel of his revered superior's engines; his response when eventually succeeding was to mix good sense with petty mean-mindedness. The GWR is a very

Duke class 4-4-0, 9083, *Comet* at Reading West in September 1943 and, top: the author at the time of the incident related here. My father's reaction to the more recent picture, left, was, 'You look like the guv'nor sat up there!"
Comet photo: M.W.Earley

popular railway among enthusiasts but unfortunately too many of them are following legend rather than reality, worshipping a kind of Camelot built around well-designed and usually high performance locomotives that, in their minds' eye, they see gleaming in the sun as popular fiction sees the Knights of the Round Table and providing a public service of fast and always punctual trains from architecturally stimulating and convenient stations.

In the 1970s I became a teacher trained to examine evidence for the reality of historical fact. Children at school now learn about source based evidence and about bias. And rightly so for researchers increasingly show that the long accepted 'facts' of history, our national history no less than that of our railways are sometimes almost pure fiction in their representation of what happpened. The process was actually begun by some of our oldest and most respected railway writers, Cecil J Allen for example, examining old performance logs and realising that what was recorded almost certainly did not happen. Over the last 15 years it has become accepted that there is still a great deal to discover and that the histories of some railway companies will come out of this process much altered. Unfortunately some people refuse to accept the evidence as with the correspondent who wrote to me three pages of close long hand to explain why my years of research among the primary sources was actually wrong and the old myths had been true all along!

The GWR was once described as being 'neither great, nor western or even a railway,' an unfair comment even when it was made. Sometimes but not always it had the best locomotives in Britain, occasionally in the world. But as H.A.L.Fisher said many years ago the advances of one generation can be lost by those succeeding it. The supremacy of Gooch's broad gauge locomotives was soon lost to the advanced technical innovations of the narrow gauge and not until the 1890s did the GWR once again reassert its strength, beginning that remarkable 30 year period in which the GWR was so improved as to be at least 15 years ahead of anything being done elsewhere in Britain and, arguably, in the world. There followed another awful period of decline which despite talented design engineers went on almost unchecked until nationalization. And behind that story are the personalities that bequeathed this situation to history. Not just the chief engineers, not just the shop fitters, the engine drivers or shed cleaners but the company's departmental heads and directors, for such a large organisation did not run on the reputation of one man or even of one department. If the Churchward locomotive was a world beater - and it was - it was the intricate network of the other departments that created the opportunity for that superiority to be displayed, or not, as the case was in some respects.

I should stress that this is not a history of the Great Western's locomotives or of its train operation. If it were an academic study it would have a title such as *Aspects of the development of the locomotives of the Great Western Railway, their designers and operatives and its influence on the history of locomotive engineering in Britain and the world*. Off-putting though that title may be, it does actually explain what I have set out to do, taken several aspects of the GWR's history and devoted myself from the viewpoint of the professional historian to investigating them as deeply and widely as possible. What was life like for footplatemen and workshop employees? The facts are sometimes inescapably unpalatable. What is the truth about Dean's fabulous 4-2-4T? The origins of Churchward's design innovations have long been known but beyond the immediate derivation little has been written about how and why, over many years these features came to be developed. Did the locomotive superintendents of some companies network their ideas and further, was GWR influence to be seen far away in such remote parts of the world as Egypt and Australia? What alternatives were there to the disastrous dieselization policies of the 1950s? I have painted a broad canvas and though, inevitably many of the known facts are covered again, I have tried to deploy this information with new research which aims at revealing the facts behind these specific issues.

Many of the sources for the GWR's history are well known and I refer readers to the Bibliography which follows this introduction. In addition to acknowledging my use of those works I must also express my thanks to the many people who have given me assistance of various kinds. Some are mentioned in the references which follow each chapter but here I want to record the names of the late David Jenkinson and Michael Blakemore, successive editor and publisher of *Backtrack* magazine where some of this work has earlier appeared. Richard Croucher and Roy Stannett of the Great Western Society have given enormous support and assistance and I am indebted to Dennis Howells, Project Manager for the restoration of 6023 for valuable technical advice; also C.P. Atkins formerly Librarian of the National Rail Museum, Ed Bartholomew (NRM), Dr C.L.Seymour, R.H.N.Hardy, Alan Jarvis, Mike Barnsley, Alan Wild, Bud Laws, Neil Burnell, Stuart Mackay, Graham Watkins (ARHS), Lawrence Waters (Photographic Archive Officer of the Great Western Trust), Dr G.M.D.Howat, Audie Baker (Kidderminster Railway Museum), William Morgan, Marion Beaton (Mitchell Library), Elaine Arthurs (Swindon Steam Museum) Tom Illingworth, (GERS), and Paul Goldsmith, (Editor GERS *Journal*), also Richard Marsden and the staff of the Science Museum Library at Imperial College. Not to forget either, those entlemen no longer with us, K.J.Cook, O.S.Nock, Anthony Sterndale, L.E.Trollope and my father the late Driver Alf Summers of Didcot. I want also to add the name of my wife, Barbara whose support and encouragement never fails despite serious illness and considerable stress.

Picture the scene. A secondary school in Didcot in September 1956. The formidable W.H.D.Robinson is starting a new term's geography with Second Year (Year 8) pupils. As all geography should, it begins with a local map, learning how it fits into Britain and the world. Why was Didcot significant? In those days only for the fact that it was a important railway junction and even that was often not good enough for it to feature in atlases which showed the arguably less important Wallingford and Abingdon. But what a junction, part of Brunel's unique broad gauge railway. Devised with scientific precision for which Brunel will always be famous and for which, paradoxically he ordered locomotives that were almost total failures from the start. And this I remember particularly, as Mr Robinson went through the words and actions, Brunel having to go to Stephenson with the request that he should build some engines for him.

"Like those over there," and only when he was leaving did he add, "Oh, and the gauge has to be seven foot!"

Not strictly accurate but WHDR had achieved the teacher's basic remit, he had fired the interest of his pupils. At least one of them anyway, the present writer, because though as a family we had always been interested in trains, it was only this lesson and this man whose inspirational teaching ignited in me a serious interest in railways. Over the succeeding 50 years I have developed that interest into a professional occupation. So if this book should be dedicated to anyone it is to W.Henry Dent Robinson, teacher and railway enthusiast. Thank you, sir!

L.A.Summers
January 2007

Contents

Chapters	Page
1 Footplate, Running Shed and Workshops the men who made the GWR	10
2 Weird & wonderful creatures and their fabulous offspring	26
3 Networking engineers and Swindon's world-wide web.	40
4 The origins of the Churchward Locomotive	55
5 The Great Western's Bonniest Engines - on the vexed subject of appearance	73
6 Churchward aftermath	85
7 The Myth of a Hawksworth Pacific	98
8 Swindon and the BR Standards	112
9 Railcars, Gas Turbines and Diesel Hydraulics	124

Bibliography

The standard works on the history of the GWR, its locomotives and operations are fairly well known and are referred to throughout this book with the reference number by which they are listed here. Sources referred to in individual chapters are given a chapter-speicifc number which is referenced at the end of that chapter. For ease of general reference those books have also been noted here. Other sources are referenced where referred to.

1) *History of the Great Western Railway* Volume 1
    E.T.MacDermot & C.R.Clinker
2) *History of the Great Western Railway* Volume 2
    E.T.MacDermot & C.R.Clinker
3) *History of the Great Western Railway* 3 volumes
    Peter Semmens
4) *An Outline of Great Western Locomotive Practice* - H. Holcroft
5) *The Locomotives of the Great Western Railway* - RCTS
    (Individual parts are indicated eg: 5/10 for the section on
        Absorbed Engines 1922 -1947)
6) *The Armstrongs of the Great Western* - H. Holcroft
7) *Great Western Locomotive Design: A critical appreciation* - J.C.Gibson
8) *Locomotive & Train Working in the Latter Part of the 19th century*
    Volume 4 - E.L.Ahrons

Other Works (arranged GWR-specific to general)
Locomotive Adventure - H. Holcroft
The GWR in the 19th Century - O.S.Nock
The Great Western at Swindon Works - A.S.Peck
Swindon Steam - K.J.Cook
Grub, Water & Relief: being tales of the Great Western - A.Vaughn
Life in a Railway Workshop - Alfred Williams
Great Western Apprentice - Swindon in the 1930s - Hugh Freebury
Memoirs of a Station Master - Ernest Simmons
The GWR Stars, Castles and Kings - O.S.Nock
Castles & Kings at Work - Michael Rutherford
Halls, Granges & Manors at Work - Michael Rutherford
A Pictorial Record of GWR Engines 3 Volumes - J.H.Russell
The Western Since 1948 - G.Freeman Allen
Pole's Book - Sir Felix J.C.Pole
Exeter-Newton Abbott: A Railway History - Peter Kay
The MSWJ Railway - T.B.Sands (Revised by S.C.Jenkins)
The MSWJ Railway - Mike Barnsley
Engines Good & Bad - A.W.Summers
The Four Great Railways - M. Bonavia
The Western Since 1948 - G.Freeman Allen
The British Steam Railway Locomotive 1825 - 1925 - E.L.Ahrons
British Locomotives of the 20th Century 3 Volumes - O.S.Nock
British Steam Since 1900 - W.A.Tuplin
Streamline Steam - A.J.Mullay
Master Builders of Steam - H.A.V.Bulleid

The Trains We Loved - C. Hamilton Ellis
The Beauty of Old Trains - C.Hamilton Ellis
Four Main Lines - C.Hamilton Ellis
Some Classic Locomotives - C.Hamilton Ellis
British Pacific Locomotives - Cecil J Allen
Essays in Steam - J F Clay (editor)
La Locomotive au Vapeur - English Language Edition
        Andre Chapelon/ George W.Carpenter
Chronicles of Steam - E.S.Cox
Speaking of Steam - E.S.Cox
Locomotive Panorama Vol 2 - E.S.Cox
The British Railways Standard Steam Locomotives - E.S.Cox
A Lifetime with Locomotives - R.C.Bond
The World's Locomotives - C.S.Lake
World Steam in the 20th Century - E.S.Cox
100 Years of Steam Locomotives - Walter A.Lucas
Express Trains English and Foreign - Foxwell & Farrer
The Concise Encyclopedia of World Railway Locomotives
        P Ransome-Wallis (editor)
Biographical Dictionary of Railway Engineers - John Marshall
The Worsdells: A Quaker English dynasty - G.Hill
J.G.Robinson: A Lifetime's Work - D.Jackson
Steam Locomotive Design, Data and Formulae - E.A.Philipson

Picture Credits

Where no credit appears the image is part of the author's own collection. Pressure on space has meant that some other credits have had to be abbreviated-
KRM - Kidderminster Railway Museum Collection
NRM - National Rail Museum
LCGB - Locomotive Club of Great Britain Ken Nunn Collection

Chapter One
Footplate, Running Shed and Workshops the men who made the GWR

An engine driver involved in the change over from steam to diesel has written: *Looking back from even a few years later, from the comfort of a diesel driver in his heated cab who could, with the merest action of the flicking of a switch, clear the observation windows of snow, ice and rain and remembering how, in the winter, my fireman and I would try to clear the spectacle windows of snow and ice and peer through them to locate signals, whilst all around was a white blanket shrouded perhaps by darkness, certainly by smoke from our engine, I knew that I never wanted to go back to those steam days.*[9] Its not hard to sympathise with this view, yet the poor arrangements for engine crews on steam locomotives was, certainly in the 1950s completely unnecessary. A rain and wind proof cab, heated if necessary, with a user-friendly layout of the controls and on the bigger engines, mechanical stokers would have made the supposed advantages of the working conditions on diesels much less attractive. Creature comforts for railway operatives have often lagged behind the times and it should not surprise us that it was so, but at the same time there are cases where, paradoxically, the men themselves objected to innovations designed to aid their comfort. As a matter of history, working conditions on the railways is a complex issue and a simplistic reaction citing a universal good or bad is just not possible.

The first steam locomotives were purely functional, they were built, designed is too grand a word, in accordance with necessity. On the very earliest engines the driver walked beside the engine rather as he would have walked beside a horse drawn wagon. When these engines were put onto longer runs with heavier loads and the driver was provided with a platform at the back of the boiler, the fireman's position was located at the front underneath the chimney. The horse shoe shaped flues of the early engines made this necessary, the firehole door had to be in that position. Many early locomotives therefore ran with the tender attached to what we would now regard as the front of the machine and thus the fireman would spend his working life being showered by smoke, soot, hot cinders and possibly nuggets of unburnt but hot coal or coke. Modern science tells us that such men would almost certainly be liable to serious carcinogenic illnesses. The invention of the straight through multiple tube boiler was therefore a godsend for more than the usually recounted reasons. Even that did not make it entirely safe to be a footplate man.

Boiler explosions were almost common. In the days before the invention of the injector, filling the boiler with water could only be done from axle or cross head driven pumps while the engine was in motion. Left to simmer for any great length of time the boiler water would be boiled away and eventually the pressure would rise to a point where the boiler plates could no longer hold it, a catastrophic explosion would then occur. Running light engine out on the line to fill the boiler was inconvenient and caused accidents. The usual practice therefore was for the driver, on shed, to stand his engine against some unmoving object, oil the rails and leave it to run slowly on the spot! Conversely, the small diameter boilers of early engines were also a problem in that the steam collector pipe was not positioned very high above the water level. If the boiler was over-filled then water would get down into the steam pipes and prime through the chimney. In worse-case situations the water would pass into the cylinders and cause the pistons to punch out the cylinder heads. While boilers remained small of girth the answer to the problem was a dome with the steam collector pipe inside and raised well above the water level.

Working conditions for the labouring classes had always been bad, whether employed in agriculture or domestic industry. They became a concern only with the development of large scale commercial industrialisation and only then when the kinship system in the cotton industry was replaced by direct labour employment. Under the kinship system the father contracted his family to the works manager and was responsible for their discipline and work. It was socially acceptable for him to secure their productivity by beating his children and possibly his wife too. When labour was contracted individually the overseer was responsible for productivity but his beating the wife and kids provoked outrage. Even then the reformers were not always welcomed because they were seen as reducing the short term wage earning potential of the family. [10] This paradox continues right through the history of the railways and is even found in the attitude of some employees at the beginning of the 21st century.

Considerations about the footplate conditions of engine crews were slow to surface partly for historical reasons. Before mass industrialisation commerce was generally small-scale, transport concerns no less than any other. Coach drivers sat at the front of their vehicles without shelter from the elements and with only a brief dashboard to protect them from the mud, stones and water thrown up by horses hooves. And travel by coach was hardly very pleasant for the passenger, let alone the driver. Passengers travelling on top had a most unpleasant time of it, as contemporary accounts confirm.[11] To sit outside on top was akin to being a rag doll shaken unendingly by a wicked child with the added possibility of being thrown clear and suffering a nasty injury. Travelling inside was only better in that one was protected from the elements. Even the most comfortable seat becomes unbearable after many hours of immobility, to spend several days on a coach as was necessary journeying from London to anywhere of note was almost to progress through a form of profound purgatory.

Another constraint on the development of better footplate conditions was the men themselves, the early footplate crews. Engine drivers in the 1830s and 40s were usually hardened men from 'the school of rough knocks', barely educated and often very conservative in outlook. The idea that such men would want to be sheltered from the elements and the exhaust of their mighty engines would have been an anathema. They were very special men indeed, and they knew it. Driving a steam locomotive was a craft skill out of all proportion to anything else that was the preserve of the working classes or, indeed, of most occupations generally. It was not like opening the throttle of diesel and letting the machine do the rest, the careful co-ordination between valve gear and regulator positions was not learned in a classroom but on the job, from hands on experience. Thus engine drivers acquired a reputation far in excess of any other vocation and until the advent of diesalization theirs was the one working class occupation which enjoyed a place in the romance of all classes of society. The men so employed could earn wages that were as much as four times that of agricultural labourers. It is said that the first driver of the German *Adler* - an Englishman - was actually paid more than the senior officers of the railway and it would be no surprise to me if that were true.[12] And of course, there are several well known examples of engine drivers who later became locomotive superintendents responsible for engine design, the Armstrong brothers no less, Edward Fletcher, and in later years the one armed J.F.McIntosh on the Caledonian. And perhaps we should also recall that Sir Roy Welensky, last prime minister of the Federation of Rhodesia and Nyasaland worked for a time as an engine driver.

The early railways were labour intensive and it would be no exaggeration to suggest that the railway revolution came along at precisely the right moment to provide employment for an expanding population, what was all too readily described in the 1820s and 30s as the 'surplus population'. Lack of education was no bar to employment on the railway for Brunel knew what kind of man he wanted; he believed that illiterate men were the best engine drivers as their minds were not liable to wander from their jobs.[1] Such thinking sounds almost culpable today but it should be remembered that there was actually little awareness of the dangerous nature of railway operation. It was only in 1830 that poor old Huskisson had been knocked down by Stephenson's *Rocket;* ignorance, not deliberate but arising out of unfamiliarity, was common at all levels. Several cases, some well-known, bear repeating. The Great Western Railway was opened throughout on the 30th June 1841. Though no particularly special celebrations seem to have marked this event, the Directors ran their own special train. Since the Bristol and Exeter which joined the GWR at Bristol was also nearing completion this special continued to Bridgwater before returning. Gooch, piloting the engines through the Box Tunnel, was nearly involved in an accident when a signal policeman allowed him to enter the tunnel without first receiving another train out of it.[1] There is a newspaper account of an accident in 1868 when a train drawn by *Iron Duke* 4-2-2, *Crimea* arrived at Didcot from Oxford on the running board handrail of which was found the remains of a waistcoat with half an arm still in it. In the waistcoat was found a pocket book with the name of a railwayman who had set out, not long before, to *walk along the line* to his home at Appleford. The story may have been sensationalised but it is certainly based in truth.[13] This type of accident was common; on another occasion Edward Gore, a signalman at Millstream Junction left his box to signal a train at a time when both up and down trains were due. Despite the red light that he carried he was knocked down and killed and no one knew anything about it for at least 15 minutes after the accident had occurred.[14]

We have already mentioned the fireman on the very early engines, standing underneath the smokestack. Unsheltered footplates were better only by degrees. On Reading station once, many years ago I was hurt by a minute cinder which escaped from the chimney of a *Hall* and lodged itself in my eye. It was quite painful for several days afterwards. So clearly, unprotected footplates were just as dangerous places on which to have to work. Yet being showered with hot cinders and wet soot smuts was not the only danger with which early footplatemen had to contend. Primitive brakes were another thing. In 1848

Michael Almond drove the Gooch 8 footer, Great Britain from Paddington to Didcot in 47.5 minutes for the 53 miles, an average speed of 67 mph and this was only the best of many such runs made in 48 to 50 minutes. It staggers the imagination to learn that the brakes on these trains were extremely primitive and airily dismissed by Brunel as being, 'tolerably useless'![1] The locomotive itself had no brakes at all, the tender wheels were braked by a handbrake, while first class carriages were also without brakes. Because of this, the fast running inherent in Gooch's reports of what was regularly being done meant that the stopping distance of a train was quite long and early brake applications would have to be made. Thus the point to point speeds required to maintain 63-67 mph averages would have been very high and suggests how reports of 70 mph plus speeds came to be made. It was not until the 1870s that safe and reliable vacuum brakes were introduced on Great Western engines.

Probably all early locomotives were rough riders, the chances are that the drivers and

The footplate of the original *North Star*, sketched by the author and based on a birthday card.

firemen, knowing no different, accepted it as very much part of the job; reports about the broad gauge engines tend to be contradictory, some sources tell us that they were 'very steady', others that they were very rough to ride on. In fact the short rigid wheelbase could not but have made the riding on curved sections of track very rough, more so as they became due for the Works. Brunel's baulk road is known to have been very solid and this too would make the riding rough; Holcroft tells us in his classic book on GWR locomotives that for precisely this reason sandwich framing was restored in new construction by William Dean, because it had a degree of 'give'.[4] If, as this suggests, the early GW engines were indeed rough riders, then the footplate crews, in addition to all the other risks that accompanied their daily work, were in a similarly unenviable situation from the fact that the only thing preventing them being thrown over the side was a single handrail. In order to see the reality of this, one has only to go to Didcot and watch the replica *Firefly* at work. The engine moves very slowly and Sam Bee sits nonchalantly on the footplate guard rail but I do not suppose he would be doing that at 45 mph! Some companies put rectangular side sheets on the footplate which certainly helped and weather boards against the elements also became a feature.

We know a good deal about the working of the first Great Western engines because the company's first traffic superintendent, Seymour Clarke reported daily to the Board.[15] His reports have survived and bear ample witness to the fact that railway service in those years was hard, risky and dangerous. We can commiserate with the unfortunate Isaac Robson whose usual engine was *Planet* but who, on the 15th September 1839, was on *Vulcan* when it burst one of its tubes: *...he fainted off the engine at the Thames Junction while she was running. He struck against the bridge and injured his skull: this threw him back and he has a compound fracture of the leg.* Clarke reports another incident on the 12th March: *. . .the 7 o'clock train down had gone as far as Ranelagh Bridge when the Hurricane and the carriages all got off in consequence of the switch from the Engine House being wrong. Goodlad, the man who was pardoned before is the person; I have of course finished his service here.* To be involved in a misdemeanour on the GWR was a serious matter indeed and accused employees were summoned to appear before the Board at Paddington. In employee parlance, this became known as being 'up before the picture' because the Directors hearing the case sat with their backs to a portrait of the GWR's most famous early Chairman, Charles Russell. Thus employees on disciplinaries found themselves eyeball to eyeball with the unsmiling features of Russell looking down from on high. The picture, not the Directors, became 'judge, jury and executioner' as far as employees were concerned; there will be more about this kind of thing later in the chapter.

When a train was late, the shed foreman would often take an engine down the line to see where it had got to. When they saw the train coming they put their own engine into reverse and ran ahead of the train back to their shed. Several accidents and near misses occurred because of this dangerous practice but fortunately the installation of the telegraph from about 1850 rendered it unnecessary. It is worth mentioning here that in the early days Brunel allowed his professional acquaintances from other railways almost free access to the company's lines and they were able to run around on engines with possibly greater impunity than the foreman did. Not surprisingly, these antics also caused accidents.

On the 4th February 1839 Seymour Clarke reported a more disastrous incident to a passenger train, apparently the result of negligence: *The Eagle engine and 9 o'clock train have all been off the line at Maidenhead, just beyond the Engine House, owing to the points being wrong. The Engine is now in the ditch, the carriages are all on the line again, not much damaged; the engine is, as far as they can tell, not much injured ... The Engineman, Almond, saw the points were wrong but could not stop in time.* More of these incidents are recorded by Ahrons[8] and also by Adrian Vaughn whose books are as equally full of interest as those from older writers.[16]

Michael Almond, who had the accident with *Eagle*, was probably the most famous of the GWR's early engine drivers for he made the record run with *Great Britain* in 1848. Born in 1807 he was reported to be a calm, practical and alert man which accounts for his involvement in the 1848 trials. What was being attempted was a degree of consistently fast running greater than had ever been previously achieved. No place for a hot tempered bone head. Almond retired in 1873 at which time he was foreman of Westbourne Park shed. *Iron Duke* was driven by John Simpson, while his brother William drove *Castor*. Jack Brown is associated with *Priam*. William Thompson, it was said, could push his engine, minus tender, unaided, which is an interesting story. Thompson was associated with *Orion*, a 24 ton *Firefly* class engine. It says something both about Thompson's strength but also about the freedom of movement of the gear on these engines that he could do this. *Lord of the Isles* was driven by Robert Patterson for many years; this was the locomotive which boys in Swindon in the 1850s and 60s considered *de rigeur* to have seen before being regarded as serious 'railwayacs'. (To later generations it was *The Great Bear* which denoted that you had 'arrived' as a railway enthusiast). Another driver, John Thompson, did not get as far as the Boardroom. Gooch himself rebuked him for driving too fast a train which carried the Prince Consort as a passenger. Prince Albert had complained that he had been frightened by the speed. Thompson's comment is interesting: "He must be a pretty fellow to be a Field Marshall and I frightened him!" Other names that have come down to us are those of Bob Roscoe and Henry Appleby. Roscoe drove *Sultan* for 20 years before taking over the *Lord of the Isles*. Appleby the regular driver of the *North Star* was said to be surly, heartily disliked by and disliking the man regarded by the GWR as its first wage earning employee, Jim Hurst.

Engine drivers were special people in the 1830s and 40s and it shows in the photographs which have come down to us from this period. Look at the men and the way they hold themselves, even when dressed in grubby overalls; the effect they create is of pride and well-merited self-esteem. At first this was due to the fact that they were very much in demand as having a rare skill and because of this they could demand high wages. The average driver earned between 5s6d and 7s6d a day which was a significant advance on the average for agricultural labourers of about 11s6d a week.[17] However, the men had to provide their own uniform, until the 1870s *white fustian clothes which are to be clean every Monday morning...* [18] Anyone who has had to wear white overalls will know that after a few weeks, the requirement to be 'clean on Mondays' would have had less and less meaning.

Jim Hurst drawn by Chris Seymour and based on the photograph in the Centenary edition of the *GWR Magazine*

Cabs first appeared on foreign locomotives and in Britain it was the Great Eastern that first fitted them to their engines, in the 1850s as much as 30 years after the first commercially viable locomotives had been produced. [19] The reference continues: *Great opposition was offered by the drivers and firemen to this innovation. They objected so strongly that at one time a strike was threatened and it was not easy to get men to take the first engine so fitted...* This correspondent calling himself "Old Buffer' was however upstaged by another writer who suggested that: *If our locomotive engineers knew a little more about the hardships of engine driving life they would have probably been more willing to provide our enginemen with* (better conditions)... But of course they did, the Armstrong's had both been engine drivers and knew exactly what footplate conditions were like. Holcroft tells us that: *The Armstrong's provided only the minimum of protection from the weather for enginemen. For a long time it was nothing more than a weatherboard with a pair of spectacle windows in it, but later on, wings were added and then a short top covering. It was not until the early 1880s that cabs were adopted generally ... I made enquiries into the reason for this and it was explained to me that the Armstrong's had been drivers in their younger days and knew full well the rigours of footplate life. with little or nothing in the way of protection, and they were inured to it. In declining to provide some shelter, they were asking no more of enginemen than they themselves were accustomed to.*[4] Another consideration may have been that enclosed cabs caused drowsiness.[20]

This peculiar backwardness in GWR engines manifested itself throughout the company's existence and the last Swindon tender engine built as recently as 1950 had no more crew protection than the first *Castle* built in 1923 and only a little more than the first Churchward 4-6-0. Another, and serious drawback to Churchward's engines was the extension of the reversing wheel shaft into the cab which meant that the driver had to drape himself over the barrel all the time that he was driving. A feature of the *Saints* and early *Stars*, it cannot but have had serious physical effects on men forced to work in this position. I remember that my father always walked with a slight limp and I now wonder if this was its cause. I am still surprised when getting up onto the footplate of a *Castle* to find that the driver and fireman have been provided with only the most rudimentary of seats and that when the locomotive is running tender first the movement of the cab fall plate, even on such relatively modern engines is potentially very dangerous to the unwary. When asked about it, ex-GWR engine drivers said that they never noticed the deficiency until the arrival of the Standard types and diesels.

Many of the Great Western's first engine drivers came with locomotives being delivered from manufacturers and it was in this way that the man reputed to be the first wage-earning employee of the GWR arrived. We know rather more about Jim Hurst than the other early engine drivers because the GWR published details of his career and a picture of him in its special Centenary Edition of the *GWR Magazine*.[21] Hurst

Outline sketch showing the driving position on the early Churchward 4-6-0s.

was born at Astley in 1811, the son of a family of hand loom weavers. At the age of nine he had started in the business himself. We are told that he could not settle to this work but it is more likely that such was the domination of the weaving industry by machines that it provided no living for him. Hurst's birth coincides almost exactly with the incidence of machine smashing associated with the Luddites and by 1820 there was little work left for handloom weavers. However, according to Vaughn[16] when George Stephenson was surveying the Liverpool and Manchester he contracted Jim and his father as guides across Chat Moss. From this start he became a construction worker on the line and later a footplate man ending up as a driver in 1834. In 1836 he was dismissed for causing an accident and was taken on by the Vulcan Foundry. It must have been on one of Gooch's visits to see the engines ordered by Brunel from the Vulcan factory that the two met. At some point Gooch lodged with the now married Hurst and the two men, from very different backgrounds appear to have become friends, Hurst later applying to Gooch for a driving position. He was taken on from August 1837 delivering the newly completed *Vulcan* to Maidenhead and later driving it, actually the first steamed engine on the line. After the opening of the railway Jim lived at Taplow and at this time he had a regular turn on the 8.00am train from Paddington.

Disciplinary complaints seem to have been a regular feature of Jim's career. He was not the most equable of men, having a quick and violent temper which almost certainly resulted from his hubristic nature. He was often reported for the 'too lively' driving of his engine and in December 1841 he was reported for refusing to work with a guard whom he did not like; in September 1842 he was accused of taking passengers for a joyride and keeping their fares. The charge was not that he took the passengers for a ride, that seems to have been perfectly acceptable, but that he stole their fares! Anyway, Jim was put up 'before the picture'. Hurst admitted the joyride but said that he had not charged his passengers for it. Gooch (who in his dealings with Jim betrays a degree of favouritism) spoke up for Hurst and he was let off with a talking-to. He was later transferred all over the system; his arrival at a new depot would presage only a short respite before a new battery of complaints were made. There was almost an informal campaign to get him dismissed such was the anger that he engendered. However he kept himself out of trouble until June 1856 when he was again up before the picture. This time he was dismissed but Gooch got him reinstated and he stayed clean until retirement in May 1876, becoming one of the first wage-earners to be given a pension. Jim Hurst died in August 1892.

The partiality which Gooch showed towards Hurst was not constrained only to one man, he enjoyed a reputation that appears to be quite genuine for concerning himself with the footplatemen's welfare. In 1862 William Cobbett, the advocate of Free Trade, introduced a Bill into the House of Commons designed to reduce enginemen's hours of work. This provoked a letter to *The Times*: *I am surprised by the motion of Mr Cobbett for the protection of engine drivers and firemen, that the Great Western men are classed with those who claim to protection of Parliament. I am. . . to say that they have authorised no one to use their names in any petition asking for the protection of Parliament as a body. Some few may have signed such a Petition but only with a view to benefitting their oppressed fellow workers on other lines, for as long as our respected and esteemed Chief Superintendent, Mr D. Gooch is at our head, we want no other protection than him, for we all know that we can get no protection so just and generous as we receive at his hands.*[22] I will not pretend that I think this letter to be entirely reliable; it has a certain dubiousness about it, yet the very fact that it can suggest conviction is an indication of the regard that Great Western men had for Gooch. Amongst the records of the GWR preserved in the Public Record Office is a driver's report of having been on duty for 15 hours directly as a result of being kept standing with a freight train outside Temple Meads station because the station lift was out of order and the staff were having to use the Midland one.[23] Gooch has scrawled across the report in blue pencil *this is not fair on the men.* The evidence is clear; Gooch knew what engine driving was like, for he had himself driven the first train to Exeter and back in 1844. Afterwards he could barely walk for two days so he knew what rigours his men went through.[24]

For those in non-operating departments in those early years life could be rather more difficult as can be learned from the highly colourful and somewhat libellous account of his railway service written by Ernest Simmons in 1879.[30] Unreliable as to certain details, his representation of how ordinary railwaymen felt has, however, the ring of truth about it. He described Didcot station as being: *like a dirty old barn with both ends knocked out to allow trains to run through; the roofing was blackened with smoke and the paint all blistered.* He then refers to the subway entrance: *the passage itself was simply filthy, the leakage from the engines above as they stood waiting caused a continual trickle of water which covered the walls in a slimy coating, sufficiently to spoil any clothes that came into contact with them.* Simmons' first job at Didcot was to issue tickets and, given no training, it was not enviable employment: *... the counter [of the booking office] was an open one without any shelter for me. In frosty weather the ink froze on my desk... The tickets very much puzzled me. Numerous as they were they did not cover one half of the stations .., it being the custom to print tickets only to those stations for which there was a frequent issue. A book was provided with a blank form of ticket, and I had to fill up one of these tickets when a passenger wished to go to a station for which I had no tickets printed. Unfortunately I did not know the names of many stations on the line. I did not know in which case to search for a ticket, for there were three cases full of them and I had nothing to refer to, to see if I had a ticket printed for that station. Further, in case there were no tickets printed, I had to hunt in three books to find out the fares and was even then unsuccessful sometimes.* To hold even a minor position in a railway company, particularly the GWR, was to be invested with very real status. Running foremen and station masters for example were personages of some power particularly as they had access to senior management.[25] This has down side in that there is, unfortunately plenty of evidence that workshops foreman at least did not always use their authority properly. Simmons too complains about it and was aggrieved that while engine crews had Gooch to look after them, other employees had no one.

O.S. Nock has drawn attention to the concern shown for the wage earners at Swindon by Gooch as confounding *...all the associated clichés of the tub-thumping, street corner politician*[26] and he has a point. The 'railway village' which Brunel constructed at Swindon for the Works employees is familiar enough to need no recollection here. However, the influx of workers made necessary by the expansion of the works meant that there was an almost constant need for new housing and streets of new houses, often built by speculative outsiders, grew up around the original railway village. Despite this, families had to be housed in temporary accommodation and over-crowding and disease were not unknown; in 1874 it was not unusual for three complete families to be housed in one six roomed house for which the rent was high.[20] These are the realities that management written railway history tend to ignore.

In other respects the GWR was in advance of most other railways. The hospital and dental service, parks and church that the company or its directors funded were significant contributions to the welfare of the wage earning classes of Swindon. Footplate and workshop men were required to subscribe to the GWR's Medical and Superannuation Fund Society and no doubt many objected but the wisdom of so doing showed in the payments they received at times of sickness when they could not work. The point about these contributions was that they were invested for growth not, as National Insurance currently is, regarded as funding for expenditure. This dated from the late 1850s; a house was provided free of rent to a local surgeon in return for his attending accidents in the works. That such a provision was necessary is clear from the fact that at this time there were many accidents 'inside' sometimes more than one a week. The Medical Officer became an important member of the Swindon hierarchy, responsible for medically examining potential employees. The office is most associated with Dr G.M.Swinhoe appointed in 1859 who lived at the company's medical establishment at Park House from 1877 until his death in 1907.[20]

We have already noted that one reason for the proliferation of accidents was that there was only limited awareness of the dangers of railway operation and to that one may add the physical properties of the material with which its machinery was constructed. Another consideration is the long hours that were worked by men at every level. In 1871 the working week consisted of five full days, from 0600 to 0815, known as the breakfast shift, the morning shift from 0900 to 1300 and the afternoon, 1400 to 1730. On Saturdays the morning shift ended at 1200. These were not long hours by comparison with other companies or indeed other industries but given the kind of heavy arduous work that was involved it is possible that for some it represented a daily challenge for which no degree of acclimatisation could compensate. The long hours worked at Swindon continued until 1919 and Holcroft who started as a premium apprentice at Stafford Road Works, Wolverhampton in 1898 reports that these same hours were being worked there. Each man clocked on with a brass check with his number on it, latecomers were stopped an hours pay and anyone failing to put his check in was fined 2¼ hours pay.[27] In the 1850s skilled men at Swindon were paid 25-30/- a week, labourers, about 10/-. Note that this was less than engine drivers received and by the 1870s had increased only to £2 and 18/- respectively. According to Hugh Freebury some artisans were still earning only £2/4/- in the early 1930s.[28]

To this writer, who has done some shift work in his life, these working hours appear somewhat illogical. How much better it would have been to divide the work gang into two and on alternate days have them on early and late shifts and also alternate the lunch break so that there were 11½ workshop hours each day rather than 9¾. For many employees the breakfast break could not have meant very much and I suspect that for some, lunch consisted of a walk to the nearest pub with the all too-obvious result.

Drink is of course the demon of the Victorian reformer and it is possible to see why. Railway navvies became a feared group of men whose arrival in a community was regarded with the same apprehension as the approach of an invading army. They were seen as ignorant drink sozzled hoodlums whose only interest in life was a rapacious hedonism. There are reports of large-scale fighting between groups of Irish and Scottish navvies and between navvies generally and local people.[16] There are, I believe simple explanations for these excesses. The first is that navvies went for long periods without being paid and then received all their outstanding wages in one go. Uneducated and untutored about the values of thrift they had little more to spend it on than drink. The rest follows on from that. Peck suggests that Swindon did not experience anywhere near so much of this problem as some places.[20] He argues that Swindon works employees were generally more intelligent and better educated and thus there was little incidence of violent crime, drunkenness or immorality. It is certainly true that the men themselves provided their own library long before it became customary for local authorities to do so. Clearly Armstrong's improvement of working conditions 'inside', thus continuing Gooch's concern for their wage earning employees inspired a degree of company loyalty that would have been impossible among navvies in any industry.

Other things encouraged this loyalty. Paid holidays

Joseph Armstrong, Locomotive Superintendent 1864-1877. Drawing by Chris Seymour based on an old photograph.

were a thing very much of the future in the 1850s but from 1849 onwards the GWR arranged what became known as 'trip', an annual day out to some watering place, the rail travel being free. In the mid-1850s more than 1,500 annually were going on these excursions. One result of this arrangement was the development of the free pass facility, a very valuable concession indeed especially for a Paddington engineman who wanted to take his family to say, Plymouth, Bristol or South Wales. In the 1950s my father had six of these tickets each year and he reserved them for long family journeys which would have been impossible without the free pass. Quarter-fare privilege tickets were first issued in 1891.

The writer aware of all this wants to know what it was actually like to work on the shop floor at Swindon and Wolverhampton and we have evidence from which we can make a pretty good assessment even though it comes from relatively recent times. Alfred Williams, the country ballad singer began his working life in Swindon Works later wrote a book about his experiences.[29] Williams refers to quite appalling working conditions and to safety procedures that were virtually non existent. I have my doubts about this. In correspondence that Hugh Freebury published in his book about Swindon Works K.J.Cook describes Williams as *a complete misfit*.[28] Though excessive as a description it has the ring of truth about it for are we not, at this point talking about aptitude? Williams was essentially an artist to whom engineering was almost certainly uncongenial, hence the extreme with which he writes. More authentic is what we learn from Freebury himself, even though written about Swindon in the 1930s. Freebury was a boiler shop apprentice and he writes that on entering the boiler shop *the clamour hit you like a gigantic hammer blow*. He says that ears rang long after leaving the shop and that boiler maker's deafness was a well-known side effect of employment there. It was impossible to hear anyone even by shouting so that boiler makers learned to lip read. Accidents were common, sometimes because the men would not wear the goggles provided to protect their eyes against flying pieces of metal hurtling off the hammered rivet heads. It is possible that the boiler shop was actually the noisiest and most unpleasant shop in which to work but even then it indicates that only men of a certain kind could have worked inside for any great length of time, particularly 60 years before this. Yet remember, life was much harder in the 19th century than it is today and the working man had a much different expectation than does the present generation.

That is not to say that there was no agitation for improvement. Lord Claud Hamilton, Chairman of the Great Eastern said that his company's enginemen did not need unions because he was there to look after their interests. Whatever the truth of that statement, the fact is that the GWR was one of the last railway companies to become unionised and given the foregoing, the reasons for that are not too difficult to fathom. Representatives of enginemen were being seen by Armstrong as early as 1876 and concessions on hours of work were slowly conceded throughout Dean's period in office.[20] The first union at Swindon was the Amalgamated Society of Engineers, Machinists, Millwrights, Smiths and Pattern makers whose branch income in 1877 was £793, no small total.[20] Other skill unions followed though little was gained until after the formation of the Swindon & District Trades Council which from about 1900 began to be noticed by senior management. As late as the 1920s the GWR General Manager was still refusing to recognise railway unions.[31] Despite this there was an awareness that they had to deal with the men's representatives and this they did. Though the GWR Board may have privately supported the Taff Vale Railway in its infamous attack on the ASRS (later the NUR) there was no similarly divisive anti-union action initiated by Paddington. Given that its Board included such worthies as Lord Cawdor, leader of the Conservative 'ultras' in the House of Lords who were willing to precipitate a constitutional crisis in order to stop Lloyd George's 1911 Budget one may express surprise at that. However whether men were actually dismissed for union activity is a moot point to which I cannot offer a satisfactory answer.

It is in some respects unfortunate that Swindon is associated with one of the very few working class men to reach cabinet rank. This was J.H. 'Jimmy' Thomas, a driver originally from South Wales who was transferred to Swindon in about 1897, he claimed, for political reasons. Thomas may be the street corner tub thumping politician that Nock had in mind in the earlier reference for he was not averse to what might now be termed 'reverse-spin' in what he said about railway service. Later in life he was General Secretary of the NUR, a Labour MP and Dominions Secretary in the first Labour government. In the 1931 crisis he was one of only two Labour ministers who were prepared to join MacDonald's National Government; he was later forced to resign for revealing the contents of a Budget though Stanley Baldwin admonished this failing, putting it down to no more than his being 'in his cups'.[32] In his autobiography Thomas claimed that fear of dismissal was the controlling influence at Swindon in the 1900s.[33] Given the stop-go nature of an industrialised capitalist economy workers might very well fear that the next down turn would cost them their jobs but I am not convinced that this statement is true in the sense that Thomas meant, and I write as one with very strong left wing sympathies. It seems to me that Thomas was good at what is now called 'gesture politics' because he does not appear to have practised that which he preached. It is not generally known that in his service on the GWR he never rose above the level of shunting engine driver and that his treatment of his fireman was pretty poor. It is reported that he was often asleep on the footplate, the actual driving being done by his fireman.[34] One might be forgiven for concluding that such behaviour deserved the threat of dismissal. Similarly, though he liked to present himself as a champion of the working class, on Swindon Borough Council he and the arch-priest of the 'boss class', Churchward, were often in agreement on policy issues.[35]

There is another aspect of this which the foregoing brings to mind. In his book about his railway service my father refers to the first driver that he worked with as a fireman, one Charlie Brown. Brown's first question to any new man that got up on the footplate to fire for him was, 'are you in the union?' Despite this, his: *value was later recognised by the GWR in that he was appointed to the position of London Division Locomotive Running Inspector. He also served the GWR in another way, as a local councillor, helping among other things, to get a supply of purer town water for use in the water columns.*[9] Such men were pragmatists, realists who recognised that while they might have to bargain hard for their men's interests, ultimately the well being of the company was a factor that they could not ignore. Had Thomas claimed no more than that, his reputation and possibly even his record might be the better for it.

I have suggested that Alfred Williams' complaints about life in a railway factory were not entirely justified. However, elsewhere, Williams refers to middle managers whose only concern was with currying favour with senior management and much the same is said by Hugh Freebury about workshop foreman.[28] For a start, your father's position in the works would determine the level at which a new employee would be taken on and those who had fathers willing and able to speak up for them were often able to swing a better starting gate. Much the worst thing was the means adopted by which undesirables were kept out of employment or of trades and occupations that the appointing foreman thought unsuitable. Undesirable did not mean an applicant with a police record or poor education but one who had no one currently employed by the company. I was astounded when I first heard from my father of the way in which the medical officer became involved in the most astonishing antics designed to provide an excuse for an applicant to be turned away. Briefly, it was alleged that he had a bad tooth and this precluded him from employment. The physician, one of Swinhoe's sons, told him that if he had it extracted during the dinner break he would reconsider his decision, guessing it would seem that a poor unemployed 16 year old would have neither the money nor the guile to get the treatment indicated. But he was equal to the task and persuaded a reluctant dentist to remove a perfectly good tooth. One feels almost sorry for Swinhoe who could not now raise any objection to my father's employment.

Freebury had a similar but less happy experience ten years later. He wanted to be a footplate man and his repeated applications for transfer out of the works were constantly turned down. At last he was referred for a medical with results that I do not need to record. Freebury, like my father, was in perfect good health and would probably have made an excellent engineman. It is not enough to say that with unemployment so high the GWR had to find a way of eliminating the excess numbers of those who applied for work, a system of more advanced academic and aptitude tests would have been a far better process and might have encouraged a progression by which men reached senior management. The patriarchal system was of course important. Sons of men already in employment might very well be considered as known quantities and a degree of control could be exercised through the older man. As a last word on this I may mention an old Didcot engineman of my acquaintance who probably started on the GWR around 1910. He was so frail looking it always seemed to me that a hard shunt would have knocked him off the footplate; that makes a complete nonsense of these activities.

One of the recurrent problems of conditions of service is that, perhaps like the navvies of old, working people are sometimes their own worst enemies. Freebury records that progress was constrained by: *pettiness, envy, divisions and strife... often existing among working class people, all in reality struggling for the same basic things in life...*[28] And it is in fanning the flames of such division that the powerful retain their control. These social questions are important. Even in the 1950s when certain aspects of railway service had improved, there was still no awareness by management that working conditions needed serious money thrown at them, except in the notion that the diesel would render all the improvement that was necessary. An engine cleaner from the 1950s has written: *When cleaning engines we got absolutely filthy, my mum had loads of grimy overalls to wash, and she never had a washing machine. I couldn't get my hands properly clean the dirt was grimed in. In those days most working people didn't bath and shower like we do today, mum was always complaining about my pillow cases being black, where I put my head you could see a black greasy mark from my hair. A lot of people in those days had a bath once a week, but in a dirty job like firing it had to be more often. I know the younger people reading this will think 'dirty so and so' but that's how it was. When I was evacuated during the war they had no bathroom, it was a tin bath in front of the fire, once a week and the same water for lots of kids. When I started firing, at first I got almost as dirty as I had when I was cleaning, but after a while I learnt how to keep myself reasonably clean. We had a bloke who sold hand cleanser, we called it 'jam', it was red and came in a jam jar with a piece of paper on top with an elastic band to hold it on. The price per jar was a shilling. Another way of cleaning hands was to soap them up a bit then add a bit of sand, this removed some of the dirt. There was some stuff you could buy called I think it was, Roslex; it was rubbed on hands before starting work and it was good stuff. When I got home from work I always had a good wash in the kitchen sink. In those days white shirts were usual when we went out dressed up. The coal dust got right into our pores, so after a while the shirt collar would become very dirty.* [36]

If this was the situation in the 1950s, what was it like 100 years before when the opportunities for personal cleanliness among many manual workers were close to non-existent? I have written further about this particular point in a later chapter, suggesting that the mechanical stoker was the answer to this type of problem that no one was prepared to consider.

It is unfortunate that senior management on British Railways, both centrally and in the regional workshops, were ignorant of the huge changes in social attitudes happening around them. The prevailing management attitude was that of men whose formative years dated back before the first world war and who had undergone little change from the imperatives of the 1920s. Thus it was that recruitment advertising for British Railways was still based on a clear cut and polarised view of society. Among my railway books is the 1958 edition of the Ian Allan Western Region Locomotive ABC and on the back is an advert headed *Leaving school?* After announcing that there's a career for you on British Railways it goes on to offer boys of 15 years and over a wide variety of *jobs* such as junior clerks, junior porters and signal lads, apprentices in several trades and so forth. However, *for Grammar and Public Schoolboys who have the right qualifications there are special training courses in* ... Of course the right qualifications are necessary for obtaining professional career appointments but by 1958 the two tier education system was already discredited as more and more secondary modern 'failures' achieved high value educational qualifications. You would not think so from this type of advert.[37] There is another example of this kind of thing in the writings of Cecil J Allen who comments somewhere that the promotion of a certain locomotive superintendent from Stewart's Lane, *an ex-public school boy* had led to a deterioration in that depot's work. I think we all know to whom he was referring and it is no insult to that man to comment that this had nothing to do with his education but to the fact that he was an enthusiast who obtained enormous satisfaction from attempting to do the best in the job he was doing. I have made a point about this because I believe that improvements to the locomotive operating staff's conditions of service could have been made with actually little outlay of funds. Mechanical stoking, steam cleaning and a proper career structure that encouraged engine cleaners to reach management level are only some of the innovations which might have improved the labour recruitment situation on

BR in the 1950s. Unfortunately a proper career structure in the servicing and operating grades has still not been introduced and now with a privatised and fractured network probably never will be.

Notes & References
9) *Engines Good & Bad* - A.W.Summers
10) *The First Industrial Nation* - Peter Mathias
11) Most school history departments will have books containing such extracts.
12) *Sunday Despatch Railway Supplement* - c1953
13) *Abingdon Herald* 10th May 1869
14) *Abingdon Herald* 22 February 1869
15) Traffic superintendent's Reports to GWR Board - Seymour Clarke
16) *Grub Water & Relief* - A Vaughn
17) More so when we learn that the weekly wage of some trades in Swindon works was still only 44/- in 1932!
18) GWR Rule Book -1855
19) *Engineer* March 9th 1888
20) *The Great Western at Swindon Works* - A.S.Peck
21) *The Company's First Engine Driver: GWR Magazine* - September 1935
22) *The Times* - 1862
23) The Report is dated 4th April 1863
24) *Diaries* - Sir Daniel Gooch
25) Not in the 1950s however; my father always insisted that they were little more than 'telephone boys'.
26) *The GWR in the 19th Century* - O.S.Nock
27) *Locomotive Adventure* - H Holcroft
28) *Great Western Apprentice- Swindon in the 1930s* - Hugh Freebury
29) *Life in a Railway Workshop* - Alfred Williams
30) *Memoirs of a Station Master* - Ernest Simmons
31) *Pole's Book* - Sir Felix J.C.Pole
32) *Baldwin* - Middlemass & Barnes
33) *My Story* - J.H.Thomas
34) *J H Thomas: A Life for Unity* - Gregory Bloxland
35) *Evening Advertiser* - Swindon - various dates from 1900 onwards
36) Steam E-List - Alan Pike
37) That someone in recruitment realised this can be gleaned from the fact that the advert in the 1961 ABC is couched in very different language.

Readers should note that the drawings on page 4 and 7 are not intended to be technically correct, that of the footplate of *North Star* in particular is almost certainly incorrect: the driver is on the wrong side and the train may be making 40 mph with the regulator in the closed position! Similarly with the Saint cab drawing, the regulator is closed and the driver is holding on to the vacuum brake handle, presumably running into a terminal station and about to make a brake application. Despite these points they convey the impression that is intended.

Two
Weird & wonderful creatures -
- and their fabulous offspring

Somewhere in a railway journal of the 1930s there is a review of a book in which the author advocates building locomotives on a 10' gauge with 18' driving wheels.[9] The anonymous reviewer comments only that the author had lost an opportunity to suggest double deck trains, a rather restrained comment, for the driving wheel sets of such a locomotive would be so heavy that they would require bracing along their length, to say nothing of the power required to be developed by the boiler to get the whole ensemble moving. Adolescent designers have put their ideas down on paper since time immemorial, my own diagram of a 4-4-6-4 double ender tank is still in existence somewhere, not many of us get such ideas into print. That said, some very strange machines have not only been designed but also actually constructed. The GWR's broad gauge *Thunderer* and *Hurricane* built according to the requirements of Brunel probably come a long way up the estimate of weirdness, though they could actually run, and at speed.[10] Among the more rational though no less wonderful machines to have run in Britain were the 9' singles built for the Bristol and Exeter Railway by James Pearson.

The broad gauge Bristol and Exeter was originally organised as a fully independent concern but difficulties in raising the necessary funds for construction led to it becoming to all intents and purposes a subsidiary of the GWR. Until 1849 the GW operated the line but from May 1 the B & E took over the working of all trains beyond Bristol using engines designed by Daniel Gooch.[5/2][11] Passenger trains were hauled by 7'6" versions of the Gooch *Iron Duke* 4-2-2s. The following year the B&ER appointed James Pearson as Locomotive Superintendent. Pearson is first known as having been in charge of the engines on the Croydon and Epsom Railway under Hensman, that company's atmospheric manager. He was later part of a large new staff of enginemen, stokers, valvemen and greasers taken on by the South Devon Railway where he held the post of Atmospheric Superintendent at £300 per annum.[12] His son was Churchward's collaborator in the design of the Swindon standard boilers.[13]

Pearson's first engines on the Bristol were some 2-2-2 tanks and a batch of 0-6-0s; he then ordered the first of his 9 footers, 4-2-4 back and well tanks from the manufactures Rothwells; eight were delivered in 1853/4.[5/2] These engines were more unusual than is often realised and Ahrons even when writing more formally than was his normal way could not avoid commenting on the fact. *They may certainly claim*, he wrote, *to have been the boldest departure made up to that time from the accepted canons of locomotive design...* [14] Among the more unusual of these peculiarities was the fact that the mainframe stopped short at the front of the firebox and was only 8" deep apart from the driving hornblocks, throughout its length. An arrangement of angle plates was attached to the side of the firebox and to the front of the well-tank, beyond that there was no frame at all and the ball and socket pivot of the rear bogie was attached to the underside of the welltank. However, perhaps the most bizarre aspect of the design was the springing of the driving axle. Considerations of space prevent a full description here but I have included the cross-sectional diagram originally published in the *Engineer*, (illustration, this page). It will be seen that both inside and outside bearings were provided and a double springing arrangement was necessitated by the light construction of the outside frame. Both inside and outside springs actually consisted of four rubber discs sandwiched between metal plates and enclosed in a casing. Pillars above the casing were linked by levers. The fulcra of these levers were fixed in a heavy bracket attached to the boiler. In photographs of these engines the outside portion of this springing is clearly visible though I cannot recall reading anywhere else any reference to them.

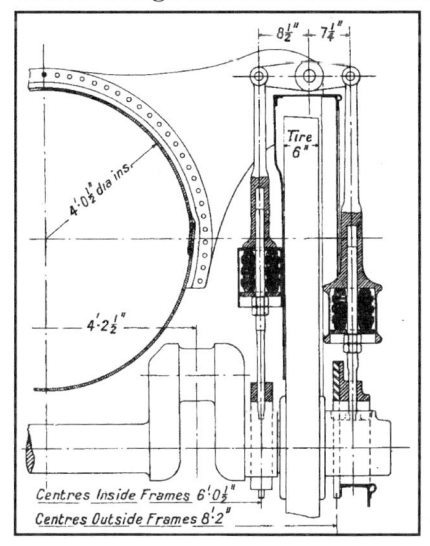

It has always been thought that these engines were employed on the Exeter expresses but Mick Hutson searching the Bristol and Exeter minute books has discovered that they were built to operate the Yeovil branch and not only were never intended as express power but never operated as such.[15] It is even suggested that the high speeds reputed to have been reached by this type were not actually achieved. The later and smaller 7'6" 4-2-4Ts (built 1859/62) did operate express trains and it may be that this encouraged Pearson to revise the earlier design for this type of work. If the question arises as to why tank engines for express trains we should note that from time to time, particularly on the broad gauge, tank engines have had a certain popularity, no doubt due to the larger availability that results from, among other things, a reduced requirement for turning. The high water mark of this tendency is probably the Billington express tanks on the Brighton though a 4-6-4T based on the *Star* would have been a very special locomotive indeed. On the Pearson engines the combination of a short cylinder stroke (24") with 9' driving wheels was obviously seen as an easier way to achieve speed though it cannot have been terribly efficient. Interestingly enough and perhaps surprisingly, they were reported to run with great steadiness.

The original series of 4-2-4Ts had short lives, all were withdrawn by 1873; the term 'renewals' given to the four members of the second series is almost certainly a misnomer, an accountants device and no more than that. Three were built in 1868 and the last in 1873. These were somewhat different to the earlier machines, with much more conventional frames and spring gear, 8'10" driving wheels, larger cylinders and inside bearings throughout. It is these locomotives which recorded high speeds, maxima of 65 mph being authentically recorded.[14] This is interesting because starting in 1869 there was an improvement in booked train times that so far as one train, the *Flying Dutchman* was concerned, remained in being for 20 years, throughout the period usually associated with general deceleration caused by declining revenue and the ultraconservatism of the GWR's Superintendent of the Line, G.N.Tyrell. In 1864 the 11.45 express from Paddington, backed into the B&E station after arrival at Bristol was booked 60 minutes to Taunton (44.8 miles) and 45 minutes thence to Exeter (30.8m).[2] In 1867 this was increased to 120 minutes but the old 105 minute schedule was restored in 1869. Two years later, in 1871 it came down to 94 minutes.[2] This is certainly fast and while there is nothing available with which strictly to compare the booking it is not without interest that I have been a passenger on a double headed steam special hauling 450 tons which ran non-stop from Bristol to Exeter in 75 minutes. By comparison with that, a B&ER 4-2-4T with say, 100 tons at the drawbar was not doing badly to make the run in 94 minutes with one stop. It is of course, in the opposite direction, exploiting the long down grade from Whiteball through Wellington that several of the GWR's speed achievements were made and the B&E authorities obviously realised this advantage. It does not stretch the credibility too much to suggest that late running expresses hauled by Pearson 8'10" locos, given their head in order to regain time could have reached very high speeds on this section. But whether a maximum of 81.8 can be accepted as authentic would now appear to be in doubt.[5/2][15] And the riding must have been horrific!

When the B&E was absorbed by the Great Western in 1876 the 7'6" and the four later engines were still at work. But not for long, on July 27 1876 No.2001 (B&ER No.39) almost new from overhaul at Swindon was derailed at Long Ashton and so severely damaged that it was scrapped. Various reasons have been given for the accident including the condition of the track.[9] Ahrons however suggests that one of the bogies parted from the engine.[8] This led to the three 8'10" survivors being rebuilt as 8' 4-2-2 tender engines by which unwittingly perhaps they became the first successful version of the traditional British 4-2-2.[11] It is interesting to recall that their axle boxes were of immense size; Ahrons, who was a premium apprentice at Swindon from 1882 to 1885 and knew them well, recorded that with slight enlargement *they would have made excellent triumphal arches*, and as their weight was naturally in proportion to their size, *the arrival of these engines in Swindon C shed was not heralded with any great amount of enthusiasm*.[8] The driving wheel set from one of these engines now stands outside the NRM in York.

The broad gauge locomotive stock of the Bristol and Exeter and South Devon companies, taken into the GWR list in 1876 comprised 95 and 85 engines respectively of which nearly half the former and all the latter were tank engines. On the absorption of the B&E their workshops at Bristol were converted for use as a loco shed and all heavy repairs and rebuilding work transferred to Swindon. There this preponderance of tank engines may well have been instrumental in encouraging William Dean to experiment with tanks for more important work on the standard gauge. The Pearson tanks in particular must have attracted a great deal of attention. It is more than likely that, despite the lack of interest by the GWR's contemporary authorities in high speed running, the record of these engines aroused Dean's interest. There can be no other explanation for his development of a 4-2-4 side tank engine intended for express running.[18] This locomotive with side tanks which ran the full length of the footplate from the front of the cab to the buffer beam was unlike anything that had previously run on the GWR.

Of the locomotive engineers employed by the Great Western, Dean is the

William Dean
Drawn by Chris Seymour and based on an old photograph.

most enigmatic, even more so than Collett, for despite long service in the Territorials, he achieved the rank of Major, he eschewed any kind of publicity about his work or private life. And though he is associated with some of the finest locomotives to run in the late 19th century, and I have been reminded, some excellent carriages, his work is littered with failures that have about them an element of obviousness. He was born on January 9 1840, the son of the manager of Hawes Soap factory and was educated at the Haberdashers School in Hoxton. In 1855 he took a premium apprenticeship under Joseph Armstrong at Wolverhampton. Nine years later he was appointed Armstrong's chief assistant and in 1868 he was called to Swindon, whence his former boss had gone, to take on the same responsibility. According to A.S.Peck in this capacity he was responsible for the design of the narrow gauge engines built at Swindon thereafter.[13] George Armstrong, senior to Dean and Joseph's younger brother was not best pleased at this move though his elder brother had no alternative if he wished to avoid the accusation of nepotism.[6]

Dean's first design was a 4-4-0T, also with long side tanks, and then in 1881 the 4-2-4T No 9, intended to be one of two similar machines; the second was to have Joy's valve gear. A feature of this engine was the outside valve gear actuated by rocking shafts from the inside cylinders, a process adopted because access to the gear, always difficult on an inside cylinder engine was made even more so by the long side tanks. In retrospect No.9 seems to have been the victim of a possibly official attempt by Swindon to remove from the record any reference to its existence. Despite the seeming sensationalism of this suggestion circumstantial evidence suggests that it is true, for the 4-2-4T was a complete failure and was kept under a tarpaulin out of visitors eyes for over two years before rebuilding as a 2-2-2 tender engine. It was further rebuilt as a conventional double framed 7' 2-2-2 in 1890 and, named *Victoria* ran until 1905 by which time it had acquired a Churchward domeless parallel boiler.

My first interest in this engine and its unhappy story was aroused by reading Hamilton Ellis while I was still a boy and perhaps over excited by conspiracy theories.[19] Then a couple of years ago, as a result of my wife's photographic work, I became aware of the potential for image enhancement and picture generation provided by the Adobe Photoshop process. Artists impressions of railway locomotives are rarely convincing because the illustration of technical equipment requires technical knowledge; just look at the mess some 'artists' make of the valve gear on a steam locomotive. Photoshop however, overcomes this problem since the image is being recreated from photographs that cannot but be technically correct. With this in mind I decided to use Photoshop to generate an impression of the GWR 4-2-4 express tank engine which may never have strayed out of Swindon works yard. Yet, in doing that I have been reminded that sometimes even the most obviously accurate information can be misleading and that the writer must be vigilant in appraising the value of his sources. In reassessing the work of all the previous researchers into this aspect of GWR locomotive history and covering again the ground of the man who finally provided the drawing that has become accepted as most likely to represent its appearance I have had access to documents and processes denied earlier researchers. Thus I have been able to both confirm and amend earlier conclusions, in a number of areas, in quite dramatic ways.

The first public reference to No.9 appears in the *Locomotive* for August 1903 but is nothing more than a couple of lines which aroused no comment of any kind. Five years later the *Railway Magazine* in serialising a transcription of David Joy's *Diaries* published what has become the main source of all we know about the 4-2-4T.[20] Like most other researchers, at first I relied heavily on that transcription but in subsequent considerations I became troubled by what appeared to be inconsistencies in the dates and actual events recorded. I decided that the only way in which to reconcile these difficulties was to obtain access to the original *Diaries*. This involved a trail from the National Rail Museum Library through the Institution of Mechanical Engineers to the Science Museum Library at Imperial College where a microfilm copy of most of this document is available.[21] The first thing that becomes obvious from examining the microfilm is that to describe the work as a diary is completely inaccurate. This is not a contemporaneous day by day record, the handwriting remains unchanged throughout the sixty years of its duration, the diagrams and drawings are too neatly executed and too detailed to have been done on the spot and, more importantly for our purposes, there are inconsistencies which indicate that this record was compiled by Joy near the end of his life from notes and records made over many years. The question arises as to why if I could see that, the *Railway Magazine's* transcribers were unaware of it, particularly inasmuch that some of their annotations to the extracts were plainly wrong.

Most observers have concluded that Joy visited Dean at Swindon once and that he witnessed 4-2-4T No.9 *tumbling over the turntable*.[5/4] There are, in fact, three visits to Swindon mentioned in the document, two during 1882 and one in 1884. The first is dated July 17 where he records that on his way to Chagford he called at Swindon *re the 6 coupled loco they were to fit* ... there the statement breaks off completely and goes on to something else. It is obvious however that the rest of the sentence was meant to read *with my valve gear*. Perhaps as a teacher I might be forgiven for suggesting that this omission is typical of someone copying from a book or some other note. The fact that the beginning of the next line has later additions - which hinder rather than aid comprehension - tends to confirm that.

The reference is to the 0-6-0T (GWR No.1833) which was fitted with Joy's gear and is recorded as having been completed in November 1882[5/4]. Yet the next note, dated December 1882 and which appears, incompletely, in the 1908 *Railway Magazine* transcription appears to contradict this completion date. It is clear too that it runs together information about two separate locomotives. The full reference reads: *Dean GW Rly asked for a free engine - six coupled 17"x28" a misshapen thing with a long stroke - but it worked out well, and they built a full size model which they told me cost £500, and on that splendid apparatus they set out the gear 1½" out of the vibrating centre, and then asked me to tell them why it did not give equal cut offs, asses!!, But she was a fine engine when they did finish her. Bar though this bit of work. I saw all about a mighty single tank engine that Dean and Charlton were building, 8.0 single and double 4.0 wheel bogies at each end. I saw drawings and all and she looked a beauty. She was intended to do Paddington to Swindon in two minutes under time and the next one was to have my gear; but the next never came. No.1 tumbled over the turntable going out of the shed and stayed there covered with a tarpaulin.*[21]

The reference to 'Charlton' is clearly an error and is obviously meant to be Samuel Carlton, loco works manager from 1864 till 1896, a mistake which tends to support the view that this record is not a day to day diary. Joy's third reference to visiting Swindon, from February 1884 says simply: *sent for to go to Swindon to see my gear fitted on model body for 6 coupled*. The microfilm shows a faint line of writing in which Joy starts to repeat the comment about the misalignment but clearly thinks twice about it and either writes no more or attempts to erase it - the film processing having recovered the words. The reader can now well understand my concern that Joy is almost certainly unreliable as to dates and the chronology of the events he is recording. Despite this I would contend that we can accept that everything that he wrote actually happened if not in quite the way he describes.

4-2-4T No.9 was completed in May 1881 and added to stock in August.[5/4] I am sticking my neck out now but I am going to hazard the guess that the February 1884 note should be dated to two years earlier, that in fact all three visits were made in 1882. This would explain a very great deal, it puts Joy at Swindon only a few months after No.9's completion when Dean and his associates were still struggling to solve its problems. Having been called in to discuss the application of his gear to the second version of the engine, he was shown the drawings and probably the engine itself in order that he might advise Swindon as to the likely cause of its instability. Sometime between then and July 17 when he was back at Swindon again, the order for the second engine had been cancelled and the decision taken to put the gear on an 0-6-0 goods engine. It was at this time that he was shown the £500 model on which the *asses* had misaligned the gear. His third visit, in December was the occasion which evoked his comment that *she was a fine engine when they did finish her*, and refers to the 0-6-0.

Readers will be aware that the content of this book is largely a revised and extended version of articles which have appeared over several years in the *Backtrack* magazine. In the article which forms the basis of this chapter I wrote: *Having indulged my boyish delight in conspiracy theory, perhaps I might be allowed to go further down the incline and argue that it is possible that the construction of the second 4-2-4T had been started and that its cancellation left the works with a partially completed machine on its hands. This might well have been the starting point for No.1833. The 28" stroke on this engine for all Joy's evident disapproval was intended to be used on the second 4-2-4T and therefore supports this contention.*[22] No one had ever previously suggested such a thing but this conjecture received an extraordinary confirmation in a communication from a William Morgan about whom I know nothing other than the name.

Mr Morgan sent me photo-copies of pages from the GWR account book in which the construction costs of locomotives were broken down under the headings, *Wages and Materials*, and further subdivided. Taken as purely an item of interest, the overall figure of £1,258 6s 8d for a 1601 class saddle tank of 1878 is interesting enough but to then be able to note the cost of materials, components and the wage cost of each employee trade group, detailed to the last penny is extraordinary. However the real point of his enclosures was to indicate that my contention that 0-6-0T 1833 was partly constructed from material rendered surplus by the cancellation of the second 4-2-4T must be correct. To quote from his letter: *...you will find very little regarding No.9, although it does give its cost as £2,667. Much is recorded for 1833 but the figures are distorted by the credit (of £500) against expenditure for 'Value of duplicate parts'. This is something I have never seen before. Normally a credit is given in the cost for the scrap, plus another for 'Profit on Manufacture' for the scrap, the latter being half to two thirds of the final figure. The total of these two is then deducted from the cost of the material only. With 1833 the £500 has been deducted as follows - £150 from wages, £100 from Factory Expenses and £250 from materials and no mention of 'Profit on Manufacture'. This is one factor supporting a sister engine to No.9 and also I think it is significant that Factory No.845 was 'saved' for 1833.*[23] While we cannot, at this time, prove that 1833 was built in part from components intended to be fitted to the second 4-2-4T, I think it is a safe assumption that this was indeed the case.

Together with the original 4-4-0 No.1 and No.9, 0-6-0T 1833 is one of the few GWR locomotive types even from those early years for which no diagram or photograph exists. We can conjecture its appearance from the photograph taken after it had been converted to a tender engine. As such it was very similar to the Dean Goods then appearing from Swindon shops, and undeniably a fine looking engine, but if, as a tank engine it had carried the second 4-2-4T's intended boiler/ tank/ cab/ bunker ensemble, cut down as necessary, it would indeed have been a very ungainly thing. 1833 was not converted to a tender engine until October 1884 so it cannot be argued that Joy's admiration dated from the alleged February '84 visit.

Going back to our own chronology, in 1908 very few people knew anything about No.9 and the transcribers of the *Diaries* made enquiries about it at Swindon. They received a response from Churchward denying that any such locomotive had existed and suggesting that Joy must have been confused with the old Bristol and Exeter engines. However, a correspondent who is unfortunately not named came forward to confirm Joy's statement.[24] This correspondent wrote: *A friend of mine worked as a fitter on the erection of a narrow gauge tank engine at Swindon 20 odd years ago ... He says she was built and tried several times but would not keep on the rails, so they brought her back and used parts to make a six wheel single tender engine.* Provided with this statement Churchward no longer denied the story, claiming that the first enquiry had not stated that the engine had been built for the narrow gauge. He now confirmed the general details adding, *it was not considered a success ... for what reason I do not know.*

One hesitates to make accusations against Britain's foremost locomotive engineer but this reply is clearly a whopper. Churchward was at Swindon at the time having been lately involved with 'Young Joe' Armstrong in the development of the vacuum brake and continued there as an inspector of metals. He could not have been anything other than aware of the locomotive and its faults. Whatever senior management does to cover its tracks, people talk and if 'the engine that wouldn't keep on the rails' was the gossip of the Swindon pubs for years, which it must have been, then Churchward must have known about its failings. That he would feel the need to deny the story twenty years after the event is rather difficult to understand though Swindon's secrecy about its every action is well known and was maintained almost to the final closure of the works.

The next reference to these engines appears in Ahrons *Railway Magazine* series.[8] As already noticed he was at Swindon in the early 80s' and was thus in a good position to recall what was happening there. He refers to No.9 specifically as having a bogie at each end, the wheels having Mansell wooden centres. Most observers have always been under the impression that this was the only reference to No.9 before, in 1940 the first comprehensive attempt was made to work out exactly what it looked like. I hesitate to say that 'I have discovered ...' because the reference I have found in Ahrons *British Steam Locomotive 1825-1925* has been there for anyone to read ever since the book was published. However, the fact remains that I can find no reference to it in any subsequent source that I have consulted. And what it says is in some respects, quite devastating.[14]

The late E.W.Twining, later to be associated with the RCTS history of GWR locomotives, writing in 1940 challenged and discarded the description of No.9 as a double bogie.[25] By this time there were only two drawings of the engine in existence, that of the boiler dated 1879 and the layout of the tanks, sand boxes, coal bunker and wheel base dated 1880 on which the driving wheels were indicated by double dotted circles. At this time Swindon was less prickly about the affair and *Mr Collett has been kind enough to loan the drawings of the tanks and boiler...* Using these drawings and the well known appearance of the locomotive as a 2-2-2, Twining was able to produce a diagram of No.9 which has long been accepted as being as accurate as anyone is now likely to be. What is truly significant is that Ahrons makes almost exactly the same claim, that Collett gave him access to these drawings. Even more significant is the fact that he agrees the one detail in Twining's conjecture which I have rejected.[14]

Twining began by dismissing the description of the locomotive as a 'double bogie' used both by Joy and Ahrons on the grounds that this would mean that the engine would have no fixed wheelbase. His diagram shows a long 7'3"

wheelbase for the front carrying wheels and he suggests that this is evidence that they were not a bogie but rigid wheels with lateral sideplay. My first reaction to this statement was to acknowledge that it was true, that as far as the GWR was concerned, this was a very long wheelbase for a bogie, not to be equalled until the building of the Dean/Churchward 4-4-0s in the 90s. However, almost by accident I stumbled over evidence that strongly suggested that Twining's diagram could only be in error in stating a wheelbase of 7'3".

At first my concern was with the remark about there being *no fixed wheelbase*. Twining reports that the Pearson engines which were double bogies had *flangeless driving wheels and* (bogies with) *rigid centre pivots without sideplay ... flanged No.9 could not have worked like this,* he adds. I cannot see that this can be true, given the long fixed wheelbase common on later 4-6-0s, there was no reason why a 4-2-4 with a flanged driving wheel could not have been operated in this way. Again, if the reference to there being no fixed wheelbase applies to No.9 it applies equally to the Pearson engines. (And indeed several other examples that leap to mind, the Norris 4-2-0s for example.) That such an arrangement might not be very stable gives a hint at least in part of what was wrong with No.9. Twining's suggestion that the leading carrying wheels were rigid with some sideplay is therefore open to question. Both Ahrons and Joy, who was shown drawings of the engine, were engineers with an interest in their work, I cannot believe that either man would have missed this important detail.[26]

And indeed, there is evidence that strongly suggests that Twining was wrong. He obviously had no access to any other drawing than those loaned to him by Collett nor was he able to inspect the Swindon Drawing Office Register.[27] This document is now among the records kept at the National Rail Museum and it makes fascinating reading. Locomotive types were referred to by their Lot numbers, the 4-2-4T was Lot 54 and under date February 1881 there is a reference to a drawing of: *frame plan leading and trailing bogies Lot 54*.[27/1] I believe this confirms beyond doubt that the leading wheels were contained in a bogie. At this point I was happy to accept Twining's 7'3" wheelbase for the leading carrying wheels/bogie. Then something quite remarkable happened. I have already mentioned my wish to construct a picture of No.9 exploiting the Photoshop system. The obvious starting point was Twining's diagram and the photograph of No.9 as a 2-2-2, which was in fact where he started. As soon as I had transferred a cut-out of the driving wheel/valve gear ensemble I knew there was something wrong because the connecting rods on the 2-2-2 were much longer than those on the Twining diagram.

Consider, No.9 was a total failure which cost over £2,000 to build and against which there had been no revenue recovered. Such a sum would have been a great deal of money in 1882, perhaps as much as £250,000 in present day terms. Any rebuild would have to be undertaken with the minimum possible expense. We are told that this involved the reuse of a section of the frame, driving wheels, valve gear and cylinders;[5/4] but why lengthen the connecting rods, why go to the extra expense of such a manoeuvre when keeping cost down must have been a primary consideration? Turning the question round and asking why Twining decided to shorten the connecting rods in his conjectural diagram revealed another interesting point. If the longer length connecting rods of the 2-2-2 had been employed on the 4-2-4T they would have tended to foul the rear set of the leading carrying wheels. For that reason Twining had obviously decided that on the tank engine shorter connecting rods had been employed. But had they?

I agonised for a long time over these points. I checked the scales of the photographs being used and the possible distorting effect of the camera. However, given a broadside taken with the very large format (8" I believe) plate camera used at Swindon, we can accept that very little or no distortion occurs. I have checked the scales of the diagram. I have reread and reconsidered every interpretation of my notes made from the article in *The Locomotive*. But two things convince me that the stated length of 7'3" for the leading wheelbase is inaccurate. The first is the Registry entry already referred to entitled *frame plan leading and trailing bogies*.[19/1] I originally considered that this merely confirmed that No.9 was a double bogie engine but it could also be a suggestion that both bogies were identical. A mirror copy of the rear bogie brought forward and lined up on the centre line of the leading wheel fits snugly under the smokebox where it should be and avoids all but a minimum of conflict with the longer connecting rods. (I return to this point later) I therefore believe that in some way Twining made a crucial error in reading the material he was shown at Swindon.

But did he? In order to push that conjecture we now have to consider Ahron's statement confirming Twining's reading of the workshop drawing. Is it possible that both men made the same mistake in reading the diagram? Is that possible? Twining tells us that the diagram of the tank ensemble showed the wheelbase but does not say whether this actually showed the wheel centre lines apart from the driving wheel shown by a dotted line. Can we assume that Twining accepted Ahron's figure without checking it, possibly because the drawing with which he was provided was unclear? The point is that if my contention about the length of the leading bogie wheelbase is accepted then several conundrums detailed in this chapter now have answers.

Which brings us to the actual design of No.9's bogies. Holcroft tells us that Dean converted three Wolverhampton 2-4-0s to tank engines but that the axle loading with the tanks of the desired capacity was considered too great and they were converted back.[4] This led to the design of No.1 (Lot 46) which had outside frames and long tanks extended right forward to the smokebox. The particular interest in this locomotive is in the leading bogie which had a normal wheelbase but to quote Holcroft was: *centre-less and consisted of a frame outside the wheels carrying the axle boxes and laminated springs. Attachment to the main frame was through the long spring hangers, which were anchored to a bracket in the form of a large loop bolted to the frame.*[4] The attachment was only indirect, the weight of the front end was carried to the bogies through the loop bracket referred to by Holcroft which was reportedly only 4" deep and ¾" thick attached via the spring hanger to the bogie sideplates 5" deep and ¾" thick. Vertical strength was maintained by three cross stays in the attachment plate. The bogie moved only laterally without any normal torque movement. It proved most unsatisfactory, being far too light for the weight of the front end;[5/6] a feature of its failure, not highlighted by previous writers, may well have been the full weight of the water in the forward extensions of the side tanks and we will refer to this again.

I have devoted some space to a description of this bogie because Twining reports that 'someone at Swindon' told him that the bogie(s) of No.9 were similar to that on No.1 and it is now possible to confirm that this was so. The Drawing Office Register[27] shows that all the drawings expected for a new locomotive were actually completed though unfortunately none of them is now available. But just by examining the evidence that the catalogue alone provides suggests that Twining's informant at Swindon (who may have been asked to find all existing drawings of No.9), actually realised the importance of a Register entry that has since lain unexamined for over sixty years. Twining reported that the 1880 diagram of the coal bunker showed no arrangement facilitating the provision of a bogie pin and went on from this to hypothesise that something similar to the bogie on No.1 had been used. Looking through the Drawing Office Register I was startled to find the drawing reference: *bogie brackets and slides Lots 46 & 54!*[27/2] This confirmation of similarity at least in part of the bogies of both the 4-4-0T and the 4-2-4T tends to confirm that both bogies on No.9 were identical to those on No.1 except in the means by which they were attached to the mainframe.

If this contention is correct then the answer to the all important question of why the 4-2-4T derailed so easily is now very clear. The exceptionally long side tanks must have been a debilitating factor. The weight of water ahead of the driving wheels was large; scaling the water capacity from the Twining diagram gives something like two tons additional weight either side. It is highly likely that this had a seriously deleterious effect on the locomotive, overburdening the front carrying bogie whenever it moved out of the centre, and upsetting the bogie at the rear end by interfering with the longitudinal stability of the locomotive. A possible corollary to this may be found in the statement that on 0-6-0T No.1833 *variations in tank water level are said to have affected the working of the Joy's valve gear...*[5/5]. A more explicit explanation of exactly what is meant here would be useful. But if it suggests that there was some imbalance between the tank capacities as water was used, it would add point to the foregoing. That there were serious problems caused by the long water tanks cannot be denied, the balance was almost certainly very tight and even minimal displacement of the bogie could have upset that balance. According to Ahrons there was at one time a story circulating in Swindon that: *the late Sir Daniel Gooch ... did not like the long side tanks.*[8] Gooch would obviously have been a frequent and welcome visitor to the works that he had created and as Chairman of a company very concerned about the profit and loss account, more than interested in a locomotive that could not even have begun to pay for its construction. Can we read into this comment a possibility that Gooch actually told Dean that the derailments were caused by the long side tanks?

There are further doubts about the facts surrounding No. 9. The completion date given for 4-4-0T No.1 was May 1880 and that of No.9 as May 1881 though as already noted, it was not added to stock until August.[5/4] It is possible that the dates for No.9 are wrong. The drawing referred to previously of the leading and trailing bogies is dated February 1881, only three months before this completion date. Not impossible of course but it raises the possibility that the date of 'adding to stock' is the actual date of completion. I have attempted to settle this by reference to various committee Minutes but unfortunately there is a complete blank in the records of the Locomotive Committee for this period and contemporary Board Minutes make no reference to requisitions for expenditure on locomotives or rolling stock as they do at the end of the century and thereafter. At this distance of time it is unlikely that anything further of significance about these matters will now be uncovered. But there is no doubt that these most recent discoveries do show that we now have a clearer understanding than was previously thought to be the case.

The question of the length of the wheelbase of the front bogie is therefore crucial. Despite everything I continue to believe that it was a mirror image of the rear bogie because, as we have seen, this answers so many of the unanswered questions surrounding the engine. I would give almost anything to see the original drawings. That those seen by Ahrons and Twining are still in existence is beyond doubt, they must be part of the collection held at York which it is suggested will take years to sort and catalogue. One day then we will have these and possibly other drawings to reveal the truth about the conjectures in this chapter. Perhaps before then someone might come forward with the copy drawings that were given to Ahrons or Twining. We must live in hope.

According to David Joy[21] No.9 was expected to do Paddington to Swindon in two minutes under time. In 1880 the fastest down narrow gauge time to Swindon was 115 minutes inclusive of a 5 minute stop at Reading. Up trains were a little better, the 09.05 from Swindon ran to Paddington in 100 minutes inclusive of a 5 minute stop at Reading and a 25 mph speed restriction through Didcot.[2] Exactly what Joy meant by 2 minutes under time is unclear, it is hardly likely that Dean was proposing to run to Swindon in under even time and a cut of two minutes from the contemporary schedule was not something to talk about very loudly. For all that, the computer generated illustrations of No.9 included in this book show that the observer can only agree with Joy that Dean's 4-2-4T must have been a mighty beauty. Indeed, the engine as illustrated here is a strikingly handsome machine.

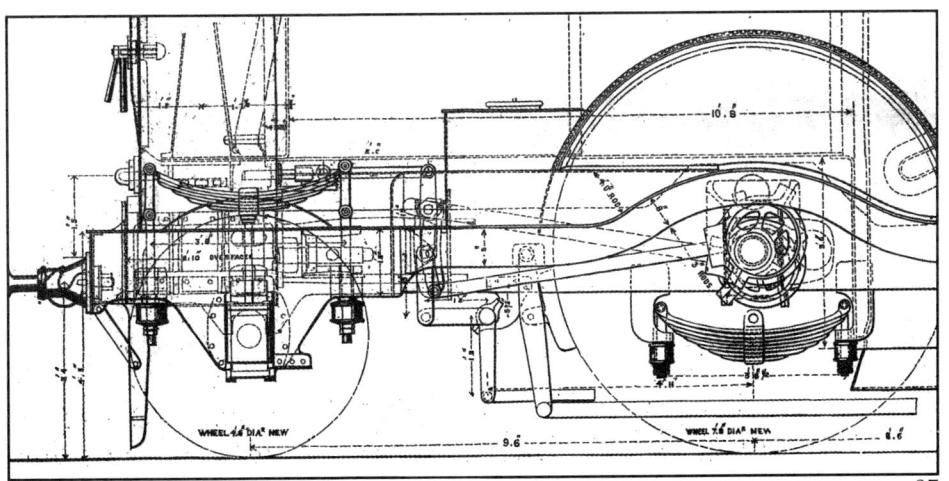

Some points about these conjectured illustrations are open to contention and I welcome constructive comments. One point about which there might still be some argument is that of the layout of the gear between the leading bogie and the driving wheel. I have laid great stress on what I believe to have been Twining's mistake in deciding upon a wheelbase of 7'3" for the leading bogie and how this forced him to conjecture connecting rods much shorter than were fitted to the single wheeler rebuild. In fact, even with the special bogie, the connecting rods are actually shorter by a few inches than those on the 2-2-2. To some extent this does undermine my suggestion that concern about expense would have made any such alteration undesirable. However, by chance I discovered in the pages of the *Engineer* a copy of another diagram of which the original is unavailable, the side view general arrangement of No.9 as first rebuilt to a 2-2-2.[28] This shows clearly the layout of the cylinders and valve gear and I believe it is safe to assume that, apart from the slightly shorter connecting rods, this represents the layout as it was on No.9.

Reference has already been made to the subsequent career of No.9, as a 2-2-2 tender engine. It worked slow trains between Swindon and Bristol for a couple of years before being booked to expresses. The rocking shafts were inclined to break but once strengthened gave no further trouble. Ahrons says that *it could pull like a coupled engine*.[8] It has always been supposed that there were only two photographs of 2-2-2 No.9 extant but another of Mr Morgan's enclosures was a totally unexpected third. Fairly obviously it is a previously unknown official picture of the locomotive and as is usual with Swindon's photographs is a first class image with perfect sharpness. It is also the other side from the two images known, but without the tender. Photographic records were continually reorganised down the years with some negatives possibly destroyed though it is not impossible that there may be lurking somewhere a copy of the photograph(s) that most certainly must have been taken of the 4-2-4T when it was first completed.

It is a great pity that No.9 was not provided with reliable bogies nor the destabilising effects of the long tanks sorted out. Had it been successful it is likely the type would have been multiplied further and that they would have taken their place alongside the *Cobham* and *Queen* class single wheelers; who knows, they could have ended their days running with Churchward domed belpaire boilers. The single wheeler express tank engine is largely unknown in Britain and it would have been entirely in character for the GWR to have been the railway that constructed one. We are left with the almost Wagnerian legend of Dean watching his engine steamed for the first time and as it derails turning on his heel and without a word walking slowly away.

Notes and references

9) *Railway Magazine* - regrettably I have lost the exact date of the reference.
10) Readers unfamiliar with these engines could do worse than examine the models of them that are exhibited in the Great Western Society museum at Didcot.
11) At one time trains for Plymouth could have run behind no less than four locomotives, an Iron Duke to Swindon, a Waverley 4-4-0 to Bristol, a B&ER engine to Exeter and an SDR tank thereafter.
12) *Exeter-Newton Abbot: A Railway History* - Peter Kay
13) *The Great Western at Swindon Works* - A.S.Peck
14) *The British Steam Locomotive 1825 - 1925* - E.L.Ahrons
15) *Backtrack* June 2004 - letter from Mick Hutton
16) Report on the Long Ashton Derailment - Colonel Yolland

17) The bogie design of Archibald Sturrock's 1853 4-2-2 for the Great Northern was rather different and not entirely successful.
18) As a sidelight to this it is interesting to recall that at nationalisation the GWR owned far more tank engines than the tender variety.
19) *Four Main Lines* - C.Hamilton Ellis
20) *Diaries of David Joy - Railway Magazine* 1908
21) *Diaries of David Joy Vol 1,2 & 4-6* Science Museum Library microfilm B238
22) *Backtrack* - April 2004
23) William Morgan - letter to the author May 2004
24) *Railway Magazine* - January 1909
25) *Locomotive Magazine* - January 1940
26) Holcroft (4) also refers to it as a double bogie engine but his knowledge was second hand.
27) Swindon Drawing Office Register No.1, 1870-1888
    27/1) GWR Drawing 3516
    27/2) GWR Drawing 3548
28) *The Engineer* - September 24th 1886

Three
Networking engineers and Swindon's world-wide web

The late W.A.Tuplin was not afraid of criticism, one could almost believe that he courted it with original, individual and sometimes extraordinary statements in the articles and books which he published over many years. Among his memorable epithets was the belief that: *there were at any one time a score of locomotive engineers all doing what was essentially the same job, each in his own different way, in greater or lesser degree influenced by the human failings of pride, self-righteousness, adherence to tradition, deliberate blindness to virtue elsewhere, and reluctance to believe that anyone else's job was quite so difficult as his own.*[9] Not such an extraordinary statement because a simple examination of the railway workshop scene seems to demonstrate that it contains more than a kernel of truth. And of course it does. However, recent research shows an equally apparent regime perhaps not of collaboration but certainly of ideas and innovations being networked between locomotive engineers. I was led to this discovery while researching material from old albums once owned by students at Culham College when I discovered among the brown badly faded photographs of mock-gothic buildings and forbidding lecture halls two astonishing photographs of locomotives and trains. What was of greater interest was the way in which this discovery, possibly not very special in itself led to revelations new to me and as they developed, astonishing.

Culham station is on the GWR main line from Paddington to Oxford, 3 miles north of Didcot, opened as Abingdon Road in 1844. Altered to Culham in 1856 when the Abingdon branch began passenger operations it was never much more than a wayside station with a goods shed, cowpens and meagre sidings. Culham village was about 1½ miles away and Abingdon itself about 3, it might just as well have been named Clifton Hampden to which it is actually closer. To this day the station remains virtually isolated except for a public house recently reopened after a long period of closure. Culham College was on the Abingdon Road about a mile west of the station. Closed in 1979 the buildings are now used as the English outpost of the *Scholastica Europea* system.

The importance of the station to the college over many years cannot be exaggerated. When the college opened in September 1853 the GWR laid on a special train from Oxford to bring the University Chancellor Designate to Culham to perform the opening ceremony.[10] And of course, for over 100 years, railways were the means by which most people travelled; so it was that students would arrive at Culham's lonely platforms, valise and portmanteau in hand to await whatever transport might be available to take them to their new and certainly in the early days, cold, almost monastic life. Many were disappointed to discover that the carriage of said valise was a 'fatigue' freshmen were expected to handle for themselves. In the student magazine for February 1899 one of their number recorded his experiences: *Scene - Reading GWR station, a cold drizzling January evening. The 5.45pm train from Paddington emerges from the darkness, and comes thundering down alongside the platform, including among its precious burdens some three dozen or more exalted sons of*

Culham.... "Hooray, Hooray, HOORAY", shouts a small ardent band of brother pilgrims already on the platform, accompanied, many of them by wholesale consignments of sisters and cousins. "Good old Culham, Hooray" those in the train send back ... The porters, especially the old hands, smile hugely. They know the cry, "tis re-assembling day up at the College" and many a 'bit o' silver' has changed hands from a Culham toff's capacious pockets to those of the obliging railway men. ... As the lighted carriage windows pass by, crowded with heads, cheers are sent up long and lusty...[11]

The journey is still there to be made, of course, though unfortunately not behind a *Queen* class single wheeler or a 4-2-2 making a stately progress along the Thames valley. What however, remains is the indelible mark of Culham's students on a piece of railway property that the many thousands of passengers travelling through Culham never see. Just north of the station is a bridge which carries a track once called Back Lane over the railway. A very ordinary GWR bridge replicated around its system so many times as to be completely unremarkable. Yet it is unique in that inscribed into the coping and brickwork are the names of many students who were at Culham in the second half of the 19th century. Graffiti is not new, it is well known that the Romans in Pompeii left graffiti which is rather more naughty even than most modern examples of the *genre*! But these are not just scratchings in the brickwork, most of the names are very carefully and fastidiously carved, such that they might have been completed by skilled craftsmen.

There were other customs associated with the Back Lane bridge as this extract from the ex-students magazine explains: *At Culham in our time, there were, I should think, about as many Northerners as Southerners, and there was not the slightest friction between them as such... never at any time was there any attempt to divide into rival North and South camps. We did divide on the occasions to which I am about to refer, but then the division was for a pleasant, not to say sentimental, reason. On the eve of the last day of the Certificate examination, we would all proceed down the lane to the bridge, and those who would on the morrow or the next day be going South would stand on the side of the bridge nearest the way they would journey, and those going North would stand on the other side. Then we would sing songs, some of a humorous and others of a "Home sweet home" and "Should auld acquaintance be forgot" character. Speeches short and to the point would be made, the Southerners would cheer as only Culhamites can cheer, for the Northerners, and the Northerners do ditto, only more so, for the Southerners, we would vow eternal friendship, and return slowly, and some of us seriously back, for we knew only too well, that many of us who had spent two years in about the closest possible relationship, would never meet again on this side of the grave.*[12] So if you happen to be near Culham station at night perhaps you will hear the spectral voices of these men singing and cheering!

Among the Archives of Culham College, now housed in the Oxfordshire Record Office are some photograph albums belonging to students who were at the college 100 years ago. Inevitably the images in these albums are brown in colour, faded and in some cases deteriorating to the point of complete disintegration. Copying them digitally and transferring the new images onto CD-Rom has certainly saved them from being completely lost. While that was the proper purpose of my day at the record office I was also hoping that some enterprising student had photographed a train at Culham station, perhaps the 5.45 from Paddington. In that I was disappointed. What I did find however, in an album that had belonged to Albert Floyd who had been a student at Culham from 1905 to 1907 when the photographs were taken, were two photographs of Great Eastern engines.[13] The means by which I identified them led me to a startling discovery. Looking through the album while my wife was doing the actual photographic work I found what I at first thought was a broadside shot of a GWR Dean 2-4-0. It was all I could do to prevent myself splitting the sepulchral silence of the record office with a shout of exclamation. But immediately I realised that such reactions were misplaced because the tender of the engine in question was clearly marked G E R. It was in fact Great Eastern T19 2-4-0 No.1038, one of James Holden's first express engines. The second photograph shows a GER train double headed by two T19s of which that nearest the camera is No.721. The two photographs are full of interest for what is happening as much as anything else.

What was striking to me was that I had mistaken GE engines for those of the GWR, Yet, coolly observed, the remarkable resemblance of the T19s to some of the Dean 2-4-0s becomes too obvious to miss. In fact the T19s were not the only Great Eastern engines that could, more than superficially have been mistaken for the work of Swindon. It looks now as though there may have been a good deal of communication between Dean and Holden in which rather than copying of ideas by one or the other, there was a definite pooling of practices. Subsequent research demonstrates that influences of this kind were rather more common than Tuplin suggests and indeed, longer lasting as well.

James Holden was born in Whitstable, Kent on 26 July 1837, the nephew of Edward Fletcher, at that time a driver on the Canterbury and Whitstable Railway but later Locomotive Superintendent of the York, Newcastle & Berwick, afterwards the North Eastern Railway.[14] Holden was apprenticed to Fletcher at Gateshead and spent some time working in Sunderland where he got to know William Armstrong, son of John Armstrong, whose brother Joseph became Locomotive Superintendent of the Great Western in 1864. In 1865 Holden was taken on by Joseph Armstrong as manager of carriage and wagon repairs at Shrewsbury. He was later promoted to Saltney as superintendent of the carriage works and from there to Swindon in 1873 as manager of the carriage and wagon works.[6][15] In this capacity he built the first sleeping cars to run on the GWR, almost the first real sleepers in the country. He also designed the eight wheeled 10½' wide broad gauge convertible clerestory coaches that figure so prominently in photographs from this time. To enable a quick return to service, the centre sections could be easily removed and narrow gauge bogies substituted for the broad. On the GER Holden reversed the process when widening some suburban stock to take six people abreast rather than five.[16] Interestingly Holden who was very junior to Samuel Carlton the loco works manager became Dean's chief assistant in April 1878. He retained the title of carriage works manager but it seems that the day to day responsibilities were actually carried out by a deputy.

Swindon in the early 80s was suffering from the dichotomy between the understandable wish to make a final abolition of the broad gauge and the nostalgic urgings of others, notably of Sir Daniel Gooch to put off the fateful day for as long as possible, a feeling accentuated by the belief (theoretically correct but not practically demonstrated) that the broad gauge was actually capable of running faster trains than the narrow. Most narrow gauge trains of this period that might be described as expresses were hauled by 2-2-2's of the *Queen* and *Sir Daniel* classes assisted by Dean's *Cobham* class. The *Cobham's* with outside sandwich framing were long term descendants of Stephenson's *Planet* type willed to the GWR through *North Star* and its fellows. For secondary duties the 2-4-0 was favoured and these made an early appearance both on the broad and narrow gauges. There was no particular standardisation between them, as usual both forms of outside framing was used, with the incredibly late resurrection in 1892 of the old sandwich framing, while several classes had inside frames for the driving wheels and double frames for the leading carrying wheel. Gibson says that his father recorded these 2-4-0s at speeds of 80 mph but gives no precise details.[7]

This inside cylinder 2-4-0 design evolved through several incarnations and the 2211 Dean variants of the Armstrong 806 class, the first of which came out in 1882 had a very simple and attractive appearance. Though the splasher and footplate layout seems to have been arrived at by a developmental process it was not unique to the GWR, variants could be found on many railways, including the Midland, Lancashire and Yorkshire and to a lesser extent, the Great Eastern, on T.W.Worsdell's G14 class. Here the splashers were combined in one deep elliptical plate and the carrying wheels had inside bearings only. The Great Eastern 2-4-0s had 7' driving wheels but the Great Western 806/2201 classes had 6'6½" driving wheels. At first the GWR engines had domeless boilers, the first in the country to be constructed in two steel rings, later they had a profusion of different types of boiler, some with the dome behind the chimney and in others in the more normal place.[5/4]

Though in later notes he is more complimentary to the G14s Ahrons initial experience with this class, on a run from March to Cambridge he described as: *one of the most solemn and funereal processions that it was ever my lot to endure.*[17] This is intriguing because some interesting figures were published in the *Engineer* when the G14s were the principle express engines on the route.[18] Diagrammatically it is shown that over 20 years GE Ipswich line trains had increased from 10 four wheelers to 16 six wheelers or by 82% in length and 227% in weight. Figures were provided by Worsdell which it was claimed showed an actual reduction in coal used per mile of 1.39lbs at the same time as overall speeds had been increased by 15%. Too much should not be read into these figures because they include every type of engine including Worsdell's notorious 'Gobbler' 2-4-2Ts on every type of job. A similar table produced for the GWR makes interesting reading. Here a saving of 4lb per train mile is shown to have been effected over a similar period. The report goes on to say, without apparently the slightest irony that: *The conditions here are somewhat peculiar, because the weights and speeds of the trains are very nearly now what they were ten years ago. It must be remarked that the Great Western trains ran at higher speeds than those on other lines even before 1873, and the other railways have only been doing recently that which the older line had already done.* The saving in fuel may be put down, generally, to two things, the greater use of Stephenson's rather than Gooch's valve gear and the encouragement engine drivers received to work as economically as possible.

Another and more telling report on the situation is to be found in the book on express trains in Britain and abroad published by Foxwell & Farrer in 1889.[19] They show that on the basis that an express train was one achieving an average speed of 40mph the GWR was far outstripped by other railways, including the Great Eastern. Indeed Great Western goods trains were booked at proportionately better speeds than expresses. They cite the best goods train taking about 200 tons from London to Reading in just two minutes more than the 12.00 express made up to only 120 tons. Their criticism of the Great Western is entirely justified, though to be fair it is only right to add that the situation was soon to change.

Holden was appointed Locomotive Superintendent of the Great Eastern in July 1885. He was a Quaker and while sharing the general opinion of railway management in which trade unions were not encouraged he does seem to have had a genuine if paternalistic approach to employee welfare. He was largely responsible for the building of an 'enginemen's dormitory' at Stratford, what in later parlance was known as a 'double home lodge' where private sleeping cubicles, bathing facilities and also a library and writing room were provided.[20] His first express engines were the T19 2-4-0s with 7' driving wheels. The first to appear, numbered 710 to 779 had three-ring boilers with the dome on the middle ring and a pressure of 140 lb. A further 20 were constructed in 1892, ten more in 1893 and in 1895. Then in 1897 the last ten came out with two-ring boilers, the dome on the front ring. This last batch had increased boiler pressure at 160 lbs and in the course of time the whole class was fitted with the two-ring boilers and increased pressure. A 5'8" version for mixed traffic, the T26 *Intermediate* class are best known to us as LNER class E4.

The T19s (known to GER man as 'standards') are often described as developments of Worsdell's G14s but I am not convinced that this is altogether correct. Although certain Worsdell features were continued in the T14s, a major departure was the use of Stroudley's cylinder layout, with the valves below the cylinders. Inclining the centre line of the cylinders downwards towards the driving centre and inclining the centre line of the valves upwards towards it enabled the valves to be directly actuated by the link motion. Holden continued to use this cylinder layout with all his subsequent designs including the *Claud Hamilton* 4-4-0s. The use of separate splashers owed a good deal to the devolved design of the GWR 2211 class and therefore the T19s it can be asserted combined elements of Worsdell, Dean and Stroudley design practice. They were good engines and fitted with water scoops ran non-stop on expresses between Liverpool Street and Yarmouth and North Walsham.

So far so not very extraordinary. But now there is a surprising turn of events. In 1886 Dean turned out a new 2-2-2, No.10, with 7'8" driving wheels. Previously

GWR engines had been built with the valves placed above the cylinders but with this engine the Stroudley/Holden layout was adopted. Not only that, but thereafter, all new Dean designs used this cylinder layout. Even though Dean continued to build double framed and sandwich framed locomotives, his last 2-4-0s, the 3232 class, a development of the 2211 class, were very similar in appearance to the Great Eastern T19s and this clearly accounts for my error in identifying the engines in Albert Floyd's album. The general dimensions of the T19s and the 3232 Class were very similar though the 7' driving wheels tend to make the GE engines look bigger.

What I certainly had not previously realised was that this similarity between the appearance and the cylinder layout of these 2-4-0s was carried forward by both engineers in a quite remarkable way. When Holden became Locomotive superintendent of the GER, that railway had 75 bogie single or four-coupled engines, by the end of 1897 their number had dwindled to 12. Again, I see here the influence of Swindon where four wheel bogies, as usually understood, were very rare indeed. In chapter two I have recounted Dean's contretemps with a special bogie that was the achilles heel in an otherwise enterprising design. The Pearson broad gauge 4-2-4Ts rebuilt by Dean in 1877 were the first engines on the GWR to have a true leading bogie and it was not until 1894 that such an engine was built by Swindon for the narrow gauge. The 2-2-2 with sideplay in the carrying axles remained supreme on the GWR until 1894. Holden pursued a similar policy, building only engines with a single leading axle, the T19s and between 1889 and 1893 single wheeler versions of the same design. It has been argued that this accorded with the needs of Great Eastern train services which in general operated short distance runs over sometimes difficult gradients.[21] I am not convinced, and an examination of the position on other, similar lines underscores my argument. The London, Chatham & Dover introduced 4-4-0s as early as 1877 and the South Eastern by 1879. Both were essentially short distance lines with sharp gradients even if not identical in operation to the GER. I therefore reiterate my belief that the absence of 4-4-0s on the latter railway was inexplicable except in relation to the similar policy adopted on the GWR.

Quite unexpectedly, in 1898 Holden changed everything that had gone before, producing a bogie single with outside frames and in place of the traditional GER stove pipe a shaped chimney with a copper cap. Some commentators have suggested that the impetus for Holden's P43 4-2-2s was the Johnson Midland 'Spinners' built successively from 1887 to 1900. I am not at all certain that this is the case. It seems to me that the full story of the express bogie singles of the last quarter of the 19th century has yet to be told, particularly the fact that in some cases they were reversions not just in terms of wheel notation but of actual design. Johnson, credited with starting the craze, went back on his previous usual form 2-4-0s and 4-4-0s with inside cylinders and inside frames to produce an outside framed bogie single. Though he had used a form of the Stroudley/Holden cylinder layout, the 'Spinners' had the valves above the cylinders. Mechanically therefore the GER 4-2-2 is not derived from Derby; the impression that it did created in the appearance of inside bearings on the bogies and the rectangular panel in the cab side-sheets is misleading. Furthermore the P43 chimney is an exact copy of the Swindon version and I will risk the ire of GER enthusiasts by suggesting that the *Claud's* original chimneys were too. No, the influence can only have been Dean's *Achilles* Class 4-2-2s built by his old chief from 1894 onwards and no less a person than that enthusiast for the GER the late C Langley Aldrich also remarked on this Great Western 'touch' in the line of the Holden 4-2-2s.[20]

I have been at some pains to test the veracity of this suggestion, studying the general arrangement drawings of all three types and, while I would not want to over stress the similarities, it can only ever be an assumption anyway, I do think that Holden's adoption of the outside framed 4-2-2 was inspired by Swindon. That is not to say that Lord Claud Hamilton did not send for his Locomotive Superintendent and say to him something like, "Look here, Holden, these other companies are running some superb looking single wheeler express engines, can't we do the same?" Nor that Holden, possibly knowing that such engines were rapidly being rendered obsolete by ever increasing train weights did not go into his chief draughtsman, Frederick Russell and pass on the order in words that may have been along the lines of, "... look at what Mr Dean's doing at Swindon, they're the best of the lot ..." Russell certainly had a hand in the designs ascribed to Holden in his later years, becoming Chief of Locomotive Design (whatever that actually meant) so this conjecture may be closer to the truth than we know.[22] Another factor not often considered is that the Midland engines had been around for much longer than the GW types and were actually quite dowdy by comparison with the sparkling appearance of engines liberally endowed with highly polished copper and brass.[23] The general dimensions of both are very similar, the driving wheel sizes being the only major difference. However, the frames of both were different. So too were the elevations of both cylinders and valves out of the horizontal, the GE machines having the cylinders much more steeply inclined.

On the GWR the Holden cylinder layout, as adapted by Dean continued to be used on all his four coupled engines and this practice was maintained by Churchward with his taper boilered 4-4-0s having inside cylinders. The continued use of double frames by the GWR, the last new such frame was constructed as late as 1909 has often been remarked. The *Achilles* 4-2-2s were not by any means out of the ordinary run of Swindon styling. But for the GER the outside framed P43 certainly was. Holden's next express design, the celebrated *Claud Hamilton* 4-4-0 had inside frames and cylinders just as did the T19s thus emphasising how exceptional the P43s actually were. These engines like most of their kind were obsolete almost before they started running. Only ten were constructed and never rebuilt they worked almost exclusively on the Cromer expresses.[24] Ahrons timed No.19 taking 250 tons from Liverpool Street up Brentwood Bank to Shenfield (31½ miles) in 32.35 minutes.[25] However they were quickly withdrawn between 1907 and 1910. Dean's *Achilles* types, successively rebuilt by Churchward remained in service a little longer, until 1915. It is a great pity that neither engine is represented in preservation.

There are several interesting points about the *Claud's* apart from the chimney. The original engines had what is described as a variable orifice blastpipe, manipulated by a rod operated from the cab. Is it possible that this is the ancestor of Churchward's jumper top blastpipe, a device designed to reduce the tendency of the fire to lift when working hard which worked automatically when the exhaust pressure was strong enough to lift a 'jumper' ring? Holcroft shows that a lot of discussion about this problem took place and implies that several devices were discussed before the final form was decided.[4] His suggestion of a separate pipe to lead away some of the exhaust steam was discarded in favour of the blastpipe device which I submit could have been arrived at by someone mentioning the blastpipe on the *Claud Hamilton's*. What is even more striking is that Wilson Worsdell fitted a variable blastpipe to his S class 4-6-0s. Patented with W.R.Preston in 1907 the purpose of this device was exactly the same as that of the Swindon jumper top blastpipe.[26]

The new roomier cab with side windows introduced with the *Clauds* which, with some modification remained the GER standard is also interesting. The impetus for this can only have been the North Eastern where such a cab had been standard for many years and clearly, Darlington and Stratford were in contact. However, Swindon rebuilt a *Badminton* 4-4-0 No.3297, *Earl Cawder* with just such a cab in 1903 at the same time as a large diameter round topped boiler was fitted. The North Eastern has been suggested as the influence behind this innovation.[27] While an obvious enough reaction it is I think incorrect. Russell tells us that the rebuild was carried out at the suggestion of F G Wright, Churchward's chief assistant and that the rebuilt engine was very similar to the *Clauds*. The first part of this statement is probably correct and the photograph reproduced in these pages shows that 3297 does indeed look like a double framed *Claud*. Yet, to point the finger at the *Clauds* cannot be right. What does seem to be without doubt is that the cab is much more Holden than Worsdell. Would it then be too much to suggest that Wright had in mind not the NER but *Decapod* built the previous year? The given raison d'etre of these locomotives was different but the principle of their design, high boiler output was not dissimilar.

Among the GWR's locomotives few are so significant yet so little known as the tiny 0-4-0T No.101 built in 1902 but which, reputedly was not taken into stock until a year later.[5/6] The construction of so small an engine, it had 13"x22" cylinders, 4½ inch piston valves actuated by Joy's valve gear and 3'8" driving wheels might well be open to debate. However, it was actually an experimental oil burner using the system developed on the GER. Holden's name is usually associated with this development but that of Arthur Morton Bell should also be noted.[28] Simply explained, the Holden system burnt waste from its oil gas plant at Stratford though in later years the oil was imported. Several locomotives were fitted with the equipment before the T19 which carried the name *Petrolea*, including other T19s. Why the GE decided that this particular engine and not an earlier one should carry the name, especially as naming was a considerable rarity on the line, is beyond me. Here then is another and perhaps astonishing example of apparent collaboration between Stratford and Swindon with the latter place prepared to pay a royalty on the Holden patent to try out the system developed by him and his associates. GWR No.101 did not however, have any effect on Swindon practice. It was the guinea pig in another experiment, coming out of the works in October 1903 with a Lentz corrugated cylindrical firebox. Later converted to burn coal it remained at Swindon as a shunting engine until withdrawn in 1911. Readers who were very young in the

47

1960s may be more familiar with 101 than they realise for a very popular train set of that period contained an engine clearly based on it.

In an industry where officers move from one company to another it is inevitable that the identity of one might well show itself on another. An extreme case of this is that of the Drummonds, Dugald and Peter who between them gave a distinctive and to all intents and purposes identical house style to no less than four major railways over a period of 35 years. Indeed, for many years a rail traveller in Scotland could catch almost any train and find it headed by a Drummond engine! More usual are the examples of engineers taking from one railway the mechanical and stylistic essentials of their former employer and combining them with the new one, Holden and Dean for example. Maunsell had no house style of his own, continuing both the Urie LSWR style and that which he had originated on the SE& C but which was actually a combination of Swindon, brought to Ashford by Pearson and Holcroft and Derby, sired by Clayton who, incidentally had earlier been at Swindon where he had been heartily disliked.[29] The influence of W.A.Stanier on the LMS needs no repeating here. Not so well known is the case of J.G.Robinson usually associated with his long tenure as CME of the Great Central.

Robinson served his apprenticeship at Swindon under Joseph Armstrong.[30] His father was Loco, Carriage and Wagon Superintendent at Bristol and Robinson's first job was to be appointed as his assistant in 1877. Seven years later he went over to Ireland, joining the Waterford & Limerick Railway. Great Western influence was strong in Ireland, both on what became the Waterford, Limerick & Western and the Great Southern & Western which later took it over. The GWR, anxious to maintain its influence, provided loans and rebates which gave the troubled Waterford line a stronger degree of financial security than might otherwise have been the case. There were also working arrangements between the GWR and the W&L for the Milford Haven-Waterford service. Robinson's predecessor had been Henry Appleby, another Swindon trained engineer whom he succeeded as Locomotive Superintendent in 1887; he recruited a further Swindonian, William Wood as his chief draughtsman and when he left to go to the Great Central in 1900 he was succeeded by William Gadd, yet another Swindon output. If from this the reader concludes that the WL&W was a 'little Great Western' that would not be far from the truth, certainly as far as its locomotives were concerned.

Robinson's first engines for the WL&W was a 2-4-0. With inside frames and cylinders but double frames for the leading wheels, a copper capped chimney, large brass dome and cab all reminiscent of Swindon, externally at least they would have looked completely at home across the Irish Sea. The driving wheels were 6' in diameter and the cylinders 17"x24" representative of the 717 class Armstrong engines built in the 70s. Eight were eventually built up to 1894 and enjoyed Ahrons good favour which was no mean achievement.[17] He recorded No.48, *Granston* as reaching 64 mph and added that they were usually rostered to the best trains on the Waterford - Limerick section and had a good deal in hand, *making the fastest running which I experienced in Ireland*. Among further Robinson engines for the WL&W were some 4-4-0s built in the mid-90s in which the Swindon influence was also very strong. A photograph in which this class figures looks to even fairly close study as though it was taken somewhere on the GWR.

Another aspect of the influence that Swindon had on Robinson's work was his use of components standardised not just on one particular class but across similar types. It appears that he was still receiving advice from his father while in office at Waterford but later on he came under the influence of S.W.Johnson. Thereafter the predominance of Swindon diminished. Interestingly he remained in touch with the GWR through his brother J.A. who was Divisional Loco superintendent of the Northern Division. Holcroft relates that a problem with the blastpipe first fitted to the 3601 class 2-4-2T inspired the 'Jar' as he was known to approach his brother for a solution. J.G. recommended a modification tried on 3629 but unfortunately it made no difference to the steaming of the engine.[4]

Of course there was another, more infamous association between Swindon and an Irish railway, in the person of E.A.Watson, recruited by Dean in 1896 as assistant-works manager. More is written of this gentleman elsewhere and it suffices here to say that in 1911 Watson became works manager at Inchicore on the Great Southern & Western Railway to which R.E.L.Maunsell had been newly appointed Locomotive Superintendent. Maunsell and Watson do not seem to have got on very well. Watson appears to have been continually declaring Swindon's pre-eminence in all locomotive matters prompting Maunsell's well known retort that 'Mr Watson seems to think that all Swindon geese are swans.' His chance to prove this came when he was appointed to succeed Maunsell in 1913. Previous to this date the largest GSWR express passenger engines had been 4-4-0s but Watson went straight to a four cylinder 4-6-0. There is no doubt that a six coupled locomotive had its appeal. Greater traction with a potential for greater power at less axle weight is not easily ignored. A brief examination of the GSWR operating situation suggests that a mixed traffic 4-6-0 with 6' driving wheels, two outside cylinders and outside valve gear, with high degree superheat to compensate for the low quality coal available in Ireland and designed so as to be available to work all but the lightest routes would have been economical to operate and provide potential for accelerated schedules. Unfortunately that is not how Watson saw it.

The fact that he had previously been at Swindon is often quoted as the origin of the four cylinder 400 Class, the first of which came out in 1914 but the influences of the American Locomotive Company where he received his training and the Pennsylvania Railroad on which he worked initially have been ignored. Though No.400 was reported to be fast and powerful and able to handle satisfactorily loads of up to 360 tons, the truth was that the design was a mess, the reason for which, as far as I can see, no one has provided any explanation. The relationship to the *Stars* was in some respects very strong but the defects had nothing to do with Swindon. The cylinders were laid out in the same de Glehn fashion and the general dimensions of the boiler which could obviously steam were not dissimilar. However, rather than the finely curved taper boiler/belpaire firebox of the *Stars*, the 400 Class had a domed parallel boiler with a belpaire firebox which was quite different. The superheater on 400 was twice the size of the Swindon superheater contributing to an overall heating surface that was about 9% greater. However, while the *Star* boilers were pressed to 225 lbs/sq.in., the 400 class were set at only 175 lbs, completely contrary to Churchward practice. The only explanation for this figure that I can see, was a wish to avoid the use of thicker boiler plates and thereby keep the weight down.

The worst aspects of the locomotive were in the steam distribution channels and valve design. The steam and exhaust pipes were concealed within the smokebox and frames and there were several complicated bends and joints which led to fractures and leaks. Reversing the layout of the gear, placing it outside the frames and driving the inside valves from rocking levers was a considerable improvement. But the cylinders, at 14"x26" and the 8" short travel piston valves hardly made for efficient running and indeed the 400 class were heavy on coal and water. The observer is entitled to ask how such an appallingly ill-designed locomotive could possibly be associated with anyone so closely familiar as Watson was with Churchward practice. There are two possible answers to that question. The first is that Watson left the detail design to the Inchicore Drawing Office and beyond broad outlines gave them a free hand with the job. Given what we know of the man that seems unlikely and leaves only the possibility that Watson, arrogant as he is supposed to be, did not believe that Inchicore could deliver the sophisticated machine that the Churchward locomotive certainly was and therefore ameliorated the principles to the level that he thought they could reach. Strange then that after he had gone, the GSWR acquired from the Woolwich Arsenal sets of unsold locomotives built there to the Swindon derived designs of R.E.L.Maunsell, advanced boiler design and all.

An even more extraordinary example of the form and style of Swindon being translated intact to another organisation was that of Frederick H Trevithick, son of Francis Trevithick who did his apprenticeship with the Cornish company of Hayle & Co before employment 'inside' at Swindon. He eventually became carriage & wagon superintendent of the London Division and then in 1883 was appointed chief traction engineer of the Egyptian State Railways.[14] From the start, with some double framed 2-2-2s built by Kitson's in 1889 he built locomotives so strongly redolent of Swindon that they might almost have been direct copies. Only the open sided sun-shade cab betokened a warmer clime than Wiltshire. Even more extraordinary were the batch of Trevithick 4-4-0s delivered by North British in 1901 which can only have resulted from close collaboration with Swindon. They were almost identical to the original Dean *Duke of Cornwall* class, the first of which had been built in 1897. The leading bogie had inside bearings and the cab roof was more appropriate to the climate of Egypt but apart from this the similarity is more than marked. The extended smokebox with its replica GWR copper capped chimney placed towards the rear of the smokebox, also a feature of the *Duke* class is staggering. Later versions with belpaire fireboxes and more conventional cabs were delivered from Henschall in 1906.

It is possible that Swindon also influenced the work, far away in Austria of that master engineer Carl Golsdorf. This was first aired in one of Hamilton Ellis's books[31] and, referred to by no one else, indeed, categorically denied by E.S.Cox,[32] I wrote and asked him about it. CHE replied: *My first inkling of the Churchward-Golsdorf connection came at Salzburg in 1930 when, not for the first time I visited the sheds. Though I was but 21 they were awfully interested to have an Englishman who knew anything about engines and wanted to know all about the* Englische Westbahn. *There was a taper-boilered Golsdorf engine by way of immediate scenery and that started the conversation. The young Chef said he knew there was a connection but who began it? I said that Americans began it.... He said, "But doktor Golsdorf and Mr Churchward knew each other." Much later I .... accompanied Sir William Stanier in a BBC broadcast and let him talk. I forget now what I knew already as opposed to what was new but the gist was this... Golsdorf visited England and homed on Swindon to see what Churchward was up to. The two men got on well. Golsdorf"'s first 2-6-2 express engine, with the taper boiler... came out in 1904, just when Churchward's Cities were bursting into flaming-fire.*[33] It would indeed be interesting to know more about this.

There are other cases, one which is fairly well known is that of Hugh le Fleming who, Swindon trained became a District Locomotive inspector on the Federated Malay States Railway and from 1929 to 1941 was an assistant to the chief mechanical engineer. In a long series of articles published in *The Locomotive* he reveals that several features of GWR origin found their way onto that system, some clearly at his suggestion. Much the most significant however, actually from 1914, long before he reached Malaya, was the construction of four six wheeled steam rail motors which he states were based on the GWR types.[34]

Astonishing though it is, Swindon influence even reached Australia through the work of Ernest E Lucy who had been a Swindon apprentice and became CME of the New South Wales Government Railways in 1911. The railways of Australia are a fascinating study in themselves and not just because the many railway museums around the country contain locomotives that are virtually identical to those that ran in this country and have long been scrapped or which, certainly in the case of New South Wales and ignoring the different loading gauge, could have been translated to these shores without anyone being very aware of their origin. This is not the place to go into that in detail but the reader will find most interesting the story of how the Metropolitan 4-4-0T was developed into a 4-4-0 express engine and laid the basic shape of the NSWGR locomotive, 4-6-0, 2-6-0 and 2-8-0 alike.[35] Thus it was that when Lucy arrived at Eveleigh Works in Sydney he found a situation that could not but be very familiar, engines with outside cylinders and inside valve gear, belpaire boilers and tall steam domes. His first engines mirrored these characteristics but the NN or 35 class as they were later designated were clearly intended to be different.

Their large belpaire fireboxes, short cone taper boilers, drumhead smokeboxes and inside valve gear differed from that used at Swindon but despite this they had more than a passing resemblance to Churchward's locomotives. Gifford H.Eardley wrote: *One recalls with pleasure the first glimpse of No.1027 ..... as it stood outside the Eveleigh coal stage one frosty morning in July 1914. For official photographic purposes this then new engine, on one side only had been painted Battleship Grey, set off by a black smokebox and chimney.* [No prizes for guessing where that idea came from.] *This striking ensemble was quickly replaced by a coat of regular black and for the next ten years or so the NN class engines handled most of the southern main line passenger traffic, being known* as the 'racehorses of the system.'[36] 'Racing' was relative of course since their maximum speed, officially at any rate was only 70 mph. Lucy made none of the mistakes that Watson did; the theoretical horse power of the 35 class at 60 mph was very high, backed by a steam pressure of 180lb but 2,782 sq ft. heating surface and a grate area of 30.8 sq ft, actually in excess of what Churchward provided for the 4 cylinder *Stars*. However, the secret of the success of the 35 class was almost certainly that most important aspect of Swindon design which Watson forgot, large diameter, long travel, valves; 10" and 5¾" respectively. The latter figure is not as great as came to be adopted on GWR 4-6-0s but at a time when valve travel generally was not more than about 4½ inches it represents a notable advance.

Eardley continues: ...*these engines were allotted to operate the famed* Caves Express *between Sydney and Mount Victoria in the 1930's. The late Malcolm Park timed these trains at 80 mph as they passed through Toongabbie, much to the disgust of the station newspaper vendor as he retrieved his stock in trade, blown in all directions by the slip stream!*[36] Despite this obvious success story there were several drawbacks to the design, some of which are interesting in the way they relate to Swindon engines. Neil Burnell tells me that: *the smokebox design was such that the accumulated ash blocked off some rows of tubes naturally reducing the heating surface and the steam supply, the inside Stephenson valve gear was a pain to both enginemen and fitters, the driving wheel balance gave a poor ride and consequently high hammer blow, the "fan" effect from the driving wheel spokes was like a vacuum cleaner drawing in dust into areas, for example, like the valve gear, and the ashpan design left a lot to be desired.*[37] From 1937 they were rebuilt with new frames and other alterations, the last was withdrawn from service in 1966. From 1925 the 35 class were replaced on the heaviest trains by Lucy's 36 class 4-6-0s, 75 of which were eventually built. On these engines the boiler pressure was raised to 200 lbs but for some reason they were originally built with round topped boilers, the more characteristic belpaire boiler being put on only from 1955 onwards. Interestingly no one whom I have consulted can offer a reason for this break with normal policy. Burnell continues: *strangely there is not a single mention* [in published sources] *as to why the belpaire boiler was not used which is so odd that I rang a friend in Sydney who used to work on the Dynamometer Car, to find out but he nor anyone else can answer your question as to why this change.*[37] It is interesting to read that in their later years the manual screw reversing gear was a subject of some union agitation, it being regarded as very awkward to use. One locomotive was fitted with a Giesl oblong ejector and has been subsequently preserved. In their later guise they resembled parallel boiler versions of Stanier's LMS 4-6-0s.

It may be that what is being related here is obvious enough. An engineer trained on one railway would inevitably take that concern's mechanical and stylistic forms to another. Yet it is a process that has been consistently denied over the years, with commentators emphasising the competition between workshops and the determination of most engineers to pursue an entirely independent line. The Association of Railway Locomotive Engineers, a purely private organisation quite separate and different from the Institution of Locomotive Engineers is often quoted as having achieved nothing but an agreement about fusable plugs. That is to deny the very real advantages that accrue from any form of discussion between professional peers. Probably none of them would admit that they got an idea from someone else whilst out walking on a ARLE excursion but I am more than prepared to believe that it happened. To take that further, there are cases of near litigation because of just that kind of thing, Gresley's conjucated valve gear, so similar to Holcroft's gear as to be the same, falls into precisely that category.

There is actually more circumstantial evidence to suggest this networking of ideas. The unrebuilt GER T19s were all scrapped between 1908 and 1913. The *Intermediate* engines, because they were so suitable for light branchline work remained in service much longer, surviving into BR days, the last, not taken out of service until 1960 has been preserved as the last 2-4-0 to run in Britain. Between 1902 and 1904, 21 of the T19s were rebuilt with larger boilers which gave them a very top heavy appearance leading to the appellation of the nickname 'Humpty Dumpties'. A further 60 T19s were rebuilt as 4-4-0s with larger boilers between 1905 and 1908. They continued to run as LNER class D13 until the last was scrapped in 1944. On the NER Wilson Worsdell carried out a similar process in 1906 rebuilding one of the old Fletcher 901 class with a large seemingly oversized boiler and a second engine as a 4-4-0. No more were rebuilt in this way but it is not out of the question that Holden's T19 rebuilds were the inspiration for these developments. Worsdell also used what I have called the Stroudley/Holden cylinder/valve layout in his R1 4-4-0s with piston valves. I think its a fairly safe assumption, on the evidence to conclude that a good many of the old locomotive engineers were in contact, the evidence of their work leaves no doubt about this. Further than that Swindon's 'web' was not just countrywide but world wide!

Notes & References
9) *British Steam Since 1900* - W.A.Tuplin
10) *Jackson's Oxford Journal* June 11 1853
11) *The Return of the Prodigal - Culhamite* - February 1899
12) *Customs connected with the bridge* - 'Bertie' Winfield - *Culham Club Magazine* June 1896
13) Albert Floyd: born 1886, a teacher in Potters Bar he was also a Company Sergeant Major in a volunteers regiment. Died 1965.
14) *A Biographical Dictionary of Railway Engineers* - John Marshall
15) *The GWR in the 19th century* - O S Nock
16) *Four Main Lines* - C. Hamilton Ellis
17) *Locomotive & Train Working in the Latter Part of the 19th century* - E.L.Ahrons
18) *The Engineer* - January 23rd 1885
19) *Express Trains English and Foreign* - Foxwell & Farrer
20) *Locomotives of the Great Eastern Railway 1862-1962* - C Langley Aldrich
21) *Backtrack* July 2006 - letter from Lynne Clifford
22) *The Trains we Loved* - C.Hamilton Ellis
23) Anyone who doubts this contention should go to Didcot on a sunny summer afternoon and look at the burnished metalwork on the GWR engines preserved there.

24) No.12 ran for a few months with an extended smokebox.
25) Quoted by Cecil J Allen in *The Great Eastern Railway.*
26) *The Worsdells: A Quaker English dynasty* - G.Hill
27) *Pictorial Record of Great Western Engines* - Volume One - J.H.Russell
28) *Backtrack* July 2006 - letter from
29) *The Great Western at Swindon Works* - A.S.Peck
30) *J.G.Robinson: A Lifetime's Work* - D.Jackson
31) *Pictorial Encyclopedia of Railways* - Hamilton Ellis
32) E.S.Cox - letter to the author - 18 April 1974
33) C Hamilton Ellis - letter to the author - 17 July 1974
34) *Malayan & FMS Railway Locomotives* - H.M.le Fleming - *Locomotive Magazine* 1954/ 56
35) *Some Classic Locomotives* - C.Hamilton Ellis
36) *Locomotive Guide: Thirlmere Railway Museum* - Gifford H. Eardley
37) Neil Burnell - correspondence with the author - September 2006

The portrait of James Holden is a computer generated wash drawing based on an old photograph.

Four
The origins of the Churchward Locomotive

George Jackson Churchward was born on 31 January 1857, at Rowes Farm, Stoke Gabriel, in Devon. He was the son of George and Adelina Churchward, descendants of two families who had been leaders in the county for many generations. Will Churchward was a Juror of the Court Baron of the manor of Paignton and in 1644 was fined 20/- for *opposing and disturbing the court*. At the same time that Will was making a nuisance of himself, Gabriel Jackson was a fellow juror and the two families have close family ties over the next two centuries. However, G. J. Churchward's family was only distantly related to the squires of Stoke Gabriel who lived at Hill House (now the *Gabriel Court Hotel*) and not as has been stated, a direct relative. The man who later became locomotive engineer of the GWR had two sisters, Mary, born in 1863 and Adelina, born in 1865. Strangely enough, none of the three ever married and all lived to very old age. Mary Churchward died in 1940 and Adelina in 1951. After education at Totnes Grammar School, the young Churchward became a premium apprentice on the South Devon Railway.

Today, Stoke Gabriel is considered to be one of the beauties of Devon and tourists flock in their thousands to see one of the most unspoilt parts of Devon. The visitor who knows something about the GWR will also go to the outskirts of the village, just off the Paignton Road, where Rowes Farm is still to be seen. Looking at the thatched roof of the farmhouse where he was born, with its white stucco walls, set in the middle of hedge lined fields, it is not

Rowe's Farm, Stoke Gabriel, photographed in 1974.

inappropriate to wonder what motivation brought a son of this house not only into engineering but to the very apogee of achievement and renown. All the traditions of the Churchward family were rooted here in this rich Devonian soil and it seems entirely out of character that this man should be any different. Yet it is possible to make a considered guess at what moved him. In the 1860s and 70s railway engineering, like advanced scientific research in the 21st century, was the career with a future for bright young men. The evidence is that the plodding nature of the countryside had no appeal for him and this is clearly implied in a letter that he wrote to a friend in the early 1890s in response to an invitation to a wedding reception. He is very dismissive of a place whose attractions he surmises have changed very little since his childhood and are, we can be of no doubt, hardly worth his attention.[9]

There are few records available which can tell us with any certainty just what form Churchward's apprenticeship took. However, enough has been written in the first chapter to indicate that it was little more than a process of familiarisation with workshop practice based on little in the way of co-ordinated planning. The long accepted method of locomotive repair was for individual engines to be allocated to a gang under a chargehand and they would go through all the stages of the job from stripping down to finishing except for specialist work such as valve setting. Apprentices would be allocated to one of these gangs and work with them, at first being only required to watch what was being done before being allowed to tackle successively larger jobs. Then would come a period of footplate work on the line before the really skilled jobs referred to were explained to the apprentice and he was trained to do them. Finally, came a year in the Drawing Office, where the pay was low, but which was the starting off point for appointments of responsibility in the department.[4]

The Grenville Steam Carriage as it is today.

It was during this period, in fact in 1875, that the 18 year old Churchward collaborated with another premium apprentice, Robert Neville Grenville in the design and construction of a steam road vehicle which happily, still survives in Bristol. How much of the design was due to the one and how much to the other is unknown and may even have been unknown to its builders who just worked together, completely indifferent to any claim on any part of the work. Since the Grenville-Churchward steam carriage is often mentioned but rarely described, a few words about it will be of interest. It was a three wheeled machine based on a frame of 2" 'I' section girders with a vertical boiler pressed to 120 lbs/ sq.in. lagged with mahogany strips and topped with a brass cap. There was originally a single vertical cylinder 5"x6" mounted on the boiler worked by conventional Stephenson link motion through a slide valve. The rear wheels were 4' in diameter and formed from sections of teak rimmed with iron. The 2'6" single front wheel steered by a tiller from the driving position almost directly above was of similar construction. An account exists which shows that it burned about 6lb of coal per mile and ran at an average speed around 6 mph. This, it should be remembered took into account any stops en-route, for example to take water or for 'blow ups'. It continued to be used until 1897 though perhaps not surprisingly Churchward seems to have lost all interest in it.[10]

The outline of Churchward's career over the next few years is well known; after the SDR was taken over by the GWR he was transferred to Swindon and soon put with Joe Armstrong, son of the late Locomotive Superintendent on the design of what, with modification, became the standard GWR vacuum brake. 'Young Joe' as he was always known is himself an interesting study in personality. Joe's talent and ability are often mentioned. Holcroft tells us that his papers show an original and enquiring mind and that he anticipated many of the later developments in chimney and blast pipe design.[6] Though as far as I am aware no one has subsequently seen these documents, his appointment as Assistant Locomotive Superintendent of the Northern Division of the GWR and Manager of the workshops at Stafford Road, Wolverhampton, at the early age of 29 tend to suggest that he did indeed have exceptional ability. The historian must be careful in judging personality but it is possible that Armstrong himself could not cope with his own ability. He was a convivial man but unmarried and plagued by ill-health, all suggestive of some kind of personality defect. It follows, and there is evidence to support this, that be could not get on with his aged uncle George Armstrong, the dominating Northern Division Locomotive Superintendent.[11] The outcome was an appalling tragedy. In the early hours of 1st January 1888, Armstrong committed suicide on the line near the bridge over Stafford Road. Some of this has been known for many years, particularly when Holcroft's book on the Armstrong family was published in 1953 but at that time, members of the family who had known 'Young Joe' were still living and Holcroft omitted to mention the suicide. What has never been revealed before but which throws an altogether different light on this tragedy is that Joe took out an insurance policy on his life immediately before the suicide. We can only conclude that the full details of Joe's personality disorder will never positively be known; maybe the 21st century would have treated him with a little more kindness. Interestingly, the fact of the suicide circulated in anecdotal form on the GWR as late as the 1950s and occasionally even became connected with Churchward himself who died in a similar way, though entirely accidentally, in November 1933.

'Young Joe' Armstrong
Drawn by Chris Seymour and based on the well-known photograph.

"If your Uncle Joe had lived, I should not be occupying this house today, he was a far cleverer man than I."[6] Thus did Churchward speak of Young Joe; if, as seems likely, this is more than just Churchward being generous to the relative of a friend it raises many interesting questions. It was widely assumed that he and not Churchward would succeed Dean as Locomotive Superintendent but it is impossible to make any assumption as to what kind of engines he would have designed.

In 1882 Churchward became Assistant Carriage Works Manager and in 1885 succeeded James Holden as Manager, staying ten years before being appointed Assistant Locomotive Works Manager and four months later, Manager. In recent years a good deal has been written about this change-over period. Churchward was appointed chief assistant in 1897 but before this date, for twelve years after Holden had left Dean acted without such an officer. We now know that Dean's mind had been going for some time and that the Board, aware of this, in an act of surprising magnanimity allowed him to continue in office but with Churchward taking the major day-to-day decisions, even though he continued to attend Board and Committee meetings and, to all intents and purposes, hold full office.[12] It was not unusual for the locomotive superintendent to be a figurehead, 'Wainwright's locomotives' are said to have been designed, in actuality by his chief draughtsman, Robert Surtees[13] and even Stanier's, according to some authorities, largely by T.F.Coleman. Dean's retirement and Churchward's succession are not even formally acknowledged in the Minutes of the company's Locomotive Committee and this tends to suggest that as far as the Board was concerned Churchward was already the Locomotive Superintendent. Churchward's behaviour during this period was beyond criticism, the situation had all the ingredients for a major display of frustrated impatience but there is not the remotest suggestion of this in the evidence available to us, rather the contrary.

In accordance with normal procedure Churchward moved into the house that had become accepted as the Loco Superintendent's official residence, the large dwelling known as *Newburn*. It has long been thought that the house was originally built for Joseph Armstrong but Peck believes that it was actually built for Archie Sturruck, Gooch's assistant.[12] In the event since Collett declined to live there, Churchward was its last occupant remaining in residence until his death in 1933.

It is quite clear that Churchward's design policy evolved out of the conventional Swindon practice of the day and was not as is sometimes suggested a sudden revolutionary break with the past. Previous historians have traced Churchward's influence at Swindon back to the incorporation of the belpaire firebox into the *Badminton* 4-4-0s of 1897 and I am inclined to accept this as pretty well true. Nonetheless I do not believe that when he was transferred from the carriage works to locomotives he had any more idea of how to progress than any other young forward thinking engineer. It may have been seeing Dean's unsure design work which drove the young GJC to make a study of practice elsewhere, in particular, in the USA and Europe. But I am not convinced that this influence was crucial in the formative stage. What was crucial was Churchward's ability to weld together the talents of his subordinates to form a team of outstanding innovators. This has been mentioned before but it is worth noting again especially in view of the last paragraph. The names usually associated with Churchward are those of H.C.King, works manager from 1902 to 1913, G.H.Pearson, son of the Pearson who built the Bristol and Exeter's 9 footers and J.W.Cross, these two forming a very important and as it was to turn out, crucial test team. G.H.Burrows was chief draughtsman and C.B.Collett works manager. E.A.Watson had received his training in America

Newburn

G.J.Churchward in the lounge at *Newburn*.
A date for this photograph is unavailable but his appearance suggests that it is from early rather than later in his term of office.

with ALCO and had worked on the Pennsylvania Railroad but just what he contributed to the development of the Churchward locomotive is unknown. There is some reason to believe that he was unpopular at Swindon and that senior management were relieved at his departure for Ireland.[14] The name that tends to be missing from accounts of these developments is that of F.G.Wright who was actually appointed Churchward's chief assistant in 1903. Holcroft tells us that: *Churchward interested himself in locomotive, carriage and wagon matters, leaving the rest to Wright*[4]. This gives the wrong impression because Wright was instrumental in at least one major locomotive experiment and was responsible for the design and construction of all the Churchward running sheds including that at Old Oak. More will be written about this gentleman later in this chapter and in the next.

However unlikely it may seem, it is, I submit, possible that Churchward would have continued to build double framed locomotives but for the fact that the layout of cylinders and frames on express 4-6-0s was virtually preordained by certain unavoidable facts, underpinned by his experience with the 'Kruger' 4-6-0. This was a period of rapid change both in Britain and abroad. Increasing train weights were matched by a demand for greater speed set off in part by the Scottish races. The development of other forms of transport were putting steam on its mettle; as early as 1901 a German electric locomotive attained 101 mph and this achievement was soon surpassed.[15] The requirement for locomotives larger and more powerful than the standard British 4-4-0 and 0-6-0 was unavoidable. That meant, at base, the development of more powerful boilers. The Caledonian *Dunalastair* is often predicated as the harbinger of this transformation, a contention with which I do not agree. It was actually smaller than the Gooch *Iron Duke* and by virtue of its poor grate area was a veritable coal gobbler. I would pick out the Jones Highland 4-6-0 as the starting point for the new form of passenger engine. It is true that the Jones Goods was not a great deal bigger than the original *Dunalastair* in terms of boiler dimensions but, in that it was a six coupled locomotive it was the real indication of the way development had to go. It also had outside cylinders which as we shall see were more or less essential for express passenger 4-6-0s.

Interestingly the next 4-6-0 was Dean's double framed freight engine, No.36 unofficially dubbed 'Crocodile' completed in 1896. In this strange combination of broad and narrow gauge practice the grate area was 30½ square feet, quite a significant figure for the time and possible because the inside frames stopped short of the firebox permitting the use of a 5'6" wide box. We have no reports of any work done by this engine and it was scrapped after less than ten years in service but I suspect that it steamed well and performed effectively. Three years later came 4-6-0 No.2601 which has come down to us as the 'Kruger', so named by railwaymen incensed by imperialist anger at the activities of the Dutch Boers in South Africa and only too ready to apply their hated enemy's name to perhaps the only truly ugly locomotive the GWR ever built.[16] The cylinders on 2601 were an early trial with piston valves and longer stroke; a 28" stroke gave throws of 14" and failures of its crank axle convinced Churchward, already thinking in terms of 30" that the cylinders should be outside where the crank could be placed straight onto the driving wheel. There was another reason why outside cylinders became necessary and it is the underlying reason why there is a marked similarity in the appearance of the early two cylinder express 4-6-0s built in Britain.

Among such locomotives built around this time were Worsdell's S class (1900) Peter Drummond's *Castles* (1900) and the McIntosh Nos. 49 & 50 later associated with *Cardean*, built in 1903. The Caley engines were by far the bigger with an overall engine length between six and ten feet longer than the others. This was a direct result of having the cylinders inside the frames. With larger driving wheels and inside cylinders the drive has to be on the leading axle, this is unavoidable, the expedient of inclining the cylinders is not possible because there is no space under the boiler to do that. The knock-on effect of driving on the front coupled axle is that the length of the boiler becomes overlong and this was undoubtedly the case with 49/50 which despite a larger grate had a boiler that was simply an extension to that fitted to the *Dunalastair* class. On the later Robinson *Sir Sam Fay* type the problem was almost certainly insufficient grate area. Thus outside cylinders became the norm with six coupled express engines. That locomotive engineers did not much like doing this is evidenced by the fact that they continued to build in the traditional way when producing new classes of 4-4-0. It is to me extraordinary that the last such engine should appear as late as 1926 in the Maunsell L1.

Generally speaking, in 1900 the locomotives running on Britain's railways were small and conservatively proportioned, a situation that was replicated in almost all its colonies with the exception of Canada where American forms predominated. Even on the 5'3" and standard gauge lines in south eastern Australia medium powered locomotives typical of British practice continued to be built almost to the end of steam itself. So marked is this fact that a visitor to the North Williamstown Railway Museum in Melbourne would be forgiven for thinking he has wandered via a time warp back into Edwardian England.

The situation in Europe was very different, British design characteristics were almost unknown as was the archetypical British locomotive. At the end of the century only in the low countries, Belgium and Holland were such machines to be found. In Holland the influence of Beyer Peacock was profound and long lasting, a visitor to the Dutch railway museum in Utrecht has almost the same reaction as going to North Williamstown, for here will be found British locomotive types that have long passed away and of which no examples remain in preservation. New Dutch steam building ended early in a bar framed 4 cylinder 4-6-0 with 16½"x26" cylinders, 6'0¾" driving wheels, 200lb boiler pressure, and 34 sq ft grate, a potentially powerful locomotive especially given the Dutch topography and which looked as though it had been directly copied from a British line right down to the inside valve gear. In Belgium British locomotives were copied directly despite a generally more nationalistic locomotive policy. Following the purchase of engines of the Caledonian *Dunalastair* type Belgium built its own versions and improved and enlarged the basic design in a manner that the Caley never did though without upsetting the overall likeness. In the land of its designer the Belpaire firebox found little or no use but next door, in Holland it became standard.

These two countries did not conform to the European norm which was for larger engines, with more extensive use of 4-4-2 and 4-6-0 types for passenger trains and 0-8-0 and 2-8-0 for goods traffic, with compounding much the preferred system. The compound never found favour in Britain and we could devote pages to the reasons. The larger continental loading gauge made it easier to design well proportioned components and accounts for the fact that European locomotives in general were second only in size to those of North America but that does not explain why compounding was not deployed more generally in Britain. It seems to have been in part at least the innate conservatism of the British who like everything to be simple, straight forward and free of what is often seen to be unnecessary complexity. It was such conservatism that fatally undermined the Riddles Standard designs 50 years later. Another reason must be that French enginemen, *mechanicien* as they were termed, were much more highly trained than their British counterparts to whom the complexities of compounds built for operation in different expansion modes would have been another 'damned contraption'. Certainly there was nothing inherently wrong with the compound, the GWR's French compounds ran satisfactorily for nearly 30 years a fact often ignored when comment is being made on the Webb and Midland Smith compounds.[17]

On the continent, compounding was generally the norm on locomotives intended for fast or heavy passenger running and this was especially so after the first de Glehn 4-4-0 type appeared in 1891. This was not the first of the compounds associated with the name of the chief engineer of the *Society Alsaciene Constructions Mechaniques*, his first venture in this direction dated from 1885. However, the 4-4-0 built in collaboration with Gaston du Bousquet for the Nord in that year was the foundation stone of what within a few short years was the archetypical French express locomotive, in its best known form as a 4-4-2 but later as 4-6-0 and 4-6-2. Eventually the type spread to Germany, Spain, Portugal, Italy and even to Egypt, many of these derivatives being built outside France, particularly in Germany. The secret of the breed lay partly in well designed cylinders laid out in such a way as to provide good balance, boilers with adequate heating surface, high pressure and appropriately sized grates but also in the very ingredients which made them unsuitable in Britain, the complex arrangements for starting and running which enabled the driver to maintain high power output with an economical consumption of coal and water even in adverse conditions. Writing in 1903 Lake said: *Four-cylinder compound engines of* [the 4-6-0] *type are especially to the fore on the French railways, and some of the fastest and heaviest passenger trains are worked by them, particularly on the Eastern Railway, where the type has been developed to something near maximum proportions.*[18]

On the Austrian Railways in 1900 Carl Golsdorf was coming to the end of the first period of his term as locomotive engineer in which he turned out two cylinder compounds varying from 4-4-0 to 4-6-0 for passenger and 2-8-0 and 0-10-0 for freight work. This was before his celebrated taper boiler 2-6-2 and 2-6-4 locomotives appeared but already we can see the ingredients of good design in boiler and cylinder dimensions and note how high power was attained despite weight restrictions over most of the system.

Compounds were built by most of the pre-Reichsbahn German railways for express passenger trains, though here simple engines were often preferred for secondary passenger and freight work. Many of these German compounds were on the de Glehn principle, others had the cylinders in line abreast, the high pressure cylinders outside and all four connecting rods driving on the same axle. 4-4-0 compounds were general, the first compound atlantics had two cylinders and were introduced on the Palantinate Railway in 1898. Designed to haul heavy expresses between Basle and Rotterdam and between Berlin and Strasbourg they were expected to take 220 tons at about 40 mph on 1:100 inclines or about 55-60 mph on the level. To British eyes they are rather peculiar looking engines with inside cylinders necessitating manipulation of the front section of the frames and bogie frames. The trailing wheel was provided with a double frame while the driving wheels had a slotted valance which looks like another section of double frame. The cab had a deep 'v'-front. In Switzerland there were 2 cylinder compound 4-4-0s with inside cylinders which had more than a passing similarity to the traditional British passenger engine.

In 1902 the Baden State Railway introduced four-in-line compound 4-4-2s (IId class) with the high pressure cylinders activated by piston valves and the low pressure from side valves. With 6'10" driving wheels it was claimed that they could achieve 1,600 to 1,850 horse power. The Saxon State Railway had four cylinder de Glehn compound atlantics with different types of valve gear for high and low pressure cylinders. This was not as uncommon as it was in Britain, the Prussian 4 cylinder compound atlantic introduced in 1904 was similarly equipped. This type was compounded on the von Borries system and was fitted with a Pielock superheater, basically a box of retarding baffles located in the dome; though it was claimed to be successful very little is heard of it thereafter or of other primitive superheaters such as those located in the smokebox and subject to blockage from ash deposits.

The German 4-6-0 came onto the scene with the introduction in 1904 of the Bavarian P3/5 class which continued to be built until 1921. These were four cylinder compounds built by Maffei of Munich in that company's normal pattern, with the cylinders in line, the low pressure outside and two sets of valve gear. According to Cox they were not noted for speed though the dimensions suggest that they ought to have been capable of it: the cylinders were 13¾" and 22¼"x26", boiler pressure, 213 lbs/in. grate 28.2 sq.ft and the total heating surface 2,247sq.ft.[19] The advantage of this design was ease of maintenance made possible by the use of forged bar frames and high running boards. As a policy the Prussians built both compound and simple locomotives in roughly similar numbers until the mid-1900s when they dropped the compound altogether. This review is supposed to centre on the turn of the century but it is not irrelevant to mention the Prussian P8 4-6-0 introduced in 1906 and originally intended as an express passenger engine which, modified as experience dictated became perhaps continental Europe's most successful mixed traffic 4-6-0. With 5'8¾" driving wheels and other dimensions similar, they were very much the equivalent of the British Class 5 4-6-0.

Thinking back to some of the criticisms of standardisation made in Britain, that it was impossible to design locomotives that could be operated on more than one railway, the Prussian P8 suggests that furthermore, it would have been possible to build locomotives that could have operated successfully in most European countries, even allowing for the difference in loading gauge. It could be argued that operational differences dictated that continental railways required larger locomotives but it could be counter argued that in Britain, even in recent times we have been unwilling to raise the average speeds of our trains and utilised only medium sized motive power. If one is looking for a general contrast between continental and British locomotives that goes beyond the prejudiced complaint about the complex and fussy appearance of engines supposedly criss-crossed by pipe runs and levers, then compounding is perhaps the most important side of the story. But the other is this matter of the general dimensions of locomotives. While in Britain the norm at the turn of the century was for cylinders at about 18"x24" or 26", boilers with around 1,500 sq. ft heating surface with pressure at no more than 180 lbs and grates at about 23 sq. ft, on the continent the same components were appreciably bigger. Of course, indigenous factors all had something to do with this. A recurrent feature of steam locomotive operation is the quality of coal available and large boilers and grates were considered essential to overcome the problem of poor quality coal. Phillipson says that the good bituminous coal available in the Britain was best burnt in a deep narrow grate *with a relatively small grate area*, a contention which may explain why, at least until the 1940s inadequate grates were a recurrent failing.[20] Another consideration was a country's topography. Spain is a case in point, the 0-8-0 first appeared in the 1860s and there were eventually 100s of them, joined in the 20th century by similar numbers of 2-8-0s and 4-8-0s, the type being a response to the mountainous nature of much of the rail system.[21] The observer of the British railway scene in 1900 cannot escape the notion that as a general thing continental engineers displayed a greater enterprise than was to be found among their British compatriots.

The other important sphere of steam design was of course, North America. Here the British influence lay at the very foundation of steam locomotive development, in the Bury locomotives exported to the USA in the 1830s. Norris took the basic Bury 2-2-0 with its bar frames, inclined outside cylinders and haycock firebox and developed it into the 4-2-0 and later the 4-4-0. Joseph Harrison's *Hercules* of the Beaver Meadows Railroad built in 1837, a direct development of the Bury/Norris design laid the foundation of the typical American 4-4-0 with its three point suspension which overcame the problem of the rough tracks with which many US railways were first built. The haycock firebox gave way to what was known as the 'wagon top' firebox, a cylindrical raised steam space above the top of the inside firebox. Extending above the level of the boiler top it necessitated a coned back ring to make a flush connection. James Mulholland on the Philadelphia and Reading was among the first to lower the cylinders to the horizontal position placing the valves on top driving inside link motion. Another development due to Mulholland was the 'swallowtail' firebox in which the coned back ring of the boiler was combined with a slope on the top of the firebox back towards the cab thus creating a steam space at the hottest part of the boiler. Bar frames were pretty much universally employed since rolling mills capable of turning out suitable plates were not available. Bar frames and particularly repairs to them could be made in a forge with little requirement for sophisticated equipment, hence their use. Mathias Baldwin, founder of the famous Philadelphia locomotive construction company, in 1858 initiated the front end layout in which the outside cylinders and steam chest were cast as one with the smokebox saddle. Though this did have its advantages, it meant that extension frames had to be fitted ahead of the casting to take the leading bogie or pony truck. No one aware of GWR main frame construction needs to be told about the knock-on effect of this practice, the oscillation caused by the motion interfered with the rigidity of the extension and most American locomotives featured strengthening bars running from the smokebox to the front of the running platform. They were sometimes to be seen even on locomotives with front bogies.

Thus came into being the typical American locomotive, bar frames, two outside cylinders with slide valves above and inside link motion and wagon top or taper boiler. There were very many different types that conformed to this general layout, it was developed into the 4-6-0 and 2-8-0 types and can be identified in American locomotives built even in relatively recent times. Early American locomotives were not overly powerful but by 1900 saturated boilers with around 2,500 sq. ft heating surface, pressed to 200lbs/sq.in with much larger grates were becoming common. Wide rather than longer fireboxes allowed for larger grates. The literally huge loading gauge made for rapid advances on these figures unhindered as in Europe by restrictions on axle weight. The Pennsylvania D16 4-4-0s of 1895 for instance had 23½ tons on the driving axles which by 1901 had expanded to nearly 30 tons in the E2 atlantics. However, the drive to heavier locomotives was not completely unrestrained. All-steel boilers which had the double advantage of more uniform expansion and contraction and weighed less had become common.[18] Superheating had not yet appeared in 1900 though large diameter piston valves were coming into use.

Compounding was relatively rare though the Vauclain system in which the high and low pressure cylinders drove the driving wheels through a common crosshead had wide usage at one time. Possibly as a result of reports of Churchward's doing so, the Pennsylvania imported a de Glehn compound in 1904. After thoroughly testing it the PRR brought out their E28 4-cylinder compound. Tank engines were uncommon in North America and were usually very different to those found in Europe being back and well tanks like Pearson's 9 footers. In Britain next to no attempt was made to improve the driver's view of the line ahead of the locomotive but in the USA builders tackled the problem with far greater resolve producing several types of cab-in-front locos. Indeed the Southern Pacific RR was at one time renowned for precisely this type of set up. Bulleid's *Leader* was not the only or even the best cab-in-front locomotive to have been built, examples were constructed in Europe as well as in America. What is interesting is that today, they are quite unnecessary for a well protected CCTV camera placed on the smokebox door would give the driver all the view ahead that he requires. Indeed, he could drive 'blind', without any resort to his own eyes at all. Another innovation was the 'camelback' type, with the driving cab placed over the boiler in front of the firebox. This had several variants on roads like the Erie, Baltimore and Ohio and the Leigh Valley. With this arrangement the fireman was left in the usual position but with only a scanty shelter from the elements.

Constructional finish, as one might suppose in a country where the demands of the outback made rugged functionalism important tended to be somewhat rough and ready by comparison with the highly finished products of British railways. This was one of the complaints levelled at the American Baldwin 2-6-0s imported into Britain at about this time. More importantly they were poor steamers due to inadequate grate area and the bar frames gave trouble, cracking next to the horn plates where it was difficult to make repairs.

Perhaps the most important contrast between American railways and those in Europe, particularly British companies was that in the United States railways more usually bought in their motive power from outside manufactures. Thus, though most lines lacked a corporate identity, the manufacturers supplied basically the same designs to the different railways so that there grew up a form of standardisation that was not restricted to one company. The major exception to this was the Pennsylvania Railroad which 100 years ago was one of the foremost and also most individualist of American railways. In the first place it built almost all its locomotives in its own Altoona works at Schnecterdy in Pennsylvania. Furthermore, like the Great Northern (USA) and the loco-builder, Brooks it made almost universal use of the belpaire firebox. American railways generally, right up till the end of steam construction favoured the round topped firebox with recognisably the same basic wagon top design originating 90 years previously. On the PRR however, Axel Vogt the Swedish born engineer who was head of mechanical design from 1887 until 1919 was responsible for the introduction of the belpaire firebox which as later developed into the 'Wootton' wide bottomed type marked it out even as late as 1944 in the striking Duplex 4-4-4-4 T1 class.

Beyer Peacock had been using the belpaire firebox for locomotives intended for export for some thirty years before the GWR took it up. It had first found favour in Britain with Pollit on the Manchester Sheffield & Lincolnshire clearly because Pollit's chief draughtsman William Thornley had come from Beyer Peacock whose Gorton Foundry was only just across the road from the MS&L's locomotive shops. Churchward made visits to see how foreign railways operated[4] and also encouraged his junior staff to do so;[22] we are also told that he was on terms with Alfred W. Gibbs the PRR's General Superintendent Motive Power and Axel Vogt's closest colleague.[7][23] This almost certainly accounts for the take-up of the belpaire firebox at Swindon. Churchward readily appreciated that a constraint on the trend to larger boilers was the need to provide a steam dome. The constraint on a domeless boiler was that the mouth of the steam collector pipe was close to the water level, with the ensuing difficulties already discussed in chapter one. The large steam space at the front of the square belpaire firebox compensated for the omission of the dome and with the collector pipe brought right back to this point, the usual difficulty with the domeless boiler was also avoided. However, in 1899 American influence at Swindon was, I think limited and only became significant when problems were experienced over the following 18 months with the new boilers.

No one seems to have recognised that the 'Kruger' 4-6-0, the last of the Badminton 4-4-0s, 3310, *Waterford* and 5'8" 4-4-0 3352 *Camel* all completed within weeks of each other in 1899 were not separately devised designs but actually the then current level of development for freight, express passenger and secondary passenger engines. Together with 4-4-0 pannier tank 1490 built in 1898 these locomotives represent Churchward's initial approach to a standard plan. The 4-6-0 passenger engine was clearly in his mind, but this must have been his starting point. All three tender engine designs had domeless Belpaire fireboxes though 'Kruger' with what could have been a 14' barrel was provided with a combustion chamber 3'6" in length. *Waterford* was otherwise a standard *Badminton* with the usual inclined inside cylinders and undermounted slide valves. *Camel* is significant in being the first Swindon engine to be provided with a drumhead smokebox which rested on a separate saddle rather than be combined with it. The old practice led to disturbance of the air tightness in the smokebox caused by motion vibration. As we have already noted 'Kruger' was very different, having piston valves 8½" in diameter mounted above cylinders inclined at 1:7 and with single slide bars. I am convinced that the difficulties experienced with this engine led Churchward to give American practice a closer examination. If 4'7½" driving wheels and a long stroke made outside cylinders necessary, how much more so was this with 6'8" drivers and 30" stroke. Thus the layout of the Churchward 4-6-0 was due both to experience and to necessity.

Like all good innovators should, before proceeding he examined what was being done elsewhere. We have seen that British engineers preferred to put their cylinders inside the frames where the oscillation caused by the motion could, they believed be better controlled. Another discouragement to outside cylinders was that a weakness was sometimes caused in the attachment of the cylinders to the frames causing them to work loose. Churchward could readily see that the extra fore and aft force caused by a 30" stroke might well accentuate this problem and he thus imported into Swindon the layout common in America in which the cylinders and valves on one side were cast as one, the casting incorporating one half of the smokebox saddle; the two halves were then bolted back to back. This dealt with one problem but caused another, as we shall see. While this innovation was being studied, Churchward moved cautiously forward. *Achilles* single wheeler 3021 was fitted with wooden templates on either side and run round the system to check the clearances.[4] Reassured on this point he directed the drawing office in the creation of 4-6-0 No.100. Many writers have referred to the startling appearance of this locomotive which among myriad high born ladies clothed in double frames, it appeared like a scantily clad female at a grand Edwardian *soirée*. However, this is only true in the context of Swindon. The Jones Goods, Ivatt's large Atlantics, Robinson's 4-4-2s and 4-6-0s if not Worsdell's S class all proclaimed the coming of the miniskirt.

If in its appearance engine No.100 may be regarded as the first clear sign of Churchward's locomotive development coming to fruition, then it must be added that in some respects it was a mess. The construction of locomotives with the *Camel* type of domeless belpaire boiler and the reboilering with it of older classes had continued apace. By 1902 there were many examples on *Bulldogs* and *Atbaras* to say nothing of certain other smaller classes. However, the fact of the matter is that it was not a particularly good steamer. Another problem was cracking at the front corners of the firebox and on No.100 both problems were particularly marked. Pearson and Cross were put onto exploration of these problems and it was at this point that the crucial American innovation was brought to Swindon. The steaming problems were put down to poor circulation which was corrected by introducing the wagon top or taper boiler and combining that with widened water legs in the firebox.[24] The characteristic swallowtail firebox in which both the top and the sides of the firebox were tapered towards the cab, the overall shape being very carefully designed came in with these developments. None of this is particularly new nor is the belief that the shape was derived from an Illinois Central Railroad boiler. What is not so well known is that the boiler, as illustrated by Cook[25] appears to belong to 4-4-0 No.961 built by the Brooks Locomotive Company in November 1896. This link has never been made before and I only chanced upon it at college many years ago when writing an assignment for my final exams. But it is unmistakable. 961 is a very ordinary American 4-4-0 with bar frames, half frame cylinder/ valve casting, slide valves and inside link motion but what sets it apart is a boiler and firebox ensemble which in every respect, including dimensions is that of the boiler booked into the Swindon drawing office.

Excellent boiler design was not the sole ingredient of the Swindon success story. Higher steam pressures tended to push the change from balanced slide to piston valves which could provide more rapid and economical steam use and here again Churchward went one better by replicating the American tendency towards large diameter long travel valves. Eventually Swindon's 2 cylinder engines used 10" diameter valves with in some cases 7" travel, in conjunction with large inlet and outlet ports. Setting up the valve gear became crucial and a highly skilled job. However, the first piston valves used at Swindon were not overly successful and it was 1910 before an entirely satisfactory, American, type was standardised. In one respect No.100 differed from all later Swindon 2 cylinder 4-6-0s in that the valves were placed closer together though not so close as in the ALCO layout where they were right under the smokebox saddle permitting a direct run for the steampipes into the steam chest. With the system eventually adopted by Churchward, the feed pipe ran from the smokebox via a right angle bend opening into large steam chests placed further out from the centre. It has been suggested that the introduction of direct outside steam pipes was not an improvement on this layout because the capacity of the admission to the steam chest was reduced.[26] Since the more direct steam passage is advantageous, I think we can conclude that it is a case of swings and roundabouts.

The downside to the Churchward-American cylinder layout was that it tended to concentrate weight at the leading end of the engine. More important was the break in the run of the mainframes from the front buffer beam to the engine drawbar. Just as in American practice, it was necessary for an extension frame to be fitted ahead of the casting to take the leading bogie or pony truck so on Swindon engines, a rectangular slab had to be attached at one end to the buffer beam which, running below the casting was attached to the front of the main frame behind the cylinders. This was a weakness, the slab extension could become loosened or deformed particularly on 5'8" and 4'7½"engines with a pony truck where it was not possible to fit straight extensions, and necessitated the fitting of the supporting struts characteristic of American locomotives, though on GWR engines they were not set at as steep an angle. Though I have made the claim myself this set-up does not preclude the use of outside valve gear. In North America locomotives which began life with inside gear and slide valves were converted to outside gear and piston valves while keeping their basic front-end design features.[27] It takes seconds to ascertain that this was possible on GWR engines by examining any preserved *Hall* and noting that all that is required is for the rocking shaft to be turned outwards and extended into the vertical plane of the piston rod, with the gear set up from that point, by no means an expensive or complicated change. Engines with 4'7½" driving wheels would have been a slightly bigger problem but complete rebuilding was not necessary even here.

If the earlier contention that *Waterford*, 'Kruger' and No.1490 represented Churchward's thinking in 1899, the advancements that he had made by 1903 were immense. 'Kruger' was a failure but was the initial impetus which led through No.100 to the taper boiler No.98, the ancestor of all GWR 2 cylinder 4-6-0s and also 2-8-0 No.97, as developed, arguably the finest freight engine ever built. It is unnecessary to record that these epoch making locomotives were based on the use of standardised components, one cylinder and two boiler designs. O.V.S Bulleid is said to have deprecated standardisation on this scale as being a hindrance to technical progress and the criticism is valid when laid against designs that are not very advanced. But Churchward's locomotives were something in the order of 20 years in front of anything being done elsewhere in Britain. Standardisation of components was not invented by Churchward, both Gooch and Joseph Armstrong insisted when placing orders for locomotives that templates were followed and the latter is on record on at least one occasion as upbraiding his brother George for not following them.[28] Yet, to repeat, it is in the development of advanced machines that standardisation becomes so valuable.

The other member of the trio mentioned above, 4-4-0 pannier tank 1490 was also a failure. Indeed, so much so that it was quickly sold out of service. The next design to be essayed in this area was a 2-4-2T, a type that was quite common on the North Western and Lancashire & Yorkshire but a new departure for Swindon. No.11 built in 1900 with 5'2" driving wheels, 180 lbs boiler pressure and 17"x24" cylinders had a domeless belpaire boiler, inside cylinders and frames and a high arched overall cab. Though described as such it was not initially a success. The piston valves gave trouble, leading to their replacement, and there was what might almost be called the usual steaming problem with these boilers, finally eradicated, after some fruitless fiddling with the smokebox arrangements only with the fitting of taper boilers.

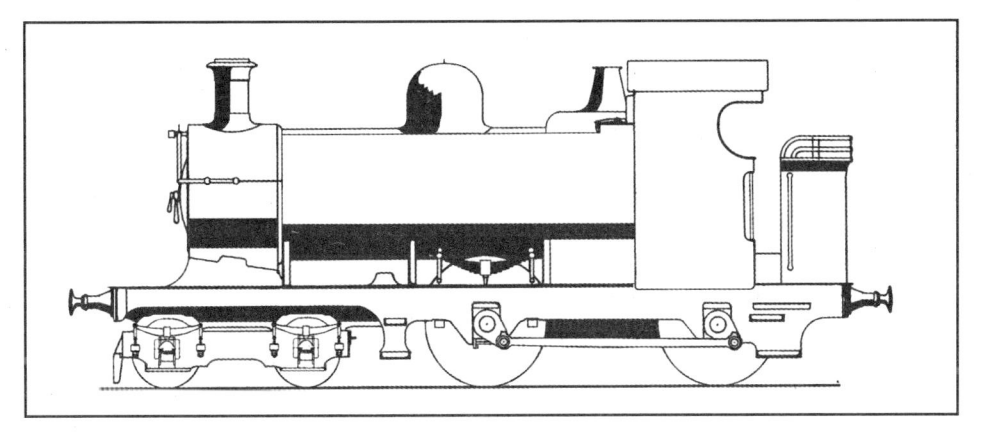

What is of interest to our examination of origins and derivations is the suggestion that the 3600 class were a half way house to the 2-6-2T. I am not certain that this was actually true. For a start, the 2-4-2Ts were intended for the same kind of work as was performed by the Armstrong 2-4-0 and 0-4-2 tanks and were essentially passenger engines. I would dare to suggest that the concept of the 2-4-2 wheel notation was 'borrowed' from Crewe and Horwich where the type was well regarded. The outside cylindered 2-6-2 tank of which No.99 was the first, was one of Churchward's 1903 prototypes developed from the same base as the 4-6-0 and 2-8-0 types. Churchward's response to the need for passenger tank engines was the 4-4-2 *County* tank with 6'8" driving wheels. An engine with the versatility to haul fast reasonably heavy trains of all kinds, what we now recognise as a mixed traffic engine had to have six coupled wheels. The 2-6-2T is not an unnatural progression from the 4-6-0 tender engine but what might have swung him in that direction were Baldwin engines which became, like the Beyer Peacock narrow gauge 4-6-0, a standard replicated over many years. This is suggested by the fact that the overtone of American practice is very much more apparent in the Swindon 2-6-2T than in any of the other Churchward designs even though side tanks were uncommon in the US.

Significant to this point are the Baldwin 2-6-2Ts the J1 (later SU23) class built from 1902-1904 for the Central Railroad of New Jersey, an important commuter line which ran west across New Jersey to Phillipsburg and across the Delaware River to Easton and Scranton. These had 18"x26" cylinders, 5'3" driving wheels and boilers with 1,824 sq.ft. heating surface pressed to 200 lbs. The mere technical detail gives no hint that these locomotives bear a strong resemblance to the Churchward 2-6-2 tank. The illustration shows an engine that but for its boiler, needs very little imagination to imply that it had come from Swindon. The link is certainly not specific but indicates how close was the standard Baldwin design to what Churchward built at Swindon.

It was while the advanced Swindon locomotive was being developed that the exploits of the de Glehn compounds burst upon the scene. Who originated the idea that the GWR should purchase one for examination is unclear, it has always been assumed that it came from Churchward himself and failing other evidence we must accept that this was the case. The Board's authorisation, given on 24 July 1902 is interesting however, only a month after he had formally assumed office. That not everyone could see the point is evident from the comment made in Swindon's local newspaper which remarked that: ... *This is an importation from a quarter by which the layman has least suspected since it has been common belief that the British railway companies have always prided themselves on the superiority of their rolling stock as compared with that of the continent.*[29] Damned frogs! Nothing changes! It is unnecessary here to repeat all the details of the comparative tests, the building of another engine with boiler pressure raised to 225 lbs and converted to 4-4-2 to make the comparison as even as possible. Since the first 'Frenchman' was named *La France*, its rival had to carry the name *Albion* but it was not perfidy that caused Churchward to write in his Report to the Board that: *In my opinion La France is capable of hauling ... one or possibly two more coaches than can be taken by our City class with the same coal consumption.* But it was not considered to be as powerful as 100, 98 or *Albion*. Churchward continued: *... it would appear that the improved type of simple engine that we are now building will prove as efficient as the compound type.*[30] *La France* had been one of a type supplied to the Nord Railway and was followed by two more derived from the PO 3001 class which were slightly larger. However according to Churchward's Report, *these were disappointing in not giving greater hauling power.*[31]

Various explanations have been advanced for the disappointing performance of the 'Frenchmen' and I have my own views on this. Gibson suggests that the shorter chimney ordered by Swindon to suit the GWR loading gauge may have interfered with the steaming; that is an interesting idea, it needs, as Ell was later to show, only the most trivial alterations to chimney size to make substantial change in boiler performance. Another consideration is that the English engine crews rostered to drive and fire them were not fully conversant with the required technique; and by the same token the running inspectors were probably no more conversant with it. On the other hand it is much more likely that the performance of the 'Frenchmen' was on a par with what they were doing in France, but that Churchward's long travel piston valve engines really were superior to the slide valve worked compounds. That the de Glehn compounds generally were not performing at their maximum potential even in France is demonstrated by the dramatic improvement which resulted from their later rebuilding by M. Chapelon.

I do not propose to detail the positive results of the trials with the de Glehn locomotives. It is well known that the very superior balancing achieved by these engines with their cylinders placed fore and aft so that the connecting rods were of equal length encouraged Churchward to build his own, simple version and to incorporate certain other components, in particular the bogie design. The result was 4-4-2 No.40 the progenitor of the *Star* class, possibly the most significant express passenger engine built in Britain in the 20th century;

I will return to a discussion of these locomotives later. It suffices here to say that the American look in Great Western locomotives continued despite the French influence which in any case, was to be seen only in the 4 cylinder types. While the enthusiast might know enough about foreign practice to identify the fact that the 2 cylinder engines were American in outline and layout it probably needed rather deeper knowledge to see the French influence. Even those able to afford to travel on the continent would not necessarily make the connection between the engines that hauled their train to Paris Nord and those they saw running in and out of Paddington.

Historians shy away from 'what if?' predictions, justifiably because nothing is ever equal, an assumption that crucial event 'x' did not happen does not mean that supporting events '$y, w,$ and z' would still occur. Despite that, some discussion of an alternative course of action and its possible results can be an instructive way of examining the past. In the Port Dock Museum in Adelaide, there is a 3'6" gauge 4-6-0 built by Beyer Peacock for the Silverton Tramway which once linked the government lines of South Australia and New South Wales. This machine, one of a batch built between 1912 and 1915, is of very great interest; it has outside cylinders and motion, a copper capped chimney, belpaire firebox and parallel domed boiler. Ignoring the difference in gauge, it represents, with the possible exception of the outside motion, an impression of what a Swindon freight locomotive of the Edwardian years could have looked like had GWR locomotive practice followed a more traditional line of development. Yet supposing that someone other than Churchward but from 'inside' had followed Dean as would certainly have happened given the usual policy on promotion, what then would have been the way of progress? Without losing sight of our initial sentence I think it is likely that Dean's successor would have been F.G.Wright, in 1900 Chief Draughtsman and from 1902, locomotive works manager and chief assistant to the CME. Although this suggests that I have ignored my own caveat and it can be argued that he was, in reality not experienced enough, it does have logic, this is the route by which Churchward himself and later Collett and Cooke made it to the top man's office. Taking that as a given, we can deduce little from what we know of his involvement with locomotive design. I showed in a previous chapter that it was at his suggestion that *Earl Cawder* was rebuilt with a large boiler; that however, means nothing, larger boilers, if not at the size put on 'Decapod' would have been necessary whoever held the reins at Swindon.

Notes and references

9) For much of the information on Churchward's family and his early life I am indebted to Mr. Richard E.Jackson, a descendant of his maternal grand father.
10) *The Grenville Steam Carriage* - Neil Cossons
11) *Wolverhampton Chronicle* - This very sad case is detailed over several editions in January 1888.
12) *The Great Western at Swindon Works* - A.S.Peck
   There are further notes in reference 7
13) *Wainwright and his Locomotives* - Klaus Marx
14) C.P.Atkins - personal information.
15) *Guiness Book of Rail Facts & Feats* - John Marshall

16) Perhaps in 2006 it would have been known as 'Saddam'!
17) Maybe Swindon should have just sold *La France* to Fowler and saved the LMS from the mess it undoubtedly got into!
18) *The World's Locomotives* - C.S.Lake
19) *World Steam in the 20th Century* - E.S.Cox
20) *Steam Locomotive Design, Data and Formulae* - E.A.Philipson
21) Why on earth the LMS with its horrendous ascents at Shap, Beatock and Ais Gill did not build 4-8-0 express engines is something I will never understand.
22) Some of the written Reports made by engineers who travelled abroad, including that written by Holcroft after his visit to the USA in 1909 are missing from the archives of both the PRO and NRM.
23) Another aspect of Churchward's association with the Pennsylvania was the stationary test plant built at Swindon in 1904. The first such plants were built in the USA and the PRR published test results from Altoona which attracted interest world wide.
24) This was not actually the first use of the wagon top boiler in Britain, as far back as 1879 there was an isolated use of the form, not repeated.
25) *The late G.J.Churchward's Locomotive Development on the GWR* - K.J.Cook
- Proceedings of the I.Loc.E vol XL
26) *Castles & Kings at Work* - Michael Rutherford
27) *Backtrack* October 2003 - letter from G.A.Davidson and subsequent correspondence with the author.
28) Locomotive Department Circular 150 - undated but probably about 1874
(PRO Rail 254/19)
29) *Evening Advertiser* - Swindon January 9th 1903.
30) British Transport Historical Records GW/18/261
31) BTHR GW/18/271

1) Archetypical of the later broad gauge scene, *Iron Duke* class 4-2-2s, *Swallow* and *Great Western* double head a west bound train through Didcot in 1888.
Photo: Great Western Trust

2,3 & 4) The development of the B&ER 4-2-4T.
2) No.44 of the original series built in 1854. The unique driving wheel suspension is clearly visible in this picture.

3) No.40 of the later series built in 1873.

4) No.40 as GWR No.2002 and rebuilt as a 4-2-2 in 1877.

2,3 & 4 are from paintings by the late P.J.T.Reid and reproduced by courtesy of the Great Western Trust

5) Dean 4-2-2T No.9 as conjectured by the author.
6) 0-6-0T No. 1833 which it is believed was built from components saved from the second 4-2-4T.
No picture of these locomotives is known to exist though it is possible that the drawings remain, unsorted, at the National Rail Museum.
7) Suggested alterations which might have made No.9 a serviceable locomotive.
8) The same engine as it might have appeared rebuilt with a Churchward domed belpaire boiler and high arched cab.
Photo credit: (5) L.A.Summers & NRM

9 & 10) No.9 as rebuilt as a 2-2-2 in 1884. (9) photo: NRM
11) *Queen* class 2-2-2, No.1123 *Salisbury* as running about 1884. 11) photo: KRM

12) Dean 3001 class 2-2-2 No. 3003 seen new at Didcot in 1892; later named *Avalanche* and rebuilt as a 4-2-2.

Note that in all four photographs the polished brass dome hardly registers.

13) Double headed Great Eastern train at an unknown location. The second locomotive is Holden T19 2-4-0 No.721. (14) Possibly at the same location is T19 No.1039. Note the fireman pulling coal forward.
Both photos: Albert Floyd, courtesy Culham College Association.

15) Dean 2201 class development of the Armstrong 806 class, No.2215 built in 1882. This is the type of 2-4-0 with which Holden would have been familiar before transferring to the GER and its similarity to his T19 class is noticeable. 16) (Opposite page) Dean 2-4-0 No.3240 of the 3232 class built from 1892 incorporating the Stroudley/Holden cylinder layout.
Photos 15 & 16: Kidderminster Railway Museum - Perkins/Wycherley Collection.

17) Robinson's 2-4-0 No.47 *Carrick Castle* built for the Waterford, Limerick & Western Railway in 1894.

18) Silverton Tramway 3' 6" gauge 4-6-0 No.A21 built in 1915 represents what GWR freight engines *might* have looked like in the 1900s.

19) Union Pacific 4-4-0 No. 75 at Omaha 1868. A typical 'American' locomotive with all the features described in this book.

Photos: 17, Mitchell Library
18, Neil Burnell

19) Holden P43 4-2-2 No.14 and (20) Dean *Achilles* class 4-2-2 No.3040 *Empress of India*. (Both LCGB Ken Nunn Collection) 21) Trevithick's 4-4-0 No. 617 built for the Egyptian State Railways (Mitchell Library) and 22) Dean's *Duke of Cornwall* class 4-4-0 No.3276 *Dartmoor*. (R.S.Carpenter) The similarity between the singles is obvious enough, that between the 4-4-0s is extraordinary.

23) *Badminton* class 4-4-0 No.3298, *Earl Cawder* as rebuilt with large round topped boiler and GE-style cab. The locomotive has the appearance of a large double framed *Claud Hamilton*.
Photo: KRM

23) Lucy's NN (35) class 4-6-0 for the New South Wales Government Railways, 1914. No.1031 as originally built.
Photo: Neil Burnell

24) The type of locomotive that Churchward grew up with, South Devon broad gauge 4-4-0ST *Zebra* running as GWR 2127.
Photo: Great Western Trust

25) The first Great Western 4-6-0 No.36 completed in 1896. Known as the 'crocodile' it was a pure Dean locomotive with no Churchward input at all.
Photo: BRB

26) G.J.Churchward. Swindon's great strength, certainly at the turn of the century was the design team assembled by Churchward which in its talent and originality was second to none.

27) The Drawing Office staff, 1899. The seated figure, centre is believed to be W.A.Stanier. It would be interesting to put names to the rest of the faces. Very large photographs showing senior management together with workshop foreman and other middle management staff were taken from time to time. Huge in size, only small out-takes can be used here. 28) is from the 1911 picture: we see, left to right, Collett, Wright, Churchward, Waister and at the extreme right, glowering at something beyond the photographer, E.A.Watson. The inset (29) is from the 1921 staff photograph and shows Stanier, Collett and Churchward.

Photo credits
27,28,29 Steam Museum, Swindon

Photo credits:
31) W. Beckerlegge (KRM)
32) R.S.Carpenter

30) 'Kruger' 4-6-0 No.2601, perhaps the only ugly engine Churchward ever built is however of very great importance, being crucial in the development of his standard locomotives.

31) 4-4-0 No.3352, *Camel*, the first locomotive to be built with a domeless belpaire boiler and drumhead smokebox. Note that the numberplate is on the smokebox, the nameplate, combined with the crest, on the cabside.

32) The domeless belpaire boiler was soon fitted to other types, in this case to *Cobham* 2-2-2 No.165 in 1906.

33) The 2-4-2T as later running with tapered boiler and top feed, No. 3612 is seen at Oxford in about 1929.

Photo credits:
35) Kidderminster Rly Museum
36) Great Western Trust

34) Illinois Central Railroad 4-4-0 No.961 as built in 1896. A diagram of the boiler of this engine was obtained by Swindon and its shape, despite the dome is the lineal ancestor of the Churchward taper boiler as seen on 4-6-0 No.98 (35). The American appearance of No.98 is unmistakable.

36) Later development of the taper boiler, seen here on *Saint Class* 4-6-0 No.2901 *Lady Superior* included a full length cone and extended smokebox. 37) The original 2-8-0 goods engine was No.97 built simultaneously with No.98. No.2857 seen in BR days carries the same boiler as 2901, with outside steampipes.

38 & 39) Although not a direct copy, the similarity in general arrangement of the Baldwin built J1 2-6-2Ts of the Central Railroad of New Jersey to the Churchward 2-6-2T is very pronounced.

40) The CRNJ 2-6-2Ts were later rebuilt with piston valves and larger tanks which both accentuated and reduced their likeness to Swindon's engines.

41) On the Western however, the later 61XX class 2-6-2Ts retained the Baldwin-American appearance of No.99. No.6159 was photographed at Didcot in 1963.

Photo: 40) Bud Laws

42) The French influence was first seen in de Glehn compound 4-4-2 No.102 *La France* delivered in 1903. 43) All three compounds were later rebuilt with Swindon standard boilers as with No.103 *Alliance*.

Photo credits: 42,44,45) LCGB Ken Nunn Collection 43) M.W.Earley

44) The French compounds directly influenced the building of the first 4-cylinder passenger engine, originally a 4-4-2, in 1906. No.40 *North Star* is seen here after conversion to 4-6-0 in 1909.
45) No. 4041 *Prince of Wales* photographed in 1935 represents the production *Stars*.

46) The first M&SWJ 4-4-0 No.9 built by Dübs in 1893.
47) After what may have been considered was a false start with No.9, Dübs supplied three 2-4-0s. No.12 is seen as GWR No.1336, the last to remain in service.
48) At Cheltenham High Street shed in 1934 4-4-0 No.1119 (ex-MSWJ No.1) carries GWR mountings on its original boiler. Standing next to it is rebuilt Dean Goods No.2517.
49) According to the author one of the most attractive locomotives ever built, MSWJ 4-4-0 No.2 as GWR No. 1120 and carrying a Swindon taper boiler.

Photo credits:
46 & 49) R.C.Riley
47) H.C.Casserley
48) G.S.Lloyd (KRM)

50) The classic GWR 4-4-0 represented by *City* No.3440 *City of Truro* as running in 1957.
51) James Stirling's Class F 4-4-0 No. A172 is hardly a very 'bonny' engine.

Photo 51) H.C.Casserley

52) MSWJ 4-4-4T No.18 as GW No.27 and rebuilt with taper boiler and high arched cab.
53) At work probably in the Kidderminster area No.27 makes a very attractive sight.

Photos: Both GW Trust

54) In terms of appearance de Caso's SNCF 4-6-4 No. 232U1 built in 1949 leaves the Riddles Standards far behind. 55) PRR Duplex T1 class 4-4-4-4 No. 5537 represents the most impressive looking locomotives ever built.

56) Churchward's magnificent pacific No.111 *The Great Bear* on shed at Old Oak and (57) after having backed down onto platform 1 at Paddington.

Photo credits:
55) Neil Burnell
56) F.Moore (KRM)
57) LCGB Ken Nunn Collection

58) 5'8" 2-8-0 No. 4701 on the '47 Road' at Old Oak in 1931. These locomotives were given little opportunity to show their real worth.

59) Standard *Hall* 4-6-0 No.4959 *Purley Hall*. This was Collett's preferred MT engine though (60) the *Grange* was possibly the better engine. No.6826 *Nannerth Grange* is seen at Didcot in 1964.

61) Probably the most famous of all the *Castles* and also one of the best performers, No. 4079 *Pendennis Castle* was among the first to be built. Happily it is still in existence and currently undergoing restoration at Didcot.

62) *King* 4-6-0 No. 6000 *King George V* on a Torquay Paddington train in 1935.
(LCGB Ken Nunn Collection)

63) In broadside the semi-streamlining on No. 5005 *Manobier Castle* worked quite well, giving a distinct air-smoothed line to the engine.

64) However, seen out on the line the after-thought bolted-on appearance of the fittings becomes obvious.

65) What Collett might have achieved had he thought about it a little more is demonstrated by this picture of NSWGR semi-streamline 4-6-2 No. 3801.

Photo credits:
62 & 64) LCGB Ken Nunn Collection
63) Computer generated by the author from a photograph by W.H.D.Robinson

66) Collett 56XX 0-6-2T No.6644 at Banbury, far away from the sphere of operation that was intended.

67) No.3625 represents the later form of the 57XX 0-6-0PT with the new version of the cab.
68 & 69) Remarkable pictures for having been taken in almost exactly the same place, at Wallingford on the branch from Cholsey. In (68) Armstrong 517 0-4-2T No.526 photographed in 1933 provides a comparison with (69) Collett's version of the same type 48XX No.1407 photographed in 1959.

68) V.R.Webster (KRM)

70 & 71) Old designs renewed: 64XX and 16XX 0-6-0PTs built from 1932 and 1949.
71) The taper boilered 94XX 0-6-0PT said to have been inspired by a comment by Sir James Milne.

72) Because of the second world war many old locomotives remained in service long after their normal withdrawal date. The last *Aberdare* class 2-6-0 ran until 1949.

Photo credit:
72) W.Potter (KRM)

73) *Modified Hall* No.6996 *Blackwell Hall* at Bristol (TM) in 1957. This was the first *Hall* to be completed under BR ownership.

74) The first *County* 4-6-0 No.1000 *County of Middlesex* in original condition.
75) No.1024 *County of Pembroke* with the later Ell double chimney.

Both photos: W.Potter (Kidderminster Railway Museum)

76 Previous page) Among the last *Castles* to be built was No.7029 *Clun Castle* turned out in May 1950. Later rebuilt with 3-row superheater and double chimney.

77) The Brown Boveri gas-turbine No.18000 on a Paddington-Bristol train when new. LCGB Ken Nunn Collectn.

78) Standard '5013' type *Castle* No. 5054 *Earl of Ducie* at Paddington paired with the post-war 'slab sided' 4000 gallon tender.

79) An unidentified *Modified Hall* battles snow and ice as it heads a train for Oxford at Didcot North Junction.

80) The BR Standard Class 3 2-6-0 carried a boiler developed from the Swindon Standard No.4.

81) *King George V* in final form, with 4-row superheater, double chimney and mechanical lubricator. Seen on an 'up' train near Steventon, the GWR 'racing ground'.

82) The *Britannia* pacifics allocated to the WR were drafted away in the early 1960s. No.70028 *Royal Star* is seen at Crewe in 1966 having succumbed to the same indignities as WR engines.

83) Class 9F 2-10-0 No.92220 *Evening Star*, a very un-Great Western engine clothed in a copper cap chimney and with Swindon-style nameplates.

84) Riddles Class 8 pacific No. 71000 *Duke of Gloucester* at Swindon in 1954 when being tested by the Ell team.

(84) Kidderminster Railway Museum: Perkins/Wycherley Collection

85) BR(W) *Warship* dh. No. D823 *Hermes*.
86) Beyer Peacock *Hymek* dh. No. D7054 at Reading.

87) Infiltrators! A pair of *Western* class Type 4 dh locomotives awaiting departure from Paddington. No.D1009 *Western Invader* (left) with a Bristol train and No. D1055 *Western Advocate* for South Wales. Surely these were the most ridiculous names ever to be given to railway locomotives.
88) The incident referred to in Chapter 8. *Hall* No. 6910 once named *Gossington Hall* limps into Oxford with a south to north express. Notice the attention of the young lad walking alongside the engine.

In paradisum

89) Scenes such as this at Oxford not seen since the abolition of the broad gauge came to characterise the WR at the end of steam.

90) But it was not the end for in 2006, *Castle* No.5051, *Earl Bathurst* was recreating the 1950s on the Gloucester & Warwickshire Railway and (91) the Great Western Society rolled out the all-but completed restoration of *King* No.6023 *King Edward II* to its 1950 single chimney condition. Given its state when obtained for preservation the restoration of 6023 has been near-miraculous.

Five
The Great Western's Bonniest Engines...
On the vexed subject of appearance

There was a time when railway books for boys started with the question, 'what is your favourite locomotive', the answers to which must have been as various as the number of people challenged with it, for as the nursery rhyme tells us: *Jack Spratt could eat no fat and his wife could eat no lean*. Therefore, to get into the argument about the best looking locomotive type is potentially dangerous and probably unrewarding. Nonetheless it is not irrelevant to look at that in the context of the GWR locomotive because it was on one occasion severely criticised in a manner to which perhaps few other railway's engines have been subject. Inasmuch that the criticism came from someone quite unqualified to be censorious impels us to a guarded attempt to establish canons of locomotive art that might be generally acceptable. That said, it is important I believe to begin with an acknowledgement that like Bertrand Russell who suggested that the pure austerity of mathematics was its supreme beauty so the best engineering artistry arises from the unadorned machinery itself.[9] Put it this way, the workmanlike functionalism of the Stanier Class 5 is far more attractive than the deliberately adorned Wainwright D class 4-4-0. I will go further, to me the original Reichsbahn 01 pacific is far more attractive, as a machine than the Midland 'Spinner'.

Paradoxically, I readily acknowledge that it is possible to take this argument to an extreme where it begets its own destruction. Raymond Lowey, the guru of streamlining had something to say about this, bemoaning the fact that many engineers were too conservative and needed 'conditioning' to see the importance of the appearance of their machines.[10] In what might be termed the brutally functional world of post-Victorian engineering any consideration of appearance tended to be frowned upon. There is a corollary here with automobiles. The late Alex Issigonis will always be associated with the epoch-making Mini but even the new Mini still looks like nothing so much as a cleaned up trade van, once the immediate engineering thrill has evaporated the car's drawbacks are immediately apparent. Issigonis has been criticised for not recognising this and it may be the reason why his name is not associated with any other innovatory car. So there is a happy medium between the austerity of pure engineering and a deliberated outcome to appearance that sets off the machine to its best advantage. Note that I stress that it sets off the machine, not that the appearance is an attraction, of itself, separate from the machine. This is important.

It is now nearly forty years ago that, in a book by George Behrend,[11] I first discovered an illustration of a type of locomotive that I had never imagined to have been built, a GWR 4-4-0 with inside cylinders, inside frames and a taper boiler. To me this was an extraordinary revelation because I had always been led to believe that the railway that pioneered the modern express passenger engine had been satisfied, throughout its history and long after other companies had given them up, with 4-4-0s having outside frames. Holcroft explains that this apparent hangover from a past age provided larger bearings and big end journals, more room for the steam chest and the potentiality for larger cylinders.[4] The last new example was completed in 1908 while No.9017, the last in normal service, was withdrawn only in 1961. My interest, all those years ago, was particularly aroused because, though it is not something that I talk about very much, I occasionally construct locomotive models. Nothing of any special note, more *Blue Peter* than *The Model Engineer*. But I had learnt very early on that GWR engines were difficult to model because in the first place, the older types had outside frames, imposing enormous difficulty in getting the axles, cranks and wheels moving together properly and that Churchward's 4-6-0s and 2-8.0s were not easier to model because with outside cylinders there was a different kind of difficulty to confront. Why couldn't the Great Western, for this once, be like other railways and build passenger engines in the traditional British manner?

And it is, of course, true that Churchward intended to build inside framed and inside-cylindered locomotives for secondary duties. Holcroft relates that in 1910 he was told that Churchward wanted to develop this layout using 10" long travel piston valves on top of the cylinders. Holcroft discovered that it was impossible to get such a layout in under the smokebox without making alterations that Churchward was not prepared to tolerate.[4] Why he did not consider having the piston valves underneath the cylinders, adapting the usual Holden-Dean layout is not something we can now know. Perhaps Holcroft, more concerned to push his own ideas did not suggest it. The upshot was the production of the Swindon 'Mogul', the first purpose-built mixed traffic 2-6-0 of which many hundreds were subsequently built by all the major British railways. It would have been interesting to see a Swindon version of the stereotype British 4-4-0, especially with state-of-the-art valve design. What would it have looked like? Unless there are drawings yet to be discovered, we cannot know for certain; perhaps it would not have deviated very much from an inside-framed version of the *Bulldog*.

Yet the assumption that the Great Western had never built such a locomotive was wrong, for the photograph in Behrend's book clearly showed that it had. Or at least, it had done so by proxy, through the rebuilding of engines that had previously belonged to the Midland & South Western Junction Railway. A secondary and certainly unlooked-for result of that rebuilding was the development of what I regard as one of the most attractive locomotive designs ever to run in Britain. Publicly at least, Churchward was not interested in the appearance of his engines. During the discussion on a paper that he read to the Institution of Mechanical Engineers in 1906 James Stirling remarked that his locomotives might be very good performers but they were ...*certainly not 'bonny', to use a Scots expression*. Churchward responded, with less acid than he might, for Stirling perpetrated probably the most dreadful-looking locomotives ever to run in Britain, *In my opinion there is no cannon of art in regard to the appearance of a locomotive. . . except that which an engineer has set up for himself by observing. . . types of engine which he has been led from his nursery days upward to admire.* An interesting comment for Churchward's nursery days and indeed, his first year as an apprentice were spent near the South Devon Railway. Having shaken off its blundering start with the Samuda-Brunel atmospheric 'caper' the SDR was operated for most of its existence by

4-4-0 passenger engines and 0-6-0 freight types the greater percentage of which were saddle tanks. The passenger engines had driving wheels between 5'6" and 5'9" in diameter and were actually quite powerful with the large grates that the broad gauge permitted and good healthy boilers. By and large they were developments of the Gooch *Corsair* class and were not dissimilar in layout to Pearson's 9 footers. The boiler provided the solidity usually associated with the main frame which in these locomotives stopped short of the crank axle, the bogie being attached via a bracket to the boiler on a ball and socket joint. One can see what Churchward meant in his repost to Stirling for his 4-6-0s, domeless and austere looked like nothing so much as an Americanised version of these broad gauge saddle tanks.

There is reason to believe that whatever he said publicly, Churchward had been stung by Stirling's remark, though it was not the first time such a comment had been made. That he was something of an iconoclast is clear. The old traditions of the GWR do not seem to have bothered him as evidence the total lack of interest in the preservation of the *North Star*, *Lord of the Isles* and the Shrewsbury & Chester 2-2-2 kept for many years at Wolverhampton. There is evidence that he would have painted locomotives black and the change of the old chocolate & cream livery to lake must have been due to him. But now, according to Holcroft, Churchward gave instructions which came down to him, to get out sketches to show how a more pleasing appearance could be given to the standard locomotive. This is interesting because Holcroft claimed to have strong preconceived notions about this and implies that the curved drop ends that became characteristic of Swindon 4-6-0s was the product of these ideas.[4] What we are not told and as far as I can establish no one has previously realised is that these 'preconceived notions' were derived from practice elsewhere, essentially that of the early Robinson 4-4-2 and 4-6-0 classes. The radii of the curves may have been different but the principle is identical and was not restricted to the GCR. Indeed, I would go further and say that it was an obvious development that did not call for much imagination.

My reaction to the appearance of the rebuilt MSWJ 4-4-0s is fully in accordance with the principle that I established for myself in the first paragraphs, the clean, uncluttered entirely functional lines of the rebuilt engine. In this case, there was also another consideration, behind the classic simplicity of appearance was an engine with a splendid reputation. Within the grandiloquent majesty of the GWR there seems to have been much about the MSWJ to suggest that it is worth more than a passing interest. Hamilton Ellis wrote: *Andover was a very remarkable place indeed; it was the southern terminus of the MSWJ Railway, of which the other extreme, improbably but truly, was Andoversford in the Cotswolds.* Which other railway in the world, I wonder, had its termini in places which, to all intents and purposes, had the same name? Hamilton Ellis continued his note about the MSWJ, *This was a small railway, with a poverty stricken history, but under Sam Fay it had nevertheless grown into a model line from the passengers' point of view. . . . Cheltenham, where the MSWJ terminated by virtue of running powers, had of course a main line through service from Paddington. But if you chose your train, travelling from Waterloo to Andover and thence took the MSWJ 'North Express', you could get to Cheltenham more quickly than by the Great Western with its wanderings round by Gloucester!*[12] And yet, at the beginning of the 21st century, very little is ever heard about the MSWJ or its locomotives. Though there have been some useful books written about it, the article in *Backtrack* which forms the original basis of this chapter was the first magazine item to appear in print for over forty years.[13][14] I hope therefore that I can be excused the indulgence of putting some detail into my admiration for the Swindon version of Cheltenham's favourite engines.

The Midland and South Western Junction Railway was an enterprising concern that developed from an amalgamation of two companies, the oldest of which was the Swindon, Marlborough & Andover running for 12 miles between Swindon and Marlborough, opened in July 1881. Right from the outset the GWR regarded the line as a threat to its interests and did everything it could to frustrate its activities. Despite this, a junction with its main line at Swindon was established the following year. Paddington's shenanigans kept the SM&A as two separate lines until February 1883 when connection end-on to the GWR Marlborough branch and a junction off the main line at Grafton enabled through running between Swindon and Andover. However, the real threat to the GWR was the Swindon & Cheltenham Extension Railway which Paddington fought tooth and nail. It reached Cirencester by December 1883 but completion was delayed for a further eight years. Lack of money and difficulty with the GWR, not least in getting running powers over its line from Andoversford, constrained further progress. Help came in the shape of the Midland Railway, ever ready to confront its arch-rival, and in 1884 the SMA and CER were amalgamated as the Midland & South Western Junction. However, the Midland never had any formal controlling interest in the MSWJ as it did with the Somerset & Dorset. Through running from the Midland's Cheltenham Landsdown station, over the GWR to Andoversford and thence to Andover, began in August 1891.

By now the MSWJ was in the hands of the Receiver, its locomotives in a poor state and unsuitable for the work being demanded of them. Trains ran so late so regularly that passengers almost knew that an advertised departure time would be exceeded by anything from ten to fifteen minutes. Among the more interesting relics that purported to earn revenue for the MSWJ was the Avonside single Fairlie 0-4-4T originally exhibited at the Paris 1878 Exhibition and notable in being one of the first locomotives in Britain to be fitted with Walschaerts valve gear. It was purchased by the SMA in 1882 and seems to have done very little work though from being unreliable rather than plain useless[14]. There is in existence a log of a run by this engine showing some very smart work between station stops which must have involved pretty brisk accelerations away from the nine stopping points on the line. It was withdrawn in 1889 when a broken spring rendered it permanently unserviceable.

The MSWJ was rescued from disaster by Sam Fay, seconded from the LSWR, serving as General Manager from February 1892, and who undoubtedly revolutionised the company's operations. Engines and coaches were borrowed from the LSWR and through working of services off the Midland onto the LSWR established. Loans from the Midland later

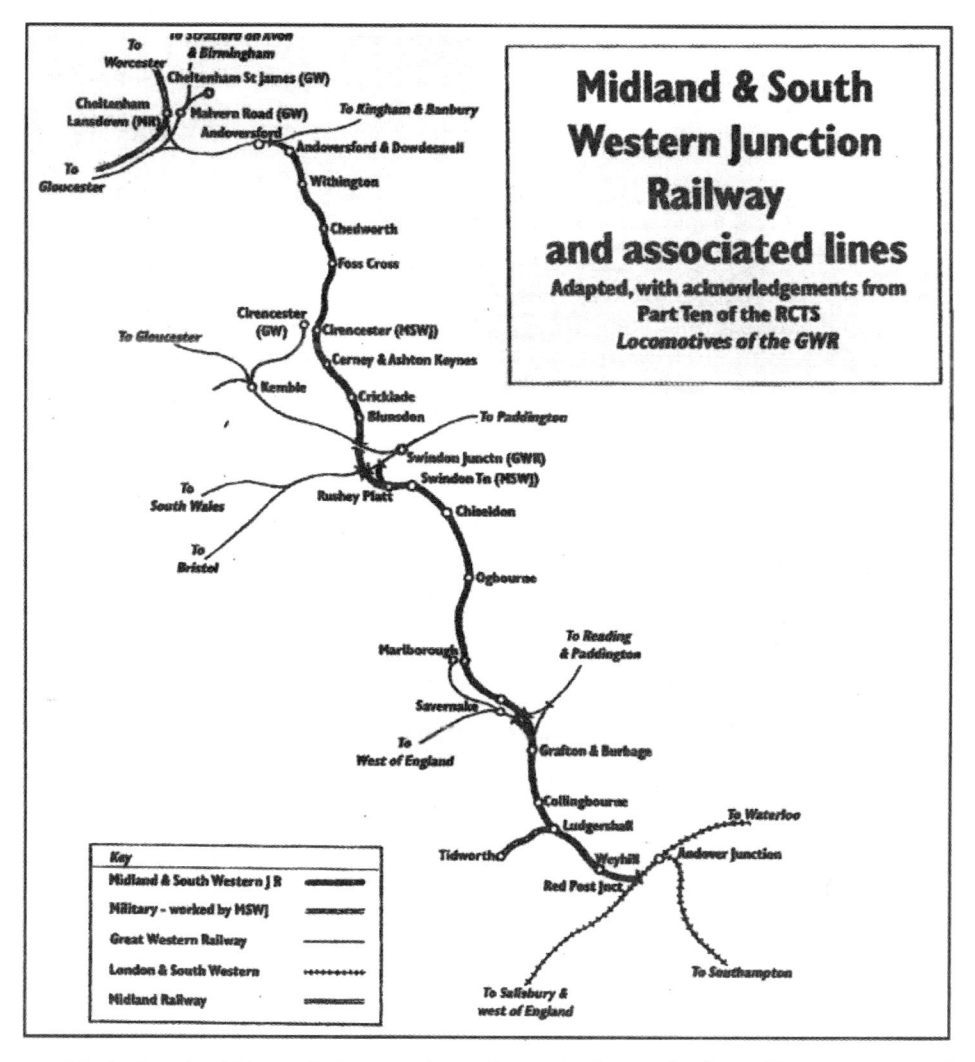

Midland & South Western Junction Railway and associated lines

Adapted, with acknowledgements from Part Ten of the RCTS *Locomotives of the GWR*

enabled the doubling of the sections from Andoversford to Cirencester and Weyhill junction to Marlborough, a total of 38¾ miles of the MSWJ's 60.8 route miles. This work greatly enhanced the potential of the MSWJ and made the punctual running of long-distance through services much easier. These services became an essential part of the MSWJ operation, with through coaches to Southampton from Leeds, Bradford and Manchester giving the line considerable importance as a north-to-south route. It was even possible to book through tickets from Edinburgh to Paris over the MSWJ. The longest-lasting section of the MSWJ, still open in the 1970s long after the rest had gone, served the War Department branch from Ludgershall to Tidworth. Such was the traffic on and off this branch that the revenue to the MSWJ was greater than for all the other stations on its line, combined.[13]

It was well understood that the apparently deliberate obstruction by GWR staff at Andoversford, Marlborough and Savernake was as responsible as anything else for the late running of MSWJ trains and this prompted Fay to build an independent line from Marlborough to Savernake and thence to its original line at Grafton. Despite GWR objection, this new section was opened in 1898.

Borrowing locomotives from the LSWR was not the perfect answer to the MSWJ's operating difficulties. In 1893, therefore, Fay took a loan from a director which enabled him to order a new engine from Dubs, (3076/93), a 4-4-0 with 6' driving wheels, 17"x24" cylinders and 170 lb boiler pressure. The new engine was, by MSWJ standards, very powerful and it has been suggested that it might have been too heavy for the track then in place.[13] A Rolling Stock Trust Fund was established by which locomotives were ordered on the security of their own value and the first to be delivered under this scheme were the three very long-lived 2-4-0 passenger engines which saw out their days as GWR branch engines at Didcot and Reading. They were moderately lighter than the 4-4-0 and shared with it the through passenger trains.[15] Under Fay's loan fund, repair shops were established at Cirencester. There were engine sheds at Cheltenham, Cirencester, Swindon Town, Ludgershall and Andover. The largest was at Cheltenham but the largest 55' turntables were at Swindon and Ludgershall.[16]

The developing train service led to the purchase of two very interesting tanks, numbered 17 and 18, traditionally designed 4-4-4s (Sharp Stewart 4300 and 4301/97), with inside cylinders, 17"x24", domed flush-topped boiler pressed to 150 lbs, 5'3" driving wheels, and overall cab. Few locomotives of this type have run in Britain and the most numerous, the North Eastern Railway D class three-cylinder type, was rebuilt by Gresley as a 4-6-2T. The new MSWJ engines were intended to work express passenger trains but quickly proved themselves to be unsuitable. It is not difficult to see why. At face value a 4-4-4 appears an ideal type to work on a winding route bedevilled with reverse curves. Unfortunately they were prone to slipping especially when the side tanks needed replenishing, a result, surely, of there being too much weight on the bogies, 28.55 tons against 30.7 tons on the driving wheels. As the water capacity reduced, so the weight on the coupled axles decreased and in wet or slippery conditions set up a potentiality for spin.[13] The 4-4-4Ts did not steam very well either and drivers adopted the traditional answer to that problem, the infamous blastpipe "jemmy"; it worked but it was the cause of an increase in coal consumption. It is interesting to see that in 1922 locomotive coal cost the MSWJ 21s 8d at the pit and 8s 3d or 9s 3d a ton carriage to Cheltenham or Swindon. This, remember, is the time when the coal industry was going through the crisis which led eventually to the General Strike.[16] Soon after the Grouping the GWR fitted No.17 (now No.25) with an extended smokebox but there is nothing to suggest that it improved the performance. This engine saw out its last years on the Swindon Town-Junction shuttle service and was withdrawn in 1927. The later history of No.18 (GWR No.27) will be recounted later. On stopping trains the 4-4-4Ts are said to have been much more successful, able to make up lost time between stops.[13]

Sam Fay left the MSWJ to return to the LSWR in 1899. He had put the company on a new footing and given it a zest for service that it never lost. His most notable successor as general manager was John Davies who was in post from 1903 till the Grouping and who came to this Cotswold outpost after six years as general manager of the Western Australian Government Railways. James Tyrell became Locomotive Superintendent in 1903. He had started out on the line as a driver in 1890 at a time when locomotive matters were handled by a foreman working under the engineer. The status of the post was raised in 1903 and Tyrell remained its sole occupant until the Grouping. His salary on his appointment was £250 at a time when the general manager's was £750 plus an incentive arrangement. Compared to a top butler in a good household earning as much as £100 annually both figures are pretty miserly, even for a small and somewhat impecunious railway like the MSWJ. It is not totally irrelevant to note that Ivatt was appointed to the Great Northern in 1895 on a salary of £2,500. Though the GNR was a vastly bigger concern and the locomotive superintendent's duties much greater, that does not entirely justify the difference. By 1922 Tyrell's salary was still only £700.[15]

By the early years of the twentieth century the MSWJ had largely relaid its lines with 87 lb rail and at the June 1904 board meeting the directors were shown what the Minutes describe as: *sketches of Bulldog and Duke class locomotives.*[15] It was decided to order a *Bulldog* type with an option on a second. I am grateful to Mike Barnsley for letting me illustrate a very interesting drawing recently discovered which was made at Cirencester on September 10 1904 and which shows the front elevation of a GWR double framed 4-4-0. *(Illustration, this page.)* Though it is not described as such, scaling the driving wheels strongly suggests that it is in fact a drawing of a GWR *Bulldog*. Clearly this cannot be the drawing shown to the Directors at their June meeting, the dates are completely wrong. However, it is noticeable that the outside cranks have been omitted and the inclusion of the MSWJ loading gauge profile strongly suggests that it was intended to show the Board that the purchase of a Swindon *Bulldog* was not a viable proposition. There is no evidence that an approach was ever made to the GWR to buy a couple of *Bulldogs* and it can be conjectured that the officers, aware that they were dealing with businessmen with little technical knowledge adopted this expedient to demonstrate the inappropriateness of the Board's June decision.[17]

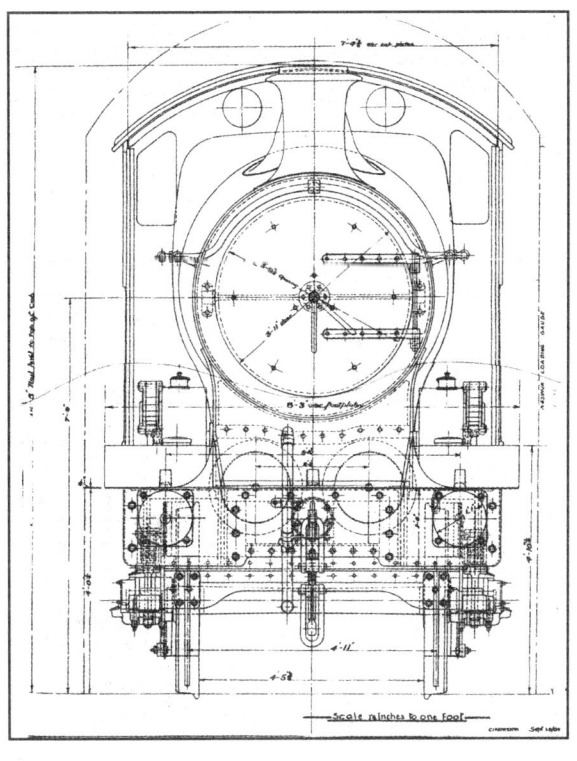

In fact, the locomotive actually delivered was, except for the wheel arrangement, as unlike a *Bulldog* as it was possible to get. An inside-cylinder, inside-framed 4-4-0 was delivered from the North British Loco. Co. in July 1905 (NBL 16817). Gibson, who started his career as a MSWJ apprentice at Cirencester says that these locomotives were more accessible than the *Bulldogs*. He describes the double framed engines as being a nightmare to work on. The space between the frames was 14" in width and it was sometimes necessary to work in this space with: *an inch thick layer of filthy black grease all around and above me*.[7] Such is the reality of railway work. I am, inevitably, reminded of the exchange between Hamilton Ellis and the unnamed driver of a Kirtley engine at Charing Cross long after their domes had been painted over. The paint had peeled off and some individual had polished the brass bright. CHE began to declaim about such engines when he was a boy but the driver interrupted him, "Yes, I remember when I was a boy, I had to clean the f------g things."[12]

Though no cost is quoted in the Board minutes a figure of £2,600 is given for an 0-6-0 at the same time and a subsequent 4-4-0, delivered in 1909 cost £2,760.[15] Eventually there were nine of these engines, all built to the same general design though with some detail differences, in 1905 and from 1909 to 1914.[18] They had 18"x26" cylinders and 160 lb boilers in two rings with the dome on the second ring. Ramsbottom safety valves were carried on the Belpaire firebox. The driving wheels were 5'9" in diameter. Coated in the MSWJ's crimson lake livery, they cut a dash in the greensward of Wiltshire and were very much the pride of the line. Official information stated that they were expected to take 300 tons up 1 in 75 gradients though at what speed is not stated.[15] However, we can formulate some ideas on their performance from examining the published timetables in conjunction with route distances.

Tables 1 and 2 have been compiled from Bradshaw for the years quoted which are more or less random choices, influenced by readings from the quoted sources. The tables show the stations at which trains stopped and the time allowed, as indicated by the timetables, between stops. [A gradient profile is available in an official document filed by the GWR in 1922.[16]] The tables indicate that the best years for MSWJ running were 1910 to 1915, perhaps not surprisingly. Overall, journey times did not change very much; the best up train was the 13.10 departure from Cheltenham in 1913 which reached Andover, with five stops, in 1 hr 50 min. In 1910 the best time had been 2 hr 8 min and in 1915 was 2 hr 9 min. A difference of 19 minutes is probably noticeable but the ordinary passenger is unlikely to notice a difference of a few minutes one way or the other. What would be of interest to such a person would be the quickest time to a particular destination. Again, rather too much of this is made by railway enthusiast commentators. The MSWJ route to Swindon was certainly far quicker than by the GWR; in 1913 the fastest GWR train was booked 92 minutes via Gloucester as opposed to 54 minutes by the MSWJ. But the situation becomes different when viewed more rationally. It is unlikely that there were very many passengers from Cheltenham travelling only to Swindon; consider, what did Swindon have that Cheltenham or Gloucester could not provide? Much more likely was that passengers would be going through to London or the south. In this context the situation appears rather different. In 1913 Cheltenham passengers catching the 10.37 MSWJ train and travelling via Andover could be at Waterloo by 14.35pm. The equivalent GWR

TABLE 1 — Trains on the MSWJR — Cheltenham to Andover 1910-1937

Miles	Station		1910	1913	1915	1921	1937
0.00	Cheltenham Spa	d	0.00	0.00	0.00	0.00	0.00
2.00	Cheltenham Sth		6.00	pass	pass	pass	5.00
7.00	Andoversford		13.00	pass	pass	pass	pass
13.50	Chedworth		23.00	pass	pass	pass	pass
20.75	Cirencester		36.00	33.00	34.00	30.00	46.00
27.25	Cricklade		49.00	44.00	pass	pass	58.00
35.75	Swindon Town	a	54.00	57.00	57.00	62.00	73.00
0.00	Swindon Town	d	0.00	0.00	0.00	0.00	0.00
11.75	Marlborough		21.00	20.00	20.00	20.00	29.00
16.75	Savernake		31.00	pass	pass	pass	39.00
25.50	Ludgershall	a	45.00	38.00	39.00	45.00	63.00
0.00	Ludgershall	d	0.00	0.00	0.00	0.00	0.00
7.50	Andover	a	10.00	10.00	10.00	13.00	14.00

Notes:
1. 1910 — 10.35 from Cheltenham, depart Swindon Town 11.47; Ludgershall 12.33.
2. 1913 — 13.10 from Cheltenham, depart Swindon Town 14.10; Ludgershall 14.50.
3. 1915 — 13.10 from Cheltenham, depart Swindon Town 14.10; Ludgershall 14.51.
4. 1921 — 15.00 from Cheltenham depart Swindon Town 16.05; Ludgershall 16.52.
5. 1937 — 13.35 from Cheltenham, Swindon Town 14.52, Ludgershall 15.47.
On the 1937 service there were three stops between Swindon Town and Andover which have not been noted in this table.

TABLE 2 — Trains on the MSWJR — Andover to Cheltenham 1910-1937

Miles	Station		1910	1913	1915	1921	1937
0.00	Andover	d	0.00	0.00	0.00	0.00	0.00
7.50	Ludgershall	a	11.00	11.00	11.00	12.00	13.00
0.00	Ludgershall	d	0.00	0.00	0.00	0.00	0.00
8.75	Savernake		15.00	pass	pass	pass	14.00
13.75	Marlborough		25.00	21.00	21.00	21.00	24.00
25.50	Swindon Town	a	43.00	39.00	39.00	41.00	47.00
0.00	Swindon Town	d	0.00	0.00	0.00	0.00	0.00
8.50	Cricklade		pass	pass	pass	pass	13.00
15.00	Cirencester		24.00	24.00	24.00	24.00	26.00
35.75	Cheltenham	a	56.00	55.00	55.00	58.00	65.00

Notes:
1. 1910 — 10.35 from Andover, depart Ludgershall 11.55; Swindon Town 12.41.
2. 1913 and 1915 — 10.56 from Andover, depart Ludgershall 11.08; Swindon Town 11.50.
3. 1921 — 11.02 from Andover, depart Ludgershall 11.16; Swindon Town 12.00.
4. 1937 — 11.09 from Andover, depart Ludgershall 11.24; Swindon Town 12.13.
On the 1937 service there were three additional stops which have not been noted in this table.

train would set the same passenger down at Paddington at exactly the same time but give him as much as an hour more in Cheltenham, departure being at 11.30.

In the reverse direction, the situation was not dissimilar, as reference to Table 2 will show. In 1913 and 1915, the overall time from Andover to Cheltenham was 109 minutes (105 net). In 1913 the passenger travelling by the 13.00 LSWR train from Waterloo and changing to the MSWJ at Andover would be in Cheltenham by 16.19pm or in 3 hr 19 min from London. By GWR the fastest train was the afternoon Cheltenham Tea Car Train which left Paddington at 15.13 and, stopping at Reading and Swindon, reached Cheltenham at 18.17, 3 hr 4 min from London. But supposing that one was unable, or did not want to travel at these times, such timings meant next to nothing. What would have been more useful would have been regular working at these booked times by all trains, something which applies as much now as then. These figures give some idea of what the MSWJ 4-4-0s were called upon to do in their original condition and some of the timings are, undoubtedly, quite good.

Most of the big and powerful railways have been accused of absorbing smaller lines and then running them down; the case of the MSWJ line on which services declined markedly after the First World War has always been taken as a case in point. However, the evidence suggests that this may be no more than partisan folklore. In truth after the turn of the century the GWR co-operated with the MSWJ, providing locomotives to haul troop trains to Ludgershall and selling them a gas cylinder car to provide gas for coaches newly acquired from the Midland. Cut backs in MSWJ passenger services were actually implemented before the GWR took over the line. Pre-war, the company had enjoyed good revenue from off peak excursion services which unfortunately they were unable to recoup at its end due to several factors of which government delay in relinquishing control was one. By 1937 services were little more than stopping trains with greatly extended running times. Long distance travel via the MSWJ was positively discouraged. The 13.35 train from Cheltenham (14.21 from Cirencester) on the MSWJ route could not be used for a connection to Paddington since the transfer from Swindon Town to the GWR station involved a wait of 82 minutes. Arrival in London was not until 18.20. If, however, the passenger caught the 12.30 from Cirencester Town (GW), the change at Swindon Junction was almost immediate and arrival in London was at 15.38. By the 14.40 from Cheltenham, the famed *Cheltenham Flyer*, arrival in Paddington was at 17.00. No-one seems to have realised that even on the basis of the timings set out here, had the GWR run the *Flyer* from Cheltenham over the MSWJ line, it could have cut 17 minutes from its booked time. A new south-facing spur off the MSWJ onto the Western main line would have been necessary but since the GWR owned all the requisite land such a construction would have been perfectly possible. A through coach attached to the train at Cheltenham or better still at Swindon would have catered for passengers from Gloucester. The MSWJ 4-4-0s would have been perfectly satisfactory motive power as far as Swindon since any 'flying' that this train did was far away from Cheltenham in the neighbourhood of Wantage Road and Steventon.

Alone of the 'big four' railways the GWR adopted a system of comprehensive rebuilding of its constituents locomotives involving the fitting of Swindon standard boilers, cabs and other equipment. On the LNER, Gresley and Thompson rebuilt constituents locomotives but by no means as extensively, nor did these rebuildings involve the use of highly standardized parts. The Southern continued to look like four railways, as far as steam construction was concerned right up till 1941 and after. Only on the LMS, after the arrival of Stanier was anything like the GWR policy considered. Cox relates that boiler designs were prepared for use on certain classes, particularly the ex-LNWR 0-8-0s and Midland compounds but that the work was never put in hand partly through considerations of cost and also its long term effectiveness.[20] 12 years after Grouping the decision was probably the right one but a *Claughton* with a taper boiler would have been an interesting sight. At Swindon a cost-effectiveness exercise on the process was never carried out but it must have had some benefit as some of the locomotives rebuilt in this way lasted well into BR days and there must, eventually, have been very considerable savings in the cost of servicing. Most of the MSWJ locomotives were thus rebuilt, the 4-4-0s in particular.

The second 4-4-4T, MSWJ No.18 (GWR No.27), was rebuilt with a standard No.10 boiler in 1925. This compilation produced a strikingly handsome engine but unfortunately its reliability was little improved and it is possible, given the earlier observation to see why. If there was too much weight on the bogies in the original design, how much worse that must have been on the rebuilt engine where the weight on the driving wheels was reduced to the point where there was actually little appreciable difference to that carried by the bogies. When in full working order the factor of adhesion was actually almost perfect at 4½ but as the tanks and bunker contents decreased so too did the adhesion factor; in a locomotive intended for high speed running that was fine but on work such as No. 27 was doing, it increased the potentiality to slipping. The 4-4-4T was sent to Kidderminster but is reported to have been out of work at Worcester from October 1926 until March 1928.[14] It lasted a few more months, being withdrawn in September 1929. Jim Russell remarks: *I have always admired this rebuild, and had ideas for making a 4 mm model but like many schemes of mice and men, it has not yet materialised.*[14] I know what he means but the old saying *handsome is as handsome does* certainly applies here. There are other examples from locomotive history of which possibly the Pickersgill *Oban Bogies* on the Caledonian must come near the top of the mark. Phil Atkins has described these engines as: *an oddity* (which) *looked like some fully-grown version of a freelance essay straight from the pages of the Model Engineer.*[22]

The 4-4-0s were of a different order altogether. Nos. 1-8 and 31 became GWR Nos. 1119 to 1126 and 1128 in the same order. The last two built, No. 4 and 31, had been fitted with boilers carrying two domes, the rear one containing a top feed apparatus which is described in the source already referred to as *GWR top feed*. This is clearly wrong but these boilers and, indeed, some of the older ones continued to be used, going the rounds of several engines, in exchange for taper boilers. The taper boiler was the standard No.2, superheated, fitted to six of the nine engines taken over from the MSWJ, the first on No. 1121 in September 1924 and the last to No. 1123 as late as August 1929.[5/10] With the new boilers, GWR cabs were also added and in this form they were extremely handsome engines indeed. And they continued to enjoy a good reputation, no adverse comment about their performance seems to have been made. Though they never worked off the old MSWJ lines, one or two strayed further on isolated occasions, never as a regular thing, it was 1938 before the last succumbed to the invasion of GWR standard types. It might be thought that given the long life of the 2-4-0 passenger engines built in 1894 and which lasted until the mid-1950s that the 4-4-0s were withdrawn early. Arguably some at least could have undertaken similar work, particularly on the line from Didcot to Newbury and Southampton and on the other railways this is certainly how they would have been employed. In fact they all had a reasonably good working lives. All of them were running for more than 20 years and the longest lasting was in service for no less than 36 years, a tribute surely to the soundness of the design; maybe also to what Gibson says was the MSWJ policy of maintaining its engines at the normal rate and not letting maintenance go as did some other railways when they knew they were to be taken over by the GWR.[7]

I suppose it can be argued that making a mess of a traditional British 4-4-0 design was actually very difficult though the example of James Stirling gives the lie to any such contention. Having also identified the Reichsbahn O1 pacific as a machine with an impressive appearance the reader might want to push me into a comment about locomotives that have left behind the easy appearance of the traditional 4-4-0. Among Great Western engines the *Star* is clearly the best looking, the lines are less bulky than either the *Castle* or the *King*. I have to add that I do not like what has been done to 6024 in order to keep it running on the main line, it now looks stunted, missing the majesty that these locomotives certainly had in their original and BR double chimney guise. In the next chapter I will add some further points about streamlining, suffice it here to say the British 4-6-0 is not altogether a suitable locomotive for streamlining, its length does not lend itself very successfully to the form. Yet the innate conservatism of British locomotive engineers has resulted in so many lost opportunities that one almost despairs. I am well aware that Riddles' pacific, *Duke of Gloucester* demonstrated important advances in cylinder design but it looked very ordinary and does so even more now, especially when compared with such as the truly imposing Norfolk & Western J class or the SNCF 232U1. Performance has nothing to do with these observations for the 1950s schoolboy referred to in the opening paragraph of this chapter would know nothing of such things. Despite the controversial performance of the type, our schoolboy might well agree with me that the most impressive railway locomotive built anywhere in the world, at any time in history was actually the Pennsylvania Duplex 4-4-4-4.

Notes and references

9) *Mysticism and Logic* - Bertrand Russell
10) *Industrial Design* - Raymond Loewy
11) *Gone With Regret* - George Behrend
12) *The Trains We Loved* - C. Hamilton Ellis
13) *The MSWJ Railway* - T.B.Sands (Revised by S.C.Jenkins)
14) *The MSWJ Railway* - Mike Barnsley
15) MSWJR Board Minutes 1900-1923 BTHR Rail 489/3 & 4
16) BTHR Rail 489/20
17) Mike Barnsley - correspondence with the author December 2000
18) Readers should note that the delivery dates quoted by the RCTS in Reference 5/10 differ from those stated in the MSWJ's Board Minutes, reference 15 above.
19) Where has that been heard before?
20) *Chronicles of Steam* - E.S.Cox
21) *A Pictorial Record of GWR Engines* - Volume 3 - J.H.Russell
22) *The Scottish 4-6-0 Classes* - C.P.Atkins

Six
Churchward aftermath

In one of his books, E.S.Cox describes what he sees as the fanaticism of GWR enthusiasts whose support for Swindon steam reaches almost to the proportions of divine worship. On top of this he states that even after the Second World War: *Swindon initiates were* (not) *prepared to concede much locomotive merit to other centres which they visited*. The final blast of damnation is put into the mouth of none other than Sir William Stanier, who we are told baited his old colleagues about their hidebound unenterprising ways *with relish*.[9] Thus is Cox condemned out of his own mouth, for his attempt to present a fair representation of locomotive development is blighted by a partisanship which these words reveal as being very close to that which he attacks. As we shall see, Swindon under Collett and to a lessor degree Hawksworth, was hidebound and unenterprising and a few devotees of Swindon are unwilling to acknowledge this. On the other hand intelligent followers of locomotive history know the truth and do not require to be daubed with a brush of prejudice which is itself infected. I cannot accept that middle ranking officers at Swindon in the late 1940s were not aware and desperately unhappy about the situation. We shall see how they reacted to this. That the followers of other railways are no less partisan is clear from the reading of any railway magazine though the example recorded by Gibson bears repeating.[7] He recalls a correspondence in which he pointed out to a commentator, proclaiming that the rebuilt *Royal Scot* was superior to the *Castle,* that since to all intents and purposes they were a new engine, they ought to be superior. And one might add that even if that were not the case, a locomotive rebuilt in 1943 should certainly be better than one that was at least 20 years older. The response was to accuse Gibson of unreconstructed Swindonian fanaticism.

There is no doubt that Churchward's production *Star* class 4-6-0 has some claim to be the most outstanding express passenger engine built in the first quarter of the 20th century. Some drivers always maintained that the *Saints* were actually better engines, a claim which despite some evidence that the two cylinder types may have been better hill climbers, cannot be sustained by any acceptable evidence.[10] I wonder if this was just a reaction to the fact that the two cylinder engines were rougher rides than the *Stars*, inevitably, and that, in the absence of speedometers, the men *thought* they were getting more out of them. It is no exaggeration to say that the four cylinder engines were real 'stars', I am convinced that most of the first generation diesel schedules on the WR could have been handled successfully by superheated *Stars* in good working order. O.S.Nock relates that the last in service, No. 4056 *Princess Margaret* was such a good runner, even in the 1950s that he confidently suggested to the WR authorities that they put it on the 105 minute *Bristolian*.[10] This is interesting and suggests that the GWR locomotive stock, certainly the *Saints* and *Stars* were superior to most of the pre-1914 services they were called upon to operate, and indeed, after that date. Booked average speeds on the GWR before 1914 were far from outstanding as can be seen by reference to the day to day schedules. In 1912 the shortest time between Paddington and

Bristol was 120 minutes for the 118.25 miles (an average speed of 59.4 mph), to Exeter, 173.75 miles, 180 minutes (57.9 mph), to Oxford 63.5 miles, 70 minutes (54.4 mph), to Birmingham via Ayhno, 110.5 miles, 120 minutes (55.25 mph) and to Cardiff 145.24 miles, 170 minutes (51.2 mph).[2] I am aware that these are overall times which take no account of intermediate station stops and that some of the routes involve heavy gradients. Also they are significant advance on the 1889 position and involve much greater train loads. For example in the summer months the *Limited* could load up to 14 bogies, nearly 500 tons gross and the Bristol trains averaged about 360 tons. Nonetheless, bearing in mind that 40 years later, in the 1950s the *Stars* were still hauling heavy passenger trains on schedules tighter than these and improving on the booked times, makes it perfectly plain that these earlier workings could have been improved. We have seen in the last chapter that something like 17 minutes could have been cut off the 1937 booked time for the Cheltenham - Swindon section of the *Cheltenham Flyer*, it is clear that much more could have been done on other trains, long before this date.

Inevitably the question arises as to why such accelerations were not actioned and there are two likely answers. The first is that the perceived demands for rail services nor the competition between railways in the years before the first world war were such that any really great increase in speed was considered necessary, (increasing train loads was another matter). It has to be remembered that the long distance travelling public was small by present day standards and that competition from other forms of transport was virtually non-existent. Life was also slower. The market for high speed trains was much less than it is today. Speed and high performance cost money, even with the *Stars* which burnt coal at a rate far below any of its competitors. This brings us to the other factor. While the GWR was not Railtrack, it was a private company committed to making a profit for its proprietors. And the evidence is that the GWR Board looked askance at the money expended by Swindon on new locomotives. Gibson relates a story in which an acquaintance enthusing about them was firmly put in his place by a director who pronounced that Churchward's engines were: *unnecessarily big and heavy, causing us to spend too much money on track and bridges and too expensive to build*.[7] This accords with the story that Churchward challenged as to why his engines cost twice as much as those of the LNWR retorted, *because one of mine could pull two of their bloody things backwards!* Clearly this is the authentic voice of British business, concerned only with short term profit involving as little investment as possible and with no interest in long term development. Capital investment in locomotive construction was cut after Lord Churchill became Chairman in 1908 and we may, I think, conjecture from this and other factors that a stronger emphasis on profit became the Board's major concern. It is possible even that this was a major underlying factor in the lethargy which came over Swindon in the 1930s. I will return to this issue several times in this chapter.

Though in their original saturated form the Churchward engines performed more than satisfactorily, the incorporation of superheaters was significant. A modern British locomotive engineer has suggested to me that Churchward was blind to the potential of superheating.[11] I can see his point. However, the description of the Swindon superheater as a 'steam dryer' will not do. While it was smaller in terms of heating area than the Schmidt derivatives introduced elsewhere, the larger Churchward boilers were pressed to 225 lbs at a time when other companies had barely risen above 180. And until they realised that with superheated steam there is a slightly greater pressure drop between boiler and cylinders, most other railway engineers reduced boiler pressure when fitting superheaters. It is therefore arguable that with the good Welsh coal that GWR engines burned, the performance of their low superheat boilers was actually superior to their Schmidt cousins on other railways. There will always be those who want to know why Churchward did not go even further and get still more out of his boilers by providing high degree superheat but the answer is clear enough. High temperature superheated steam had a deleterious effect on lubricating oils causing a build up of carbon and for this reason Churchward stayed with the moderate temperature that the Swindon superheater provided. Challenged about it Churchward gave the response adopted years later by BR when rubbishing the Giesl ejector and the Franco-Crosti boiler, its advantages were limited on well designed boilers.[12] And indeed, in the circumstances of the time that was the right response though his remarks as do others in similar situations suggest that Churchward was not good at 'thinking on his feet.' Had he talked a little bit about the effect of high temperature on lubricants, his reply would have been more convincing.

As far as this writer is concerned there are two aspects of Churchward's work that set him apart from most of his contemporaries: standardisation of components of advanced design and the constant desire to develop them further. It beggars belief that the directors of the GWR should be critical of his expenditure when under any other policy being followed elsewhere, the cost of developing motive power to meet even the demands that the operators were prepared to make might have been far greater. It was all very well to tip one's hat to Crewe's 'thrash 'em to hell' policy, but how would they have reacted one wonders to a Pickersgill, Dugald Drummond or Hughes (before he caught on to the trick of long travel valves) whose 4-6-0s were either coal gobblers or virtual failures. The crux of the matter is to design successfully for an advance on current or even foreseen needs. Bulleid was of the view that standardisation hindered developmental advance and that caveat is perfectly acceptable insofar as it is pointless producing a standardised set of components that are immediately rendered obsolete.[13] But that is not what Churchward, or later Stanier, actually did. The proper response of other engineers to what Churchward achieved was surely to have bettered it, to render his advancements obsolete before they actually were. One of the reasons that this did not happen has already been suggested, it was a long time before anyone was really aware of what Swindon 4-6-0s could do (and sometimes they did not believe it even then). It was to be 20 years before another engineer, Gresley, really approached what Churchward had achieved.

The drawback, serious in my view, to Gresley's practice is the lack of comprehensive standardisation. It is true that LNER boilers were used on more than one class, but with his undoubted ability to produce advanced designs, comprehensive standardisation along the GWR and LMS lines might well have saved the LNER a great deal of money without any detriment to performance or efficiency. There is a clue I think as to why Gresley did not do this, it was partly a sharing of Bulleid's reaction and may also have been something to do with the comment of the Great Northern's chairman in the House of Commons debate on the Grouping Bill. Sir Frederick Banbury was one of the 'characters' of the House, regarded as a survivor from a past age which, given his statement that it was impossible to standardise locomotives between railway companies was probably true.[14] It is unlikely that this remark actually originated with Gresley and that Banbury was just making it up as he went along for Gresley was involved with the sub-committee of the Association of Railway Locomotive Engineers charged with the development of standard locomotives for construction once the war was over. Though the proposals came to nothing, designs for long travel 2-6-0 and 2-8-0 types were developed. Clearly this did not represent the whole range of necessary motive power but Churchward, co-ordinating the sub-committee was clear that they fitted the loading gauge of all the main line railways.[13]

Most British engineers would have been satisfied with the two cylinder *Saints* and let them handle their company's best trains for the next 15 years. But not Churchward. What is remarkable is that even before the *Stars* were showing what they were capable of doing, he was moving on to the next stage. The full significance of this is often lost in purely narrative descriptions of his work. *The Great Bear* represented in terms of size an increase on the *Stars* of somewhere around a third as much again. 3,400 sq ft of heating surface against 2442 sq ft and 41 sq ft grate area against 27 sq ft. The proportions are enormous and might be best grasped 'at a glance' by seeing a scale model of the *Bear* stood beside a *Star*. The potential performance of the *Bear* was vastly in excess of what the GWR needed unless there was a passenger operating department with a commitment to providing the fastest possible services, willing to take a locomotive like the *Bear* and get the best out of it. Why this never happened has already been suggested, in the years before the first world war there was actually no requirement for such a locomotive. Almost certainly there was more to it than this.

Perhaps the most interesting question of all is why *The Great Bear* was built at all. There are still those who believe the old idea that the Board, mesmerised by the success of Churchward's engines demanded the construction of the 'ultimate' locomotive. But this fails the test of reality at almost every level. It is fully in accord with what we know from studying his work that he continually sought to develop and improve his designs and that this was a further movement in that direction. Knowing how Churchward thought about directors, and, on the evidence, how they viewed his expenditure is it likely, is it possible that he would put before them an outline scheme for a locomotive, the construction of which he could not justify, and guessed the Directors would block anyway? That he might have talked up the proposal privately with those who attended the Locomotive Committee meetings is perfectly possible but that still does not support the old myth of a directors ego-trip.

For me Churchward's most serious mistake was to cling to inside valve gear. Many years ago I asked my father about this and he told me that in his firing days at Old Oak, where the outside gear on the French compounds was daily on view, he had been told that it was because there was too much weight on the driving wheel, an explanation that he readily agreed could not possibly be true. I have devoted a lot of time to exploring this conundrum involving a good many other people, badgered for answers. George Davidson suggested amongst other things that the GWR Board hankered after the elegance of the Dean single and this has a ring of truth about it; being men whose backgrounds were in the 1870s and 80s, that their view was actually backward looking is not without logic.[15][16] Even so I do not think it is definitive. There is the story which appears in Gibson that it resulted from contretemps with the scissors gear fitted to No.40 (later 4000).[7] It is suggested that setting up the gear after the scissors levers had been removed took something like ten days but this was not realised until after the locomotive had started running. Churchward was being criticised by the Board for over-expenditure, and needed to correct this error without making it too obvious to the Directors that he had made a serious mistake in going for the scissors type. Thus he decided to quickly redesign the production *Stars* to take Walschaerts but placed it inside where the change could not be seen. As a conspiracy theory, this is near perfect but I am not convinced. I can accept that the redesign of the production *Stars* was carried out with a degree of urgency since only five months separated the completion of No.40 and the Board's authorisation of their construction. It would certainly have been easier to put the gear inside rather than redesign the layout to take outside motion.

That said, on the *Stars* the steam chests were outside the frames and there was absolutely no reason why outside gear, driving the inside valves through rocking levers, a reversal of the system adopted, could not have been incorporated at no very great expense. Something more however is needed to explain why the "improvisation" became a basic feature of the design. O.S.Nock's comment that GJC *had an abhorrence of outside valve gear* is just an assumption based on the fact that his locomotives had the gear inside the frames.[10] There is another reason to reject the conspiracy theory aspect of what happened and that concerns *The Great Bear*. If Churchward was being criticised by the Board as seriously as Gibson suggests, how was it that only 12 months later, in July 1907 they authorised the construction of this giant pacific? I have already explained why I cannot accept that 4-6-2 No. 111 resulted from a flight of fantasy on the part of the Board; incontrovertibly, had GJC been under any kind of cloud the *Bear* would not have been authorised. We are forced to conclude that inside valve gear was deliberately chosen after due thought, not simply from experience of circumstance. And as such it is inexplicable except in one possible respect. It can be argued that labour was cheap and remained relatively so despite the demands of industry for wage reductions; the advantages of outside valve gear did not become obvious until the costs of servicing became a serious issue. Given the GW Board's concern about money this is as tendentious a suggestion as anything else but it cannot easily be rejected.

Though I am a great admirer of Churchward I have tried to indicate that his work did have a downside which all said and done is however, small by comparison with the advances that he made in locomotive design. Five years after he had retired, advanced locomotive design at Swindon largely stagnated, a result, as most observers agree of the fact that Churchward's successors did not have his foresightedness or his comprehensive scientific approach. I also have contributed to that view which I believe to be, in the main, correct. However, there are other contributing factors which have remained largely ignored.[17] The first has already been alluded to, the Great Western Board was very concerned about the profit factor especially in the aftermath of the first world war. Some people remark that the GWR was the only company to pay a dividend on its ordinary stock during the 1930s. Perhaps the real reason for that was actually lack of appropriate investment. That is not to ignore the very real fact that the whole period from 1922 to 1939 was, for far too many people a period either of poverty or at best, insecurity. Yet even modern economists seem unwilling to accept that this was largely self-inflicted. Maintaining the currency value at an impossibly high level cut the ground from underneath exporters and had considerable knock-on effect on domestic infrastructure. There was some talk about nationalising the railways in the years immediately after the war, and given hindsight one can only comment that such a measure might well have been better than the long struggle with profitability faced by the four main line companies. Unfortunately neither conservative governments or even those claiming to be socialist were prepared to listen to progressive economists such as Maynard Keynes whose prescriptions for improvement were the making of Europe post-1945.

Another factor, paradoxically, was the nature of the railway's chief executive. Sir Felix Pole, General manager from 1921 to 1929 is often written of as being an enterprising giant who met, matched, pre-empted or defeated every manoeuvre by the GWR's competitors. I am not certain that this is true. Evidence suggests that there was very little love lost between Pole and the Board and the story of the conflict between them over the latter's attempts to drastically increase their fees tells more between the lines than on them.[18] I have long believed that the approach to him to become Chairman of AEC was far more an attempt to get him out of the Board's way as any admiration of his managerial abilities. On the other hand, he was hardly on the best terms with some of the companies senior executives either. Grierson's management plan, making the general manager the senior company executive, for all that it was the right way to proceed, was peremptorily introduced without any attempt at amelioration and caused a good deal of discontent. Nor were the demands that he made on Swindon free of mutual antipathy.[19] A real leader takes people with him, not drives them willy nilly.

Churchward's successor was Charles B.Collett, since 1919 Deputy CME and therefore probably the obvious successor, despite which the plain fact is that he *was* the wrong choice. Collett was born on September 10 1871, the son of William and Mary Collett who lived in Westbourne Terrace. His father was a journalist and obviously more than a mere hack for he was able to send his son to Merchant Taylors School where he remained until taking an apprenticeship with the marine engineers Maudsley, Son and Field. Maudsley trained men were renowned the world over, their apprenticeships were very much in demand and only the best applicants were taken on. Further confirmation comes in an interesting event. In 1893 Collett applied for a post in the Swindon Drawing Office which when it was offered, he at first turned down. Changing his mind, he applied again to Swindon and was engaged. No such second thoughts would have been granted to anyone who was not of above average ability. Some years ago I was told that Collett's actual succession to the post of CME was challenged by F. G. Wright.[20] Wright had been the commanding officer of a regiment of territorial volunteers but had made the mistake of not going to the front with them. In the appalling years after the First World War when "what did you do in the war daddy?" was a blackmail of all honour, such a decision was truly a bad career move but I am no longer certain that this happened in quite this way. Wright had been born in 1863 and was therefore, 51 years of age on the outbreak of war. While men of this age did volunteer and it may have been expected that a Major of Volunteers ought really to go with his men to the front, there was actually no compulsion, even under conscription for men of this age to do so. I therefore now think it unlikely that this happened in quite the way I had been led to believe.

Collett was married in 1896 to Ethelwyn Simon, a clergyman's daughter and they were very devoted to each other. Collett eschewed involvement in civil affairs, preferring to spend his time in his wife's company. He was a quiet man, possibly rather self-conscious and probably came to rely on his wife to a very large degree. Thus when she died he was devastated and I am convinced that it was this that determined his personality, so often spoken of as being prickly, difficult to work with, or in Gibson's words, *devious, secretive and unreliable*.[7] K. J. Cook told me that *we liked working with him* and that *he was quite accessible to his officers* but added that he was also *a stern disciplinarian*.[21] Not unusual in the 20s but it could he another indication of personal difficulty on his part. There is the story of the occasion when Churchward and Collett went together to the boiler shop to inspect a firebox. The shop was lit by gas lamps which were portable on lengths of hose. Collett instructed the Shop Foreman to "bring me an illuminant" but that person, unsure of what had been said, returned "beg pardon, sir?" Churchward interrupted "Bill, bring me a bloody gas"![19] The other side of all this is the 1911 Swindon staff photo, reproduced in this book. Here we see a man whose face betrays less of the mandarin's gimlet eye than might be expected from the foregoing. His wish to remain in office long after the normal retirement age is another indication of loneliness. Collett was involved in spiritualism reaching some prominence in the Metaphysical Society. Engineer-authors reporting these details have always tended to sneer at them but again it hints at the essential loneliness behind the facade. A complex personality therefore and in the event the wrong man to take on the challenge of keeping Churchward's momentum going.

Collett was, reportedly uninvolved in design work. So several authors tell us.[7][22] He would not have been the first locomotive engineer to have left detail design work to others but though such a contention fits in with my general theme I am not certain that I accept it. Churchward inspired very considerable loyalty from those with whom he came into contact. He was often in the Drawing Office very early each day and a draughtsman arriving punctually for work might well find the chief sitting at his board ready to discuss the previous day's work. At weekends he would often come across to the Works from *Newburn* to see how a job was coming on, progressing around the establishment in tweedy gardening clothes and a straw panama. And at *Newburn*, in an age when service was considered the normal occupation for large numbers of overworked and underpaid working class men and women, his treatment of his servants was beyond criticism; all of them were handsomely remembered in his will. Inevitably his successor would have been judged against this and it would have been a rare man who could have lived up to it. I cannot accept the bald assertion that because Collett was only rarely seen in the drawing office he was not involved with design.[23] Even if it is true that Hawksworth actually drew up the boiler design for the *King* it is much too simplistic to say that Collett was not aware or not concerned about this work. It may have been quite simply that he sent for draughtsmen or drawings when he needed them or communicated with the Drawing Office through the Chief Draughtsman.

Even so, he *was* far too content to sit on Churchward's laurels and not follow his example in constantly looking for advances. That does not mean that I join with those critics of the GWR who assert that Collett should have broken with Churchward's legacy, rather that he failed to take it on from where the master left off. There is little evidence in the available sources about the origin of the *Castles* other than to suggest that they were a hurried development of the *Stars* brought out because of demand from the publicity and operating people. In the shops, such was the demand for rapid completion that the cylinder dimensions were originally drawn on a *Star* drawing, differences being indicated in red.[7] Pole's pressurising of Swindon is strongly suggested here.

In fact the *Castle* was not the first or even seen as the ideal development of the Swindon 4-6-0. The rebuild of the *Stars* and *Saints* with the very large No.7 boiler fell foul of loading gauge factors early on. The difficulty was not intractable. A very reasonable rebuild of *The Great Bear* had been developed and was abruptly dropped. *Stars* continued to be built until February 1923, the first *Castle* took the rails in August. The design was an extraordinary compromise which I have described as achieving by some lucky happenstance one of the most outstanding express locomotives ever built in Britain. A view that has been criticised but which I still believe to be correct. Looking at the changes made it could so easily have gone wrong. The boiler is often spoken of as a compromise, the No.7 modified to allow its use on 6'8½" engines. Yet with water spaces reduced from the ideals established by Churchward, slightly increased overall heating surface area and a superheater that was no bigger than that on the *Stars*, it was expected to power cylinders that had a 1" larger bore. The theoretical horsepower increase by the *Castle* over the *Star* at 60 mph was in the order of 13% and had that been the whole story then the result might very well have been a failure. As it was the firebox was 12" longer at 10', giving a grate area larger by about 11% and that I am convinced was the secret of the *Castle's* success. Tests by Ell at Swindon established that the constraining factor in the standard No.1 boiler was the grate but in the No.8 it was the front end and this points up the conclusion I have come to.

One can sympathise with a design department harried to produce a more powerful machine as soon as possible, turning to the existing format and exploiting available components to enlarge it sufficiently to embrace new requirements. In this respect no criticisms of the original *Castle* is possible. But why oh why, as the first examples were being turned out, did Collett not instigate a renewal of the design that involved an updated valve gear layout and high degree superheat? There was a gap of over a year between the completion of Nos. 4082 and 4083. That certain modifications were incorporated into the later engines is well documented. So why not a full revision of the scheme? The problems experienced in 1926, during the prolonged coal strike when poorer quality coal was being used should also have alerted Swindon to the need to make its engines suitable for burning material of a lower calorific value. Higher degree superheat would almost certainly have dealt with this problem. In France superheat temperatures of 360-370° C had already been attained by the mid-20s.[24] The suggestion, correct enough, that it would have meant abandoning the sight feed lubrication system in favour of a mechanical lubricator is an excuse and no more. The truth is that Swindon was very complacent, certain that supplies of good coal would always be available.

These criticisms are even more profoundly relevant when it is considered that the original *King* class was a *Star* enlarged to its fullest potential and involved little new in the way of technical innovation. Once again we have the publicity people pressurising Swindon to get something out that was nominally more powerful than what was being done elsewhere. But four years had passed since the *Castle* scheme had been worked out. It is true that work in the drawing office had been very heavy during this period but why nothing further had been done in the way of express engine development is completely beyond me. The truth, almost certainly is that Collett was convinced that the *King* was fit for needs as far as could be foreseen and that in any case, further large expenditure of the kind involved in producing a new engine would have been vetoed by the Board. I will return to this point again.

It is not only in the realms of express locomotives that these criticisms can be levelled. As evidence of Churchward's continuing interest in technical development, the 1919 4701 class 5'8" 2-8-0, after fitting with the No.7 boiler, is a case in point. 'Nosing' of Churchward 2-6-0 and 2-8-0 locomotives was evident and may have been due to the frame layout, but with the 47 class it was more pronounced as a result of greater sideplay allowed in the rear driving axle boxes on account of their long, 20' fixed wheelbase. It was this effect that brought a ban on their running above 60 mph on passenger trains which, in retrospect can be seen to have been a great pity. It would have been very interesting to know just what a 47 would have done with a medium weight express train. Collett does seem to have been more in favour of front bogie engines than those with 2 wheel trucks, evidence his rebuilding of many of the Moguls as 4-6-0s. But the *Hall*, his preferred mixed traffic locomotive, though well received and a very good engine by any standards was little more than a 1900s *Saint* on 6' driving wheels. Even though not intended for the very fastest or heaviest work, by the 1920s something better was surely required, especially if a view commensurate with future needs was to be maintained. To my mind that improvement would have been provided by producing a revised 47; higher degree superheat, outside valve gear and standard axles boxes throughout but with a flangeless driving wheel set at the second or third position.

This contention, originally made in the *Backtrack* article which forms the basis of this chapter was severely criticised by a number of correspondents, none of whom it seems had done their homework. Everyone that I have spoken to about these locomotives always praised them very highly. The RCTS history does not understate the case when it says[5/9]...*they have more recently been used on express passenger trains between London and Devon in the summer, and have fully justified their original conception as heavy mixed traffic engines.* John Gibson was clear in his belief that the construction of more 47s would have been far more justified than building further *Castles* but it seems that Collett was determined on that path.[7] Cook wrote: *There has been some speculation as to whether the* [4701] *class was regarded as a failure...That was not so and some years later the Running Superintendent asked for some more and they were very nearly incorporated in the new engine building programme, but then Collett decided that although they would be a bit more costly he would rather build* Castles *which would also be more suitable for passenger train duplication at peak train periods.*[19] That really rather proves my point. It might be considered that the *Hall* could have provided the mixed traffic power for those lines and types of work on which the 47s were unable to operate and until recently I would have agreed with that, indeed my original article made precisely that argument. Interestingly, I have discovered that the contention that the *Grange* 4-6-0 was actually a better performer than the *Hall* may very well be true after all. These locomotives, regarded for accounting purposes as rebuilds of 2-6-0s were more than just 5'8" *Halls*. A new design of cylinder was necessary and that development allowed greater steam chest space thus providing a remarkably free running engine. Among some men therefore the *Grange* was much preferred to the *Hall* but it is doubtful if this information ever reached Collett.

It is untrue to suggest that no developmental work was carried out at Swindon, various schemes and designs were developed of which the Compound Castle (1926), the 5'8" 4-8-0, 2-10-2T and numerous smaller designs all provide interest for the 'what if..' merchant. Few of them were actually serious proposals and even fewer, one suspects originated with Collett rather than some mere draughtsman. Cook once upbraided me for a criticism of Collett, *I won't have that,* he wrote with reference to an unrelated matter, *that's not fair to old Collett.*[21] Yet he was no less critical of him in his book about Swindon. To quote a few lines from chapter 17, *Collett retired in July 1941 but rather involuntarily. That he stayed on so long was not in the best interests of the department... During the last three or four years of his chieftainship Collett was fully active in mind but was not using his talents for the benefit of the railway...*[19] Criticisms which he repeated in his letter to me. Volumes could be written about this period of GWR locomotive history and how this stasis in development came about. The underlying reason must be the financial demands of the Board. Capital expenditure on new locomotives was greatly restricted and new construction was made out of money set aside to take account of depreciation known as the Renewal Fund, a system which in modern parlance might be called creative accounting. This required that new building replaced older locomotives ton for ton and in building new *Castles* and *Halls*, the unnecessarily early withdrawal took place of perfectly good *Stars* and *Saints*. Indeed it is only a slight exaggeration to say that at this time the GWR was scrapping locomotives that were actually superior to those being built for some other railways.

Yet the poor economic situation is not the whole story. There was a discernible change of tone in the Boardroom. The 'in yer face' style of management associated with Sir Felix Pole disappeared, never to reappear; under James Milne the Board was clearly more in control. The speed exploits recorded with the *Cheltenham Flyer* and other trains were achieved with locomotives already in service. The very fact that these achievements were so good may well have been all the impetus those Directors interested in maximising profits needed to prevent expenditure on something new. I submit that if this was the situation then they got away with it because Collett, who it has been suggested had a lot of influence in the Boardroom was their ally in eschewing new express passenger engine development.[19] In other words, the success of the Churchward locomotive as developed into the *Castle* may well have contained the very seeds of its decline. There is an interesting vignette recorded in one of Michael Rutherford's books in which a GWR Director took Collett to see a working model of the American Baker valve gear. Collett appears to have agreed to try it on a Swindon engine. Unexpectedly the Director died. The project also quietly died.[25] Another unexplained matter is that of *Saint* No.2935, *Caynham Court*, rebuilt with rotary cam poppet valve gear. Though tests appear to have been carried out, nothing more in this way was ever done, possibly because exploitation of such a gear would have required high degree superheat with the resultant need to redesign the system of lubrication. Holcroft reports another suggestion, that the exhaust opening did not compare with that given by large diameter piston valves and that there was no saving of fuel.[4] It has been suggested to me that this conversion was done on the basis of the British Caprotti company taking the equipment and rebuilding costs at their expense.[26] There is no other explanation for it. However, *Caynham Court* never reverted to the conventional design and we might speculate as to what that tells us.

Another factor is the building of brand new versions of very old locomotives. The 57XX pannier tank was an excellent engine which, had it been available would have been a better bet for the South Wales lines than the 56XX 0-6-2T. In my view at least, the 56XX class was completely unnecessary and seriously over-produced. 200 were built, some of them by outside manufacturers between 1924 and 1928, ostensibly to standardise the locomotive stock of the South Wales colliery railways. Various factors including a decline in the coal trade meant that they were often to be seen outside their intended area of operation. Even if the pannier tank option was not available, and given that there were already a great many in service, the obvious recourse ought to have been realised, I am not certain that the construction of a completely new standard engine was really the right way forward. Engine costs are, of course a vital ingredient of operating costs and at this time the cost of coal was an increasingly major component of company out goings. The proposed electrification of the lines west of Taunton first proposed in 1931 and again in 1938 was a nonsense which can be seen to have been a political manoeuvre aimed at the colliery owners.[29] The diesel railcars are another matter and I will return to these in a later chapter. If the *Grange* was (accidentally) a good engine and the *Manor* filled a need, what are we to make of the 0-4-2T and 0-6-0 PT classes built in the 1930s to which we might add the 16XX class built under Hawksworth?

These machines have often been defended as very economical answers to given problems and while that may be true, was that really the best Swindon could do? It has been written that the construction of the 0-4-2Ts was criticised by *gentlemen of the school of thought which likes to see trains of one or two coaches hauled by a 2-6-2T*.⁽⁵/⁶⁾ Similarly, Cook went to a great deal of trouble to explain how the drawing office contrived to produce modern machines within the imposed economic constraints but failed to do so, or rather, if one reads him closely, within Collett's prejudices.⁽¹⁹⁾ My brother sometimes reminds me that a PhD in hindsight is easy to acquire and he has a point. Nonetheless it is arguable that the work of all these types could have been covered by one class of engine carrying one boiler. An examination of the weight diagrams shows that there was less than 5 tons difference in the total weight and only about 2 tons in axle weight between all of them. I can see that for branchline work the axle weight may have been important, possibly even crucial but I do not accept that this requires the proliferation of types to the extent that they were. Those intended for passenger work had 5'2" driving wheels, those seen as essentially freight engines 4'7½" driving wheels; trivial differences in wheel diameters like this have been shown to have very little relevance to performance. The 4'1½" driving wheels of the 16XX class might be different but what the need was for such engines as late as 1949 I have not the foggiest notion.

As an aside I would mention that proclaiming the 'Dukedog' as a new engine rather than what it was, a sensible reuse of components from old locomotives, was so obviously a shot in the foot that one is tempted to wonder if it was deliberate. I cannot now locate the origin of the publicity that announced the construction of this type but is it possible that this was Milne, an ex-Swindon premium apprentice very interested in locomotive affairs, aiming a shaft at Collett? Pure conspiracy theory but nonetheless not without interest.

Collett's successor as CME was Frederick W.Hawksworth who, to his credit began to move Swindon loco design forward. To what extent he actually did this will be examined in the next chapter. Suffice it here to refer to his lamentable continuation of Collett's lackadaisical development policy in regard to locomotives for lesser duties. Most amazing of all was the proposal to develop a tender version of the 16XX pannier tank!⁽²⁸⁾ What on earth would such a locomotive have been used for? The extraordinary thing is that under Hawksworth a drawing was prepared of a locomotive that, sufficiently processed might very well have covered all the requirements for which the 48,58,54,64,74 and 16XX classes were built.⁽⁵/⁹⁾ This was the pannier tank which might be described as a 2-6-0T version of the 57XXPT but with outside cylinders and valve gear. The sole drawback to the design as shown is the axle weight, heavier than the classes just mentioned but lighter than both the 15XX and 94XX panniers. I cannot believe that it would not have been possible to devise such a locomotive with an axle loading making the engine available for work on lightly loaded branch lines. A 2-6-0T would have provided a much more versatile engine, good for all kinds of work which, with its cylinders and valve gear outside would also have been economical to operate.

I began this chapter with a reference to E.S.Cox and I will end with the same source. Cox tells us that at nationalisation BR officers were *somewhat flabbergasted* to find that despite large numbers in stock, orders had been placed for more 0-6-0 tanks which he describes as *a lifelong love at Swindon* and which continued right up until 1964/5 with the construction of a 400 hp diesel hydraulic 0-6-0 intended for secondary and branch line work.⁽⁹⁾ Leaving aside for the moment the question of why they did not know about this previous to

1948, since all new construction had to be authorised by the Railway Executive, we are again entitled to ask just how fair a comment this is. Leaving aside the small engines just described, the fact is that the 57XX class 0-6-0s were very good performers and might very well have been adopted as a BR standard; if there were redundant 0-6-0s as Cox implies, some of the 57s at least could have been transferred to other regions as replacements for the antiquated 0-6-0s that continued to run all over the country until the late 1950s. If standardisation as promulgated by Riddles, Cox and Bond meant flooding the railways with LMS derived types, what was wrong with doing the same with an inexpensive GWR variant? The argument that GWR engines were out of gauge to the rest of Britain's railways does not hold good in this case, the 57XX was within the standard British profile. I have been very critical of Swindon's small engine policy in this chapter but one cannot help thinking that E S Cox was one of those individual's who did indeed prefer to see trains of one or two coaches hauled by a 2-6-2T whatever the reality of need.

Notes & references
9) *Chronicles of Steam* - E.S.Cox
10) *Stars, Castles & Kings* - O.S.Nock
11) David Wardale - correspondence with the author 2000
12) *On Large Locomotive Boilers* - G.J.Churchward - paper read to I.Mech E 1906
13) *Master Builders of Steam* - H.A.V.Bulleid
14) *A Parliamentary View of the Grouping* - L.A.Summers
  Railway Magazine - January 1972
15) *Backtrack* October 2003 - letter from G.A.Davidson and subsequent correspondence with the author.
16) On the other hand Churchward was actually much older, having been born in 1857.
17) *The Great Western, Boilers & The Great Bear* - M. Rutherford
  Backtrack - March 1996
18) *Pole's Book* - Sir Felix J.C.Pole
19) *Swindon Steam* - K.J.Cook
20) L.E.Trollope - correspondence with the author 1980.
21) K.J.Cooke - correspondence with the author 1980.
22) The late Ernest Nutty was also reported as having said something similar.
23) *Backtrack* - January 1997 and subsequent correspondence.
24) *La Locomotive au Vapeur* - English Language Edition
  Andre Chapelon/ George W. Carpenter
25) *Halls, Granges & Manors at Work* - Michael Rutherford
26) C.P.Atkins - correspondence with the author - 2006
27) *History of the Great Western Railway 1930-1939* - Peter Semmens
28) W.J.Mayo - General Manager's Motive Power Dept 1948-1960 - in correspondence with the author 2003.

Seven
The Myth of a Hawksworth Pacific

The Railway Magazine announced the appearance of the first of Hawksworth's 'County' class 4-6-0s on the Great Western Railway in the following words: *There is a peculiar interest in new locomotive design emanating from Swindon . . . For some time past, it has been understood that the first of a new class of locomotive for the GWR . . . was under construction and that the design included several outstanding features. Both in the drawing office and in the erecting shops the greatest secrecy was observed, with the result that many rumours and speculation concerning the new engine were rife.*[9] Indeed they were and, it would seem, this speculation was deliberately encouraged by people at Swindon who may well have enjoyed watching the effect they were creating, and not just among locospotters on the platforms at Paddington. At some point this conjecture became a Hawksworth Pacific and despite the attempts of historians to inject some sense into the whole story, there are still those who believe that this was an authoritative reality. There is very little real information about the proposal, the one incontestable fact is that it never had any connection with the Chief Mechanical Engineer of the GWR who rubbished the whole thing every time he was asked about it. Now, the evidence strongly suggests that it resulted from a revulsion by middle management to what they saw as the continuing inertia in Swindon locomotive design.

F.W.Hawksworth
Drawn by Chris Seymour from a photograph

Hawksworth has not enjoyed a good press. He started as a premium apprentice at Swindon in 1898, transferring to the Drawing Office in 1905 where he spent the greater part of his career. His first job was to assist with the setting up of the stationary test plant and when in the 1930s this equipment was fully updated to take the most powerful locomotives, it was Hawksworth who was put in charge of the work. As a young draughtsman he had been selected by G.H.Burrows to do the general arrangement drawing of the original Swindon Pacific, *The Great Bear*. I have been told that during his time as CME Hawksworth kept these drawings locked away and gave instructions that no-one was to have access to them without his permission.[10] He was also responsible for drawing up a substantial part of the the *King* boiler. Practical workshops men tended to deprecate Hawksworth. He became chief draughtsman in 1925 and then assistant to Collett in 1932. Cook described him to me as: *an intellectual but a not very enterprising one.*[11] From another railway R.H.N.Hardy spoke of him as *a jumped-up Chief Draughtsman*. Only now can we see that Cook's comment was probably nearest the mark. While being unmarried does not seem to have counted against Churchward, there is reason to think that it may have done against FWH. In fact he married his housekeeper when aged about 80. He was a Swindon JP and chaired the bench in a notorious obscenity case brought by the police against a bookseller.[12]

To get at the facts and indeed the story behind the legend of the so-called 'Hawksworth Pacific' it is necessary to go back more than ten years to the early 1930s when Swindon's lethargy began. Let us be clear from the outset, the previous chapter, though highly critical of Collett does not argue that the LMS and LNER left the Great Western trailing far behind; in 1930 only the A3 pacifics and *Royal Scots* held any kind of candle to the brightness of the GWR and in terms of everyday trains Swindon's locomotives were providing a very cost-effective service at a time when finances for building new types were limited.

For those studying both the published and private sources on this subject one conclusion will be immediately obvious, there is so much to study and it is so diverse that a firm definitive conclusion as to which type consistently put up the best results is largely impossible. To take just a few of the comments that have been made, Holcroft reports being told by a Running Department officer that the *Castle* was considered the best engine.[4] Gibson suggests that the *Star* was a better engine than the *Castle* but the *King* best of all, able to regain steam quickly after a hard run.[7] There is a report, though the details are sketchy that in 1938 a *King* took a 950 ton loaded goods train from Newport to Aberbeeg, not without difficulty, and with a second *King* banking, ran on to Ebbw Vale with 1,350 tons.[13] We are given no other figures and that seriously reduces the usefulness of the information but something significant occurred, warranting a report being released to the press. This is 21 miles of adverse gradients, the real bank starting just before Aberbeeg at 1:68 and continuing variously at around 1:55 for much of the way with a short section at 1:24 and 1:31. The bark from the chimneys must have been something to remember.

The many books quoted in the bibliography contain pages and pages of detailed performance data showing that all three GWR 4 cylinder locomotives were capable of consistently outstanding work which when all the circumstances are taken into account was as good as nearly everything done anywhere else in Britain. It is Kenneth H Leech who shows that the crucial point is: *when all the circumstances are considered*.[14] He reported that in 1933, No.6022, *King Edward III* worked a 575 ton train from Exeter to Paddington in 175½ minutes, very nearly even time. Now go back and read that again, what is being reported is that *a train of more than a half a thousand tons at the drawbar was hauled over a distance of close to 200 miles at just under a mile a minute*. Not a spectacular speed run but in terms of load hauled actually far more creditable than hauling say, 100 tons for a very short distance at 105 mph.

Given this kind of performance we can accept that the GWR's locomotive engineer was quite justified, at that time, in concluding that an expensive new design was unnecessary, if indeed that is how his mind worked. Nonetheless, it has to be admitted that, in the circumstances that eventually came to pass, the GWR not only passed up the immediate opportunity to really 'dish' the rest but also the long-term advantage of having on hand something that, in modern parlance, was a 'state of the art' locomotive type. Worse than this was a failure to recognise that in terms of world locomotive design the British railway company that had once led the rest was indeed beginning to trail behind the best that was being done elsewhere. Most clearly was this in comparison with what was being done in France by André Chapelon and in Germany by R.P. Wagner. However, before examining their work there is one other factor to consider, streamlining.

It is often forgotten that streamlining originated way back at the dawn of the steam age with studies done in 1825 by Charles McClaren and in 1859 by Rankine.[15] Streamline locomotives built in France in the 1900s had a 'windcutter' vee shape enclosing the chimney and smokebox front. But it was the coming of the motor car which ushered in the real age of streamlining as American automobile engineers looked for the means by which to make their products not only faster but look faster. And on railways, it was in fact on diesel and electric trains such as the *Flying Hamburger* that streamlining first appeared. The world's first streamline express steam train was actually operated by the Japanese on the South Manchuria Railway in the Chinese territory that they occupied and called Manchuckuo, the *Asia Express* which covered the 438 miles between Dalian and Changchun in 510 minutes.[15] However it started running only a few months before several north American operators of which the New York Central's *Twentieth Century Limited* was the first. Streamlining in the USA resulted from two linked impulses, the first towards ultra-modernity in appearance and the second towards achieving higher speeds by reducing resistance. The former was an integral part of the Art-deco movement which found expression in such diverse representatives as the Chrysler Tower in New York and streamlined fountain pens, still very fashionable 70 years later.

Little in the way of experimental research or trials were carried out before the streamline shrouds were designed, such research as was carried out was first done by Raymond Loewy, the fashion designer who became the great guru of modernistic design, by Bell Geddes and Henry Dreyfus.[15][16][17] For a description of this research the reader is referred to Loewy's books where he describes sitting in a locomotive with a stick to which a ribbon was attached and holding this out into the slipstream to measure the aerodynamics. Loewy describes railway engineers as needing 'indoctrination' to the benefits of streamlining and judging from these early experiments one can see why! Even so, his strictures were more right than wrong, as was shown by tests on the shape of the shroud on the S1 class 6-8-6 carried out in the Guggenheim Aerodynamics Laboratory in New York. One has only to see pictures of the standard Pennsylvania RR locomotives next to those streamlined by Loewy and the advantages of 'look good' streamlining become immediately obvious. And the device that he designed for lifting the smoke above the cab which fitted behind the chimney was more effective and less destructive of the locomotive lines than the hideous smoke deflecting 'blinkers' that adorn far too many British locomotives. Our home based engineers tended to be just as conservative as their American counterparts and very few showed any interest in streamlining either from a view of creating the ultra-modern appearance to which most Americans subscribed or as a means of reducing resistance and improving performance. Gresley who, whatever else he might have been was a first class innovator, took the first steps in this direction. This is not the place to describe his work but I consider that it was the Yarrow boilered 4-6-4 No.10000 that set him off on this particular track.

It seems that as soon as the LNER announced that a streamline express locomotive was being designed at Doncaster, the GWR Board wanted Swindon to do the same, and as quickly as possible. Given the attitude of its members to investment in new design the commentator can only express complete mystification at how they intended this should be done. In fact Collett was their man, as on other occasions. It was not to be expected that he should be anything other than thoroughly opposed to the scheme and therefore devise something that was cheap and ridiculous. In fact, in his hubristic response to the Board he actually created a very narrow near-miss. The story of the plasticine smeared over a paper-weight *Castle* which was then sent into the Drawing Office for the streamline shapes to be worked out is very attractive but I think probably a myth. Collett had only to ask for a weight diagram of any 4-6-0 and to draw on it the shapes that he wanted in order for a draughtsman to detail them, and I think this is more likely to have been what happened. Most people are familiar with the semi-streamlining fitted to *Castle* 5005 and *King* 6014 but few can bring themselves to admit to enthusiasm for it. Freebury relates, perhaps not surprisingly that Swindon workshop men regarded them as *bodged up jobs* which I suppose is exactly what they were.[18] And that is a pity. Had Collett thought about it a little more, the GWR could have had a semi-streamlined locomotive that would have really gripped the imagination and perhaps stolen the LNER's thunder much more than was actually achieved briefly by the appearance of the two conversions. This form of semi-streamlining appeared on several classes of locomotive in the United States, on the New York Central, New Haven, Norfolk and Western, in Europe and in New South Wales where the lovely 38 class pacific, 3801 can still be seen on regular runs in steam. The extraordinary thing is that the Collett streamlining, if we are permitted to call it that, actually predated all of these locomotive types and it is possible, one dare go no further than that, to suggest that 5005/6014 were actually the initial impetus for this form of shrouding.

In Britain performance-enhancing streamlining was considered to have been debunked by wind tunnel tests done for Bulleid at the National Physical Laboratory which showed that only at speeds in excess of 90 mph did it have much benefit.[16] These figures are open to doubt and were challenged at the time, Bulleid's methods of testing being seriously questioned.[17] European locomotives were somewhat less air-smoothed than standard British ones but Wagner demonstrated to the Institution of Mechanical Engineers that the reduction in drag at that speed could be as much as five times more than Bullied claimed.[18] On the SNCF successive engineers also took a similar line.

Yet it was not streamlining that offered the best means of improving steam performance in the 1930s as the scientific examination of the process of raising and using steam. This work is most often associated with André Chapelon but he was not alone, just the most significant of the engineers at work at this time. Those readers interested in the full details will do no better than read

Chapelon's own words, now thankfully translated into English.[22] Perhaps I may be permitted to quote a line from the translator's introduction: (Chapelon's research) *resulted in the maximum power of certain locomotive types being doubled within existing overall dimensions, as in the Paris-Orleans compound pacifics rebuilt as 4-8-0s in 1932...* How was it done?

Interestingly we can read as good an outline description as any in a paper prepared at Swindon in May 1939.[23] It begins: *The object of the post-war development of the compound locomotive in France has been to increase the power available with the least possible increase in the weight and leading dimensions. The effect has been to increase the ihp per ton weight from 23 to 37.* (The corresponding power to weight ratio for GWR King class engines is 20.4 taking the maximum ihp as 1,814, as recorded in the trials of 6005 in 1931, the highest figure so far obtained.) *This 61% increase has been achieved by the following comparatively slight modifications: fitting Kylchap double blast-pipe, increasing the degree of superheat, increasing the size of all steam passages.* The first point to note is that the ihp/ton weight of the *King* was already less than that of the PO pacific before it was rebuilt. And this was the engine that could haul 575 tons for nearly 200 miles at close to even time. Thus can it be seen how misplaced, in reality was the satisfaction with current operations among the hierarchy at Swindon and Paddington.

This paper is of very considerable interest and only recently have I discovered that it was actually the work of Geoffrey Tew who with Gilbert Scholes, later Chief Draughtsman at Swindon was very interested in Chapelon's work and who attempted without success to translate his book.[24] Despite this, Tew maintained that interest and following an article about it in an engineering publication drew up this paper which was submitted to the CME. It is in fact a damning indictment of contemporary GWR locomotive practice as a few extracts will show. *...the blastpipe fitted to [6005] was incapable of fulfilling its principle function, that of maintaining equilibrium between the demand and supply of steam. The increased back pressure associated with an increased rate of steam consumption should result in a smokebox vacuum sufficiently high to maintain the rate of fuel consumption necessary for the increased rate of steam production. During the trials of 6005 in 1931 this equilibrium .... could only be maintained by use of the blower... Until King class engines are provided with some means of maintaining a smokebox vacuum at least double that at present possible they will never be able to burn sufficient coal to produce steam at the rate necessary for a high power output.* The Swindon superheater again comes in for criticism with the comment that in the French type steam temperatures 3½ times better than that recorded with the *King* were achieved. It is of course well known that after his contretemps on the LMS Stanier advised Collett to go for higher degree superheat and there is a reference in this paper to a study done by Scholes earlier in 1939 which showed that there were indeed advantages to be gained from so doing. The paper goes on to show how increased superheat increased power output at the same time as being economical in terms of water consumption.

The recommendations in the paper were explicit: *...there is no reason why the power of GWR locomotives would not be greatly increased by similar treatment. Apart from the blastpipe it appears that particular attention should be paid to* the provision of at least 50% more superheater units, more direct and larger steam pipes from superheater to steam chest, larger outside steam chests and larger passages for exhaust steam. Still more economical use of the increased power thus available could be made with an increase in the area of admission and exhaust ports. It is unnecessary to say that these recommendations engendered no response at Swindon. Alan Wild is of the opinion that Collett never saw them, that Hawksworth, mainly responsible for the *King* boiler and through whom Tew's paper obviously had to go, shoved it in a drawer away from the CME's eyes.[24] I suppose we can understand that reaction, we are all capable of human frailties, but what a terrible pity.

In 1941 Collett was finally prevailed upon to resign, reluctantly, as has been noticed.[25] Hawksworth succeeded him. Though much younger than the old chief, his capacity to effect any great design innovation was restricted throughout his term of office first by the Second World War and then by the control that the wartime railway authority continued to exercise until nationalisation, after which he could do hardly anything without permission from the 'Kremlin', as British Railways headquarters was called.[26] During the war, diagrams of boilers and boiler equipment were booked into Swindon Drawing Office over several years. Much the most surprising, in May 1943, was that of the Southern *Merchant Navy* boiler. The acquisition of these diagrams is sometimes taken to confirm that several schemes for interchanging boilers between the locomotives of different railway companies was given active consideration.[5/9] It takes less than ten seconds to realise that interchanging of boilers between the MN and the *King* was a non-starter, frankly a silly suggestion, but an 8F boiler mounted on a *Hall* or a 28XX is another thing altogether. This is where the linkage actually occurs. Swindon was involved in building the Stanier LMS 8F and obviously needed the drawings to do so. The construction of these engines at Swindon is said to have been the impetus to the development of the higher degree superheat boilers fitted to the *Modified Hall* (1944), to the *County* 4-6-0 (1945) and, later, to the 5098-type *Castle* (1946). It was suggested to Hawksworth that an 8F boiler be fitted to a *Hall* but he was unhappy with the raw proposal, even for test purposes on the stationary plant, and 13 schemes were outlined eventuating in a new engine, the *County*. The *Halls* had been steadily multiplied throughout the war; the 6959 type was the first with plate frames and this innovation was incorporated in the new *County*. That the *Modified Hall* was seen as a 'provisional' design is suggested by a scheme to build fifteen *Halls* with the *County* boiler (Lot 359), ordered even before the first *County* was delivered. This was later cancelled. Another proposal was to fit outside valve gear both to the *County* and to the *Halls*. Neither scheme materialised and the reader is entitled to ask how it could possibly be acceptable to continue to build locomotives with inside valve gear during and after a devastating war when the exigencies of operation demanded the easiest and most economical maintenance arrangements. As we have seen, the Churchward cylinder layout did not preclude the use of outside valve gear but once it had been jettisoned there was no longer even that as an excuse not to do it. The argument that GWR depots were set up with maintenance provision for inside valve gear is just not good enough. What is perhaps even more difficult to understand is how it happened that the new *County*, at least as first built, left so much to be desired.

The *Railway Magazine* went on to describe the *County* as being: *not quite so revolutionary as imagined in certain quarters,* which leads the observer to wonder just what had been imagined.[9] There can be no doubt that the double chimney fitted to No.1000 was intended to give an impression of advanced design on the GWR and yet it is difficult not to see it as just a publicity stunt. By 1945 double chimneys were hardly revolutionary; even in Ireland Bredin's *Queen* 4-6-0s were so fitted. It appears to have been a last minute decision. The final version of the *County* layout shows a single chimney and it is clear that the decision to fit a double exhaust was taken at a very late stage in the development of this design. In March 1945, the smokebox diagrams from the taper boiler *Royal Scot* and the *Duchess of Abercorn* pacific were recorded in the Drawing Office schedule. These are of interest because both incorporated double chimneys and only in the spring and early summer of 1945 did Hawksworth draw out the diagrams for the double chimney equipment fitted to *County of Middlesex*. Unfortunately these drawings are no longer available but scaling a first class modellers diagram made by the late Colonel Templar suggests that the dimensions of the original *Royal Scot* double chimney were followed closely.

What is extraordinary is that Hawksworth appears to have completely forgotten the recommendations made by Tew in his 1939 paper. Even if his pride had been hurt by its tone and content, why did he not resurrect its ideas as his own when designing the *County* smokebox? Hubris is one thing, allowing it to stand in the way of progress is hardly the response of an intellectual. Tew's report contains a full description and diagrams of the Kylchap double exhaust and we can only assume that it was the cowls above the blastpipe on this device which the LMS had found a hindrance to servicing that impelled Hawksworth to discard it. Apart from that the report recommended a larger superheater, more direct and larger steam pipes, larger outside steam chests and larger passages for exhaust steam. The *County* cannot be said to have represented even a slight reference to these recommendations. The fact that they were specifically aimed at the *King* does not disbar the two cylinder engines from the general observations but it was not so; the original *County* boiler represented very little increase in productive capacity over the *Hall* and on test it was found that it would not maintain pressure at high steaming rates. Considering that the boiler pressure was set at 280lbs but with little extra productive capacity over and above the conventional 225lb boilers that cannot be said to be very surprising. Tew recommended trivial modifications to the damper controls and when actioned these greatly improved performance.[24]

I think we can assume that he was encouraged by the positive response to these recommendations because he now put in a new report suggesting changes along the lines recommended in his first, 1939 proposal. Some men would have foreseen what happened next; as soon as Hawksworth received the proposal, Tew was moved onto work that had nothing to do with locomotives. Clearly Hawksworth saw him as an nuisance. And if that is to be regretted, it is not completely incomprehensible. However, Tew's second paper is of vital interest to the main point of this chapter, as we shall see.

The *County* class could do good work particularly on inclines and Gibson sent a log of a run to Cecil J Allen which was published in the *Railway Magazine*.[7] On January 3 1948 No.1010 *County of Carnarvon* was rostered to the up *Torbay Express* and left Exeter 13 minutes late with 495/ 452 tons at the drawbar. It ran the 24.5 miles from the Westbury cut-off to Savernake, adverse gradients for most of the way in slightly more than even time and overall, the 105 miles from Taunton to Reading West in 106 minutes, being stopped by signals 5 minutes before the booked passing time. But once the *County* was in service there were other problems, complaints of a fore and aft 'hunting' motion and of heavy hammer blow on the track, reports that were regarded as serious. In March 1946 an unsigned report to Hawksworth recommended that in order to reduce the hammer blow it would be necessary to reduce the boiler pressure to 225lbs, rebalance the coupled wheels and it was also suggested that the piston head and rod, back cylinder cover, crosshead and connecting rod should be changed for those fitted to the 4901 class. This it was said would bring the hammer blows into line with those for both types of *Hall*.[27] The report is marked on behalf of Hawksworth: *no action* but a year later another letter notes that the wheels of all 30 engines were being rebalanced to reduce the hammerblows.[28] Despite this, complaints of heavy riding continued. There is no evidence that the other modifications were ever carried out.

The late L.H.Trollope, who was Drawing Office Registrar at the time told me that he remembered the conversations about these problems and of someone's suggestion that they could be overcome by the fitting of an inside cylinder and a trailing axle.[10] Could this be where the myth about a Hawksworth pacific started, with private conversations engendered almost certainly by dissatisfaction with the new engine? There is no real evidence to support this contention but the one real conundrum about the *County* is exactly what work it was intended to do. Officially described as a mixed traffic engine, Cook tells us that it was an express locomotive and the 6'3" driving wheels tend to confirm this.[25] In that case, it is possible that the difficulties with the *County* led someone in the Drawing Office, Mattingly, the Chief Draughtsman is most likely, to set about the development of something better. The comment in the *Railway Magazine* about revolutionary design is unlikely to have been a reference to a pacific because even the little that we know about this proposal dates from after the magazine item was published.

Two pieces of documentary evidence support the contention that a pacific design was actively considered at Swindon. Firstly, the outline drawing published in the RCTS history of GWR locomotives.[5/9] This was drawn by Mr L.Ward of the RCTS and is noted in the book as being *reproduced from official drawings*. The original Swindon drawing on which this diagram was based is no longer in existence but that it did exist is beyond doubt; though it was not recorded in the Drawing Office Schedule, several people have attested to its existence and the late Anthony Sterndale told me that he remembered Harry Flewellyn drawing it.[29] Swindon had a very elaborate system of producing its drawings involving special inks and covering with vellum, the fact that the pacific drawing was no more than a pencil tracing indicates that it was, at best, a very early scheme indeed. Of rather more interest, and actually still extant in the NRM library, is a packet of calculations signed by H.Tichener which refers specifically to a 4-6-2 engine. This proposes a wide firebox boiler not dissimilar to that carried by the SR *Merchant Navy* class.[30]

It is not too difficult to see that this document started life from a study of the MN diagram already mentioned as being booked into the Drawing Office in 1943 and it is the only component for which detailed information about this proposal, beyond the general layout, is available. It clearly shows a boiler pressure of 250 lb/sq in and calculations for fitting either one or two thermic siphons, a real departure for Swindon. A greatly enlarged superheater is indicated but with the temperature estimated at 250°F, still a great deal less than Chapelon had achieved. However, the fact that a wide firebox boiler is proposed raises a serious caveat. In a report to Hawksworth dated February 11 1946 dealing with a proposal to fit larger superheaters to the *Castles*, Ell showed that a narrow firebox could, in the right circumstances, steam as effectively as a wide firebox with a larger grate area.[31] Perhaps more significantly Chapelon in his 4-8-0 rebuilds of the Paris-Orleans pacifics, demonstrated that the narrow firebox was perfectly capable of steam generation on a par with what was possible with the wide firebox. If that was so, was a pacific actually the right way forward for the GWR? This is a hugely important question because it seems that widely differing propositions were being made; Ell's test results bolstered the GWR's long-held belief that a 4-6-0 was actually more suitable for its requirements than a pacific. While enthusiasts and engineers alike seem to think that the pacific represents the high water mark of British steam locomotive layout, Swindon's practical experience suggested otherwise. Why then devise such a locomotive if it did not represent that practicality?

Thus far we have recorded all that is known about the pacific proposal and not a little speculation. There is little else to add of the former and a great deal more of the latter! One of my earliest memories is of hearing my father upbraid my elder brother for sticking a picture into his school exercise book which obscured a photograph of *The Great Bear*. "There aren't very many pictures of that engine," he told him. In fact, there are probably just as many pictures of the *Bear* as of any locomotive that ran for sixteen years. Despite that when I asked him, probably at the same time, about this, his explanation that there had only ever been one GWR pacific, or "an engine with a wheel under the cab" as I remember him describing it, I learnt that crucial fact as effectively as only a young child can. And when, nearly ten years later, O.S.Nock revealed that indeed there had been another proposal for a pacific, I was exceedingly astonished.[32] It is not, I think an exaggeration to say that I have devoted almost a lifetime's study to this particular project probably because of the confrontation at an impressionable age between what I had always been led to believe and what I was now being told was the reality. Whether Nock's revelations were the first public reference to a Hawksworth Pacific I cannot say, I have never heard of any reference that predates this publication and I would certainly be interested if there were any. Interestingly, nearly 50 years later we can see that just about everything that Nock wrote on that occasion, and repeated many times, was inaccurate.

In 1958 he said: ... *the one really big new project was stillborn. This was Mr. Hawksworth's great Pacific express locomotive, schemed out during the later years of the war. It was hoped that a prototype could have been built, and tested, and that batch production could have commenced when the time came for post-war reconstruction. But. . . construction was vetoed by the wartime Railway Executive Committee. . . The new Counties could be described as a synthetic design. . . with a trial of the boiler pressure of 280lb psi that it had been hoped to use in the new Pacifics.* The next reference that I can find is in Cecil J.Allen's book about British Pacific locomotives and dates from 1962.[33] Allen wrote: *There have often been rumours of a Swindon Pacific, designed there during the middle 1940s, and I have actually seen an outline drawing of this engine.* Allen wrote to Hawksworth, now in retirement, and received a famously dusty answer, as did several other people. Hawksworth said: *I can say quite categorically that anything you may have read or heard about a proposed Pacific type design ascribed to me is pure conjecture and completely without foundation. Such a design was not even discussed.*[33] Around the same time I wrote to Swindon and received a two-line rebuttal from someone in the Mechanical Engineer's department. But that, it was later suggested, was not surprising. The reference by the *Railway Magazine* to secrecy at Swindon was no more than the norm; it was how they worked 'inside'. It was perfectly possible that the person to whom my letter had been referred just did not know anything about the proposal. The real eye-opener was the publication of the RCTS diagram to which reference has already been made.[5/9] This was also in 1962 and for many years was regarded as the proof that, indeed, a pacific had been designed at Swindon during the 1940s. In 1970 Nock added some further details to what was known about this design: . . . *Those concerned have told me that they had only the sketchiest of directives, from F.C.Mattingly (Chief Draughtsman). They were asked to put forward their ideas for a Pacific, and the only positive instruction issued in those early stages was that the boiler pressure was to be 280lb psi. . . A good deal of work was done on the boiler. While bearing in mind all the basic features of Churchward's classic development, the restriction in steam flow that to some extent handicapped the Kings was eliminated, and a very high degree of superheat provided for. Two different schemes were worked out, using five-row and six-row superheaters respectively. . . . While preliminary work was thus done on the boiler, another draughtsman had taken the King front-end and completely streamlined the ports and steam passages in the Chapelon style. Then, alas, those concerned had another visit from Mattingly . . . and then to tell them to stop work.*[34] Note the reference to the two schemes for the superheater using either five or six rows of elements, a statement completely contradicted by the Tichener paper. Interestingly, in a later paragraph Nock himself questions some of the things he had indicated as facts in his 1958 article.

An imaginative drawing by Victor Welch and based on the RCTS diagram appeared alongside these entries. Quite the most fascinating thing about this drawing is that it contains a strange inaccuracy. The bogie illustrated is that fitted to the *King*, with the infamous 'outside to inside' framing, and it could be argued that this was justified by the outline on the RCTS diagram. However, Nock himself, in the first part of this book, shows that the *King* bogie was an anachronism almost before it was designed. As a result of failures of the riveting on the standard bogie it was decided to change over to a plate-framed variant and it was this decision which made the extraordinary *King* bogie necessary. However, shortly afterwards it was realised that the bogie failures were due to weakness in diagonal bracing and that with this remedied, there was no reason not to continue with the standard bar-frame bogie. *Had this decision been reached a little earlier, the Kings would probably have had the standard Churchward bogie.*[34] Several questions occur at this point. Firstly, if that was the case, why did the pacific layout show the *King* bogie? It is, surely, to be expected that the draughtsman responsible would be aware of developments on so important a component as this. We are left wondering if the Swindon tracing just indicated where the wheels would be and Ward assumed that the *King* bogie was appropriate. We can assume that Nock had little or no detail control over Welch's interpretation of the RCTS diagram but I would like to have known whether he had anything to say about what must have been, to the book's author, so obvious a mistake. He was not above making pungent comments about how publishers handled his work and I hope that he did so on this occasion because Welch's drawing clearly contradicts his text. A second point is that the standard Swindon bar frame bogie would probably have been better completely redesigned either in 1927 or certainly when the true cause of the failures was discovered.

During the 1970s various writers published books or articles which contained references to the Hawksworth pacific without adding anything new to what was known. I have recently rediscovered a letter that I received from O.S.Nock in 1977 in which, responding to doubts that I was having even then about this proposal he wrote: *The pacific was very definitely Hawksworth's, strongly backed at the Board by Captain Hugh Vivian. FWH was very upset when he was not allowed to go ahead. .. I never spoke to him myself, about it, but heard most of the details from Sam Ell who did the boiler and Geoffrey Tew who did the internal, streamlined front end.*[35] This letter is almost complete nonsense. There is no evidence that Ell did the boiler, it is clear that it was worked out by Tichener. But look at that reference to: *Geoffrey Tew who did the internal streamlined front end*. Tew certainly did no such thing, not in regard to any proposed pacific design be it official or otherwise. His paper was aimed at improving the *County*, and for daring to make those suggestions he got the chop, or at least promotion out of 'harms way'. The late Hugh Vivian was a director of a Swansea copper works and at one time a director of both Beyer Peacock and of the GWR. I have attempted to verify the reference to this gentleman by speaking to his family but unfortunately they have no means of confirming it. In any case it is strongly contradicted by other evidence. The last Assistant General Manager of the GWR, K.W.C.Grand, was still alive in 1981 and, known to be an enthusiast for everything Great Western, I also wrote to him. Grand was quite clear that Hawksworth had never made a proposal for a pacific and that he would certainly have known about any such proposition. What was instructive was that Grand remembered Hawksworth saying that the GWR had no need of such an engine.[36] We can conjecture all we like on what evoked this comment, someone, Grand himself, perhaps Hugh Vivian, drawing Hawksworth's attention to what others, Bulleid for instance, were doing. Furthermore, in his book Cook makes no mention of any pacific and when I asked him what he knew of it, almost as an aside he replied that a pacific may have been devised but that he knew nothing about it.[25]

I have published two articles on this particular project[37][38] and after the second appeared a very long and interesting comment was received from Mr E.Davies drawing attention to further imponderables. In short Davies highlighted the contradictions between Nock's statement of the intended dimensions of the pacific and those evident from the Ward diagram and also with those in the Tichener paper repeated here. The most telling of these comments relates to the 280lb/6'3" Nock contention which suggests a factor of adhesion of 3.2 which he rightly suggested is not very likely. Furthermore he drew attention to the fact that scaling the dimensions of the Ward diagram gives a barrel length of about 20', itself contradicted by the Tichener paper. The suggestion that the 280lb/6'3" and the 250 lb/6'6" suggestions were separate schemes for the pacific proposal can be completely disregarded; the former, I believe was never part of this proposal and that belief is based on the fact that of Nock's informants, one, Ell does not appear to have been actively involved on it and the other, Tew who did indeed make certain Chapelon derived proposals was almost certainly occupied on something else when this project was alive in the drawing office. Even supposing that these men, Ell, Tichener or Tew were actually involved with the pacific project, if Mattingly, the chief draughtsman was the authority to whom they reported, then they might very well have been completely unaware that it had not been authorised by the CME.

I think the reader will begin to see a picture developing that actually shows certain people in a bad light, though perhaps from good intentions. As far as that goes I will leave him to *construe according to his wits*.[39] It is clear now that the 1946 Swindon pacific was an unofficial job, started and progressed completely without the authority and probably without the knowledge of the CME. It is clear, at the very least, that Hawksworth did not authorise any work on a pacific design; his consistent and categoric rebuttal of this suggestion, whenever questioned, is all the proof of that which is necessary. It is possible that he discovered what had been going on; his reference, in his letter to Allen, to a draughtsman's dream might be very telling. Nock's information that Mattingly told the people working on the project to stop, immediately, may have been FWH, having found out about it, telling his chief draughtsman that it did not represent any inclination that he had about future design work. (Rather as Collett had sent Stanier out very smartly when he had gone in to propose a compound Castle). Another story is that at some time in the early 1960s Hawksworth, hearing that Allen (despite his letter) was nosing around at Swindon, went into the drawing office and destroyed with his own hands the pencil tracing from which Ward had - fortunately? - already copied the RCTS diagram.[35] I have conjectured that this was the final proof that FWH wished to disassociate his name from a scheme for which he had given no authority and of which he certainly disapproved. Since Nock's death in 1994, when this tale has become more well known, doubt as to its veracity has arisen. Again, Nock was only reporting what he was told by someone 'inside' and it is quite possible that something less dramatic actually occurred; nonetheless, the fact remains that the original drawing is no longer in existence.

Very little information of significance has been added to what was known when I published my first article in 1981. What I find vexing, however, is that despite the work that I and others have done on this topic, writers continue to state, definitely, that Hawksworth made an official proposal to build such a machine at Swindon. On the basis of the evidence currently available, this is just not true; indeed, the evidence points in a diametrically opposite direction, that he was opposed to any such proposition. As a Great Western enthusiast I would be delighted to see evidence that tended to show that my conclusions were wrong but I see no possibility that this will ever happen.

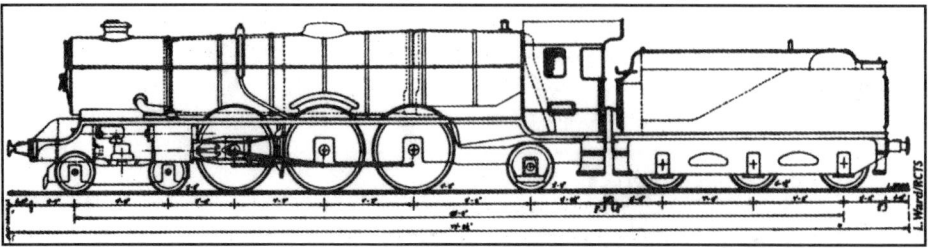

Of the many questions that remain unanswered the most important concerns the provenance of the drawing from which the RCTS diagram was copied. If it is to be taken to represent what in 1946 was the currently advanced thinking in locomotive design at Swindon, then it is a very poor thing indeed and I do not believe that it does. The original was a pencil tracing with none of the elaborate finish that Swindon applied to its drawings; it seems rather obvious that, at best, it represented no more than a very early and basic scheming out of a proposal, possibly intended as a framework into which to fit the outline dimensions of the boiler on which work was being done. Bear in mind that even this proposition is open to question for the reasons already stated, it supports very little and contradicts a great deal in the one source that remains in existence.

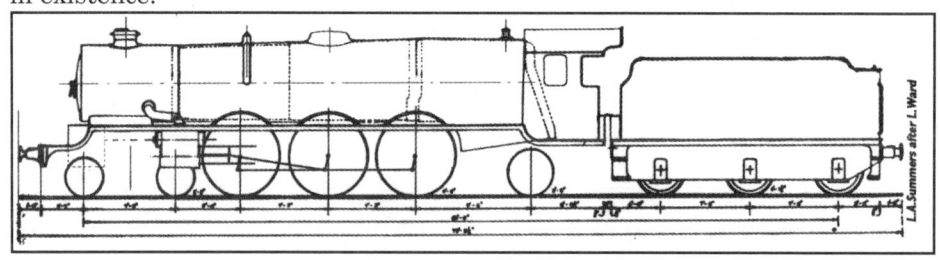

However, without forgetting this caveat, I have, in the accompanying diagram, attempted to 'de-elaborate' the Ward/RCTS Pacific diagram and suggest the detail that the original tracing may have contained. In the absence of the real thing no other conclusion about its detail is possible.

The pacific diagram as drawn up for the RCTS. The standard bogie is shown rather than the *King* type but apart from equally imaginary name and number plates no other alterations have been made.

110

Notes and references

9) *Railway Magazine* - November/December 1945
10) L.E.Trollope - correspondence with the author 1980
11) K.J.Cooke - correspondence with the author 1980
12) *Nude Ego* - Royé
13) *Railway Magazine* - July 1938
14) *SLS Journal* - May 1962
15) *Streamlined Steam* - A.J.Mullay
16) *Industrial Design* - Raymond Loewy
17) *The Locomotive - Its Aesthetics* - Raymond Loewy
18) *Great Western Apprentice- Swindon in the 1930s* - Hugh Freebury
19) *Master Builders of Steam* - H.A.V.Bulleid
20) *Lineal Testing of Streamlined Outlines* - F.C.Johnansen
    Procedings: I. Mech. E. 1936
21) *High Speed and the Steam Locomotive* - R.P.Wagner
    Procedings: I.Mech.E. 1935
22) *La Locomotive au Vapeur* - English Language Edition
    Andre Chapelon/ George W.Carpenter
23) *Report re The Loocmotive in France* - Swindon GWR - May 1939
24) Alan Wild - letter published in *Great Western Echo* -autumn 2006 and subsequent conversation with the author
25) *Swindon Steam* - K.J.Cook
26) W.J.Mayo has told me that at this time there was a great deal of acrimonious correspondence between the WR and BR headquarters.
27) *1000 Class Engine: Proposed reduction of boiler pressure and hammer blows*
    Swindon Drawing Office - 14th March 1946
28) F.W.Hawksworth - letter to A.S.Quartermaine 21st May 1947
29) Anthony Sterndale - correspondence with the author 1962 and 1980
30) *Proposed Boiler for 4-6-2 engine* - Swindon Drawing Office 26th July 1946.
31) *Proposed Higher Superheat Castle Class Engines* - Swindon Drawing Office February 11th 1946.
32) *Post War Locomotive Development at Swindon* - O.S.Nock - Trains Annual 1958
33) *British Pacific Locomotives* - Cecil J Allen
34) *The GWR Stars, Castles and Kings* - O.S.Nock
35) O.S.Nock - letter to the author 1977
36) K.W.C.Grand - correspondence with the author 1981
37) *The Myth of a Hawksworth Pacific* - L.A.Summers - *Railway World* 1981
38) *Fact, Speculation & Fiction about Mr Hawksworth's Pacific*
    L.A.Summers - *Backtrack* April 2000
39) from - *The Man for all Seasons* - Robert Boult

Eight
Swindon and the BR Standards

Holcroft's words are brief and succinct: *The General Election in the autumn of 1945 brought into power a Socialist Government whose policy promised State ownership of industry, and a plan for the unification of the four railway groups under Nationalisation was one of their first tasks.*[4] In his last letter to me, shortly before he died in 1994 O.S.Nock said that he regarded the Labour victory in 1945 as a disaster and the subsequent nationalisation of the railways as a tragedy, adding that though he thought *Riddles was an honest man, he had to follow the party line...*[9] Despite unapologetic left of centre views I am willing to agree with that to the extent that had railway nationalisation been carried out with a little more forethought and preparation some at least of the ensuing problems would never have occurred. The major problem was a distinct lack of strong leadership at the top with the result that certain officers were able to push their own agenda. It is clear from the evidence now available that among these R.A.Riddles figures prominently.

I remember very vividly some time in 1951 or '52 my father coming home and telling me that there was a new type of engine working the early evening stopping train to Swindon. What was particularly noteworthy about this engine was that, according to him, it had "all its works on the outside" and I conspired to be taken, at the earliest opportunity, to see this locomotive from what was then a narrow piece of field lying between Station Road and the cutting at the west end of the station. Imagine, then, my disappointment to discover that this new engine was not bereft of boiler plates and that its tubes were not open to the elements, that what my father had meant was that it had outside valve-gear! Yet, how else could he have described to a very young boy the new Standard Pacifics then coming into service on the WR? It was to be some years before I started to read railway magazines seriously and to discover that the engine I had insisted upon being taken to see was, with its co-types as controversial as anything else built then or at any other time, though it is only in more recent times that questioning the construction of the Standards has become more general.

This book is about the locomotives designed and built at Swindon, particularly those for the GWR, but since both the workshops and drawing office were involved with the introduction of the Standard classes it would be inappropriate to exclude these types from our review, particularly in as much that there is now strong evidence to suggest that left to its own devices, Swindon could have produced developments of its own designs that would have been superior to the Standards and probably cheaper to build and run.

Whatever were the opinions then, and now, about the wisdom of having a publicly owned transport system, the fact is that from January 1948 ownership of the railways, for better or worse, was transferred from the previous City companies to the Government, in trust for the country. Under the British Transport Commission, the administrative authority for all the state transport concerns, the Railway Executive, was charged with the operation of the railway network. There were nine members of this Executive including three from outside the industry, one of whom was a distinguished former General and Viceroy of India! Robert A.Riddles, the former LMS Vice-President of Engineering, was the Executive Member responsible for mechanical and electrical engineering. To Riddles fell the task of developing the new motive power that the intended rejuvenation of the railways would require. Why Riddles? There seems little doubt that it was because of his period attached to the wartime Ministry of Supply where he impressed a good many people with his competence and political ability. In that sense Riddles was perhaps, the obvious appointment but that does not make it the right one. That he himself was insecure about it is the only real conclusion that can be deduced from the fact that he surrounded himself with assistants from his own backyard. Of five chief officers, four came from the LMS, R.C.Bond (Chief Officer, Locomotive Construction and Maintenance), E.S.Cox, (Executive Officer Design) and E.Pugson who held a similar post to Bond covering carriage and wagon design. It has been said that he needed his principal assistants to be men that he could trust; another view might be that the mechanical engineering department of the LMS, for all its achievements, was held in pretty low regard by the other three railways and that he was protecting his back. The implication that Swindon, Doncaster nor Brighton had anyone sufficiently talented to contribute to the design of new locomotives is crazy. The regional locomotive engineers sat in on the RE's M&EE Committee meetings but that was not the same thing as being intimately involved with their design. It might have been better had the most senior appointment gone outside the railway companies to someone brought in from the locomotive manufacturing industry. That is not to support the destruction over the last 20 years of the publicly owned railway workshops. It is however, an acknowledgement of the fact that however well Riddles, Cox and the rest kept themselves informed of foreign developments an infusion of practical experience of those developments might have been beneficial.

The first task of the new locomotive engineering directorate should have been to plan for the future, both in the short and intermediate term bearing in mind remits that I believe were inescapable, the need to continue with steam, the need to make nationalisation look good - and successful - to improve working conditions, to conserve expenditure, to bridge the gap to the successful introduction of alternative traction, to decide, qualitatively what that new traction should be. On the most important point, that of whether to continue building steam there could, in 1948 be no argument, the foreign capital necessary to import oil was just not available and seemed unlikely to be so for some years to come. There is another point which is often forgotten. A great fuss is made of the government's programme to enlarge the GWR's limited conversion of its engines to oil burning. In 1946 the railways were asked to reduce their consumption of coal by one million tons annually by such conversions.[10] Within six months the fuel supply situation had so dramatically improved that this request was withdrawn. In fact oil burning was not then, nor subsequently I believe, the way forward. Bond maintains that oil burners steamed better than those using coal but firebox maintenance costs were higher which strongly suggests that the two and half times quoted cost of using coal was thus much reduced. Steam, burning indigenous fuel was therefore the correct policy to follow. Despite this, later on, in 1957 a number of 57xx pannier tanks were converted to burn oil. The first, 3711 was converted by Robert Stephenson & Hawthorn at Newcastle, it is believed following supply by RSH of oil-burning 0-6-0STs to the Northern Division of the NCB. Several others were converted at Swindon. Attempts to find out more about this work have not been successful and further information would be most interesting.

Riddles is known to have been opposed to the diesel and I have to say that on that matter I believe he was right.[10] Diesel shunters had obvious advantages over steam shunting locomotives but despite the great hullabaloo about them, main line diesel power was not then the overwhelming success that its acolytes claimed. There was undoubtedly a continuing struggle between the advocates of bridging the gap to alternative motive power with steam and those who believed the propaganda and saw a short term advantage in going quickly to the diesel. This undoubtedly polarised opinion with the result that neither 'side' appears now to have given proper consideration to what was the best way to go forward. The immediately necessary decision was the form that new build steam was to take; the supplementary question, about the form of the new traction will be discussed in the next chapter.

The policy of continuing to build major steam locomotives meant the construction of motive power units with a long working life, generally regarded as about 35 years for steam. Thus engines built in, say 1951 would run until the mid-1980s to gain the normal full return on investment in their construction. Such longevity would have permitted the continual updating of these units as was recommended again and again by Chapelon and carried out, amongst other administrations by that in West Germany. Having established that the correct policy was to continue construction of steam locomotives, three courses of action were open to the new design team, flood the system with LMS types, let the old design centres Derby, Doncaster, Swindon and Brighton carry on as before or create an entirely new range of 'standard' classes. At a very early stage Riddles appears to have decided to build a series of completely new or nearly new locomotives. This is suggested by the fact that even before he assumed office he was revealing his intentions to those who were to be his closest lieutenants. The decision was justified by Roland Bond by stating that the alternative, to allow the regional design centres to continue to provide for their own needs *would not have been acceptable as conforming to the philosophy of complete unification implicit in the Transport Act*.[10] To this writer that view does not justify anything, it is a romantic philosophy defending practical unreality. Viewed dispassionately the general requirement for standardisation was absolutely correct. Two of the four railways had well-developed systems of standardisation to which any new scheme could only be a diversion and Ivatt at least, recognised this, openly advocating that the former company design teams continue to operate virtually as before. Ivatt was right, effort and money designing a new two cylinder 4-6-0 for example was a complete waste when the various regions were well-stocked with proven types such as the *Hall* class, the B1s and 'Black Stanier'. *He saw the new standard engines as odd men out in sheds accustomed to and holding spares for the existing engines*.[11] The excuse, that changes to practices had been visited on railway companies by Grouping and in some cases even by the appointment of a new CME was hardly a cogent reason on for doing exactly the same thing again.

While yet this clear intention was in the minds of those at the top of the engineering pyramid, other recourses suggesting an entirely different approach were pursued. Concurrently a series of locomotive exchange trials was undertaken which captured a good deal of public and enthusiast attention. The results, however, were far from conclusive and have long been called into question. Former GWR types did not show well against the others except for the 2800 freight engine which had a slightly higher coal consumption than the LNER 01 which came out as 'best'. There was little scientifically proved by the test results achieved, in fact the discrepancies had more to do with operating technique than any quality of the coal used or of the design. In the light of subsequent testing carried out under the system devised at Swindon by Sam Ell many of the test figures were shown to have been unreliable. It is only fair to add that none of the professional people involved actually claimed that the results were infallible. However, they served the purpose of those who had organised them in justifying a policy of going for new 'standard' designs.

Another of Riddles intrigues, for that can only have been its purpose, was a committee, one of seventeen, set up to recommend pre-nationalisation types for continued construction. A.W.J.Dymond, then an assistant to the Western M&EE chaired this committee and, to quote Bond: *As might be expected, with the members different company loyalties, the committee did not feel justified in selecting one only of the companies standard types in each traffic category for (further) construction ...*[10] Bond is here showing a refreshing degree of honesty. A committee which consisted entirely of engineers from the former railway companies, passed over or unavailable for appointment to the new administration, were unlikely to agree which of their former rivals' products they regarded as suitable for extended construction. Precisely the answer Riddles wanted, the way forward for the pursuit of his own designs had been opened. That Swindon, Derby and Doncaster, to say nothing of post-Bulleid Brighton could have done the job equally well in their own regional interests is now clear. The Standards were an imposition that, certainly as far as the WR was concerned, was very largely unnecessary.

Since this is an important factor in the history of WR locomotive operation I am going to devote a little more attention to it. As a stop-gap to the Standard classes, the building of new pre-nationalization types was continued; the last Swindon 4-6-0 No.7829, *Ramsbury Manor* came out in December 1950, the last actual ex-GWR type, 3409 in October 1956. Concurrently with this, new mixed traffic *Britannia* pacifics were allocated to the WR which, arguably, had no need for them. Going on from that, when I read in Cox[12] that further *Clans* were to be allocated to the WR I can only comment that it would have been laughable were the proposition not so inappropriate. Think about it, just what were five completely foreign Class 5 pacifics to contribute to a region which had hundreds of its own Class 5 4-6-0s performing at worst, adequately? It was claimed that there were no modern equivalents to the Class 2 and four 2-6-0s and their 2-6-2T and 2-6-4T derivatives but this justification hardly bears examination. In reality there were already extant or in preparation designs perfectly suitable for the work these locomotives were intended to do.

This last point applies particularly to the Class 9F 2-10-0. Whether the 9F was ever justified in the quantity built is a very open argument given the powerful 2-8-0s operated by the WR, E&NER and LM Regions, there were even doubts about that at the highest level, Bond for example reckoned that a 2-8-2 would have been more useful.[10] Once the acceleration of diesalization had been decided, for better or worse, further steam construction should have been immediately cancelled. But to take the example quoted, that ignores the question as to whether in the first place 220 large freight locomotives were actually needed by BR. Some of the 9F 2-10-0s completed in 1960, even on the basis of the original modernisation plan could only have an envisaged operating life of 12 years. That none actually worked for more than 8 years and some had even shorter lives is a public policy blunder of staggering proportions.

The now well known contretemps over the decision to allocate these locomotives to the WR and Paddington's insistence that its own 2-8-0 was preferable is of great interest here. Bond actually went to the extreme of outlining a 2-8-0 specifically for work on the WR, yet despite the age of the 28xx design it was still capable of good work and of further development. It is on record as having hauled very heavy loads satisfactorily on severe gradients, an early 1950s version with the boiler off the *Modified Hall* or the modified *County*, outside valve gear and a modern all-over cab would have been perfectly adequate for the WR's needs, would have cost less since little design work and few new tools would have been required and would have had the added advantage of pleasing men known to be happy with the performance of their own regional engine.

An examination of the allocation, region by region, of the Standard types shows that a heavy proportion of what was built went straight into LMR service and this destroys utterly the argument in favour of building them. If there was such need for new engines on the LMR, and there certainly was, why not just continue to build the machines already available and with which the crews were familiar? The apparent disregard for Swindon products by the new design team may be contrasted with the fact that the WR had fewer Standard locomotives allocated to it than any of the other regions, never more than 10% of the whole build. (The E&NE Regions, too, had relatively few Standards). By 1963 the WR allocation was maintained only by ex-Southern depots in areas transferred to it by Regional changes. One does not have to be the kind of raving GWR enthusiast scorned both by E.S.Cox and in this book by the present writer to detect an element of fractious jealousy in the way in which the 'Kremlin' dealt with Swindon. Bulleid alone was regarded by Riddles people with a greater degree of scorn and that was despite borrowing his frame design.

It is a moot question as to what form Swindon's locomotive policy would have taken after 1948 had the railways not been nationalised. Not everyone at Swindon was satisfied with what was going on there. The unofficial work on a Swindon pacific discussed in the previous chapter demonstrates that lower down the ladder there was frustration with official policy and I hazard the view that this coloured what was said by certain middle-ranking draughtsmen and others to those with whom they shared seats in the dynamometer car. The official opinion was represented to me by K.J.Cook who succeeded Hawksworth in 1949. In his view the types then at work were performing satisfactorily. Given the problems being experienced with the quality and supply of coal and other problems affecting locomotive operation this could be regarded as a touch

Swindon's principal officers in 1947
Left to right, standing: H.W.Gardner; F.C.Mattingly (Chief Draughtsman); A.W.J.Dymond (Assistant to CME); Dr A.W. Bennett (MO); R.W.Dawe (Chief Chemist); R.W.Woolacott (Assistant to CME); Front: K.J.Cook (Loco Works Manager); M.Macdonald (electrical assistant); I.C.Hall (CME's principal assistant) F.W.Hawksworth; W.N.Pellow (Loco Running); W.H.Bodman (Staff Assistant); H.Randle (C&W Works Manager).

unrealistic. Problems of shed maintenance, increased time between routine servicing to say nothing of general cleanliness were serious and worsening. Nonetheless he was fully aware of the problem of coal supply mentioning in correspondence with me the need for some means of screening coal before it was put on the locomotive.[13] It was this problem rather than a desire to produce high speed locomotives that underpinned the developmental work done at Swindon.

In 1951 Riddles shuffled Cook off to Doncaster in exchange for Alfred Smeddle. The exact purpose of this exchange is not altogether clear especially as Cook was told that it would: *enable changes that he wanted to make elsewhere*.[14] One suspects that Riddles thought that the exchange would break down the perceived insularity of each place and though Cook was clear that it was, to him at least, a waste of time, he may very well have been right. Certainly Cook made some significant improvements at Doncaster and then spoilt it with the silly business of the copper capped chimney that he put on a V2. Despite the wholly justified criticisms of Swindon locomotive policy in the years after 1927, there is no doubt that its design team in 1949 was equal to that anywhere else. Smeddle must have recognised this because he threw himself enthusiastically behind the research and development that was being undertaken there. It may very well have been this influence that kept Swindon at the forefront of steam development in Britain. It was the arrival of Stanley Raymond at Paddington in 1962 that finally killed off this work and may even have killed Smeddle himself.[15]

As we have seen in the last chapter, three and four row superheaters were introduced on ex-GWR locomotives and appear on the evidence and despite some early contretemps with the mechanical lubricators to have made a significant contribution to the steam raising capacity of these engines. It should be noted that Swindon was still only getting superheater temperatures lower than those achieved in Chapelon's boilers; however, the crucial modernisation was done in the smokebox. Out went the jumper top blastpipe which restricted draught and the rate of steaming. Through several incarnations the blast pipe dimensions were altered to give an increased steamrate that was more than 60% up on what had been achieved pre-war. Further improvements, cutting back pressure were effected by fitting double chimneys, to the extent that the grate rather than the front end became the limiting factor on steam raising. While these were certainly significant improvements, what is not often mentioned is that even after 1948 no thought appears to have been given to the streamlining of the steampipes despite the fact that at least the basic research had been done.

Dennis Howells, who has been involved for many years as Project Manager on the restoration of 6023 believes that such innovation was, in a sense, unnecessary.[16] The outside steampipes on the four cylinder engines were redesigned to increase the radii of the curves but that was as far as it went. There was a school of thought which deprecated the idea of streamlined steam pipes but if Howells is right, then that becomes an irrelevance. The remit with the redevelopment of GWR locomotives was not necessarily to increase power but to increase the economics of their operation. Given that the coal consumption of Swindon 4-6-0s had been significantly better than those of other railways this suggestion might raise an eyebrow. But remember, this is the post-war world where WR engines had to burn coal of low calorific value and which according to some reports was, too often, rubbish not far removed from slack containing slate and rock.[17] Higher boiler performance was the aim and the high temperature superheaters and double chimneys were designed to provide that, not to develop 'racers'. This is, at least a partial answer to the question why when some of the *King* class had new cylinders and new half frames welded on at the front the opportunity was not taken to fit thoroughly modern cylinders with enlarged valves and ports and improved lubrication.

It is not out of place here to note Kenneth H.Leech's critique of the original and rebuilt *Castle* class engines published originally in 1962.[17] He writes about what others have also remarked, that the performance of the *Castle* was wider in variety than with any other engine with which he was familiar and that speeds above 85 mph were not easily achieved without hard work by the engine. He records that the best of the batch were the four row superheater/ double chimney engines though the margin was small. A good original engine was usually better than an average three row type and as good as an average four row. This is very interesting because of the best of the lot was probably No.7018, *Drysllwyn Castle* as rebuilt with four row superheater, double chimney and a mechanical lubricator with increased oil flow. It was this engine which made the famous 93.5 minute run from Bristol to Paddington. To mere observers from outside BR this seemed sound enough proof that a 100 minute timing for the *Bristolian* could have been worked but there may have been other considerations such as constraints created by the signalling system.[17] The variable performance of the *Castles,* already noted, may have been another.

The long term results of Ell's work manifested itself not just on GWR locomotives but those of other companies and of the BR Standards themselves. The case of the LMS Ivatt 2MT 2-6-0 which was found to steam less effectively than a Dean Goods is well known and continually deprecated by partisans. Nonetheless, it is a fact that redraughting by Swindon produced a very significant improvement in its steam rate. GWR partisans who crow about this might do well to consider that similar tests on No.7818, *Granville Manor* and resulting trivial alterations to the exhaust dimensions produced a maximum steam rate twice that previously recorded. Of far more important consideration are the falsehoods, for they are no more than that which surround the design of the *Duke of Gloucester* 4-6-2. How this locomotive came to be built is well known. The reader is justified in asking how a single locomotive could have been authorised and part of the answer is that it was not expected to be the sole representative of its class. If Riddles belief that steam should bridge the gap to electrification was to be realised then locomotives of this power range would certainly be necessary. It is clear that not everyone shared Riddles desire to go for an virtually new engine. Bond said: *I have often thought what a magnificent locomotive a Mk 2 Britannia with three cylinders could have been.*[10]

The *Duke* was designed and built at Derby and rolled out in 1954. Almost immediately it was sent to Swindon for testing on the stationary test plant. Unfortunately these tests showed that while the engine design was highly successful, the boiler was a considerable disappointment. Subsequent research by the Duke of Gloucester Locomotive Society (DGLS) has shown that the grate was inaccurately constructed and the fitting of the correctly proportioned component has made significant improvement to its performance. So far so good. But the internet hosts at least one website, not the official DGLS site let it be said, that contains the astonishing statement that part of the problem with the boiler was that Swindon insisted that it be fitted with a double chimney based on its own designs rather than the Kylchap type recommended by the design consultant for the valve gear. This is just not true though it is not too difficult to see how the misconception arose. O.S.Nock relates that Ell told him that the *Duke* had: *two Dean Goods blastpipes side by side.*[18] As Nock makes clear, this may have been Ell's recommendation but it was not taken up, the blastpipe orifices on the *Duke* as originally built were 4" in diameter as against the Dean Goods 4½". So, if the original exhaust arrangements on the *Duke* were deficient, and Cox is certain they were not,[12] then the responsibility lay with Derby not Swindon.[19]

I am bound to add that there is another factor in connection, certainly with the *Duke* and probably is just as applicable to the *Britannia* class as well. We have already discussed the publicity value of streamlining, there can be no doubt that whatever were their drawbacks, mechanically, the original Bulleid pacifics grasped the public imagination in a way that had not happened since before 1939. The BR Standard classes did not do this. Yet, all that was necessary, very largely, was for certain integral parts of the locomotive to be built in drag reducing form; apart from a curved bufferbeam apron and fairings, the main frame need not be changed and so access to the moving parts would be unaffected. Some version of this concept applied to the bigger BR Standards would have improved their appearance out of all proportion.[21] Another improvement would have been to remove the necessity for those appalling smoke deflectors which by breaking up the lines of the boiler and footplate seriously detract from the appearance of far too many steam locomotives. The BR team was looking for efficiency, robustness and economy of operation and quite rightly. But so too were engineers on the continent, perhaps more so. Yet the post war locomotives of the SNCF looked hugely more impressive than their British counterparts.

It is clear that Swindon originally envisaged the continued use of steam beyond the mid 1960s. That is the only conclusion that can be drawn from the fact that at the end of 1961 the *King* class was intact and *Castles* were still being rebuilt with double chimneys, the last, No.5078, was outshopped in December 1962. The first *King* was withdrawn in February 1962 and the last four were taken out of service in December. More extraordinary is the fact that two double chimney *Castles* rebuilt right at the end of 1961 were withdrawn within a year of being outshopped, No.5082 only nine months later. By January 1966 all ex-GWR engines save a few pannier tanks had been withdrawn. I remember the last six months, from July 1965 to the beginning of 1966 very well. I had spent the previous 13 months abroad. When I left Britain in June 1964 the diesel inroads into WR steam were deep and many of the engines with which my childhood and adolescence was associated, were no more. When I returned to this country in July 1965 I was appalled. Not only were most of the WR's steam locomotives in an atrocious external condition but a small number of thefts had evoked an edict that engines were to be stripped of their nameplates and in many cases the numberplates also were removed. The result was diabolical, not so much because of the act itself but because of how it was done. As far as I could see only Banbury shed took the nameplate brackets off as well. Most engines ran with the brackets in place providing to all the evidence of the couldn't care less attitude that lay behind it.

The first regional General manager of the WR was K.W.C.Grand, former Assistant-general manager of the GWR; Grand was an enthusiast for everything Great Western and his general policy was to continue, as far as possible the traditions of the old company.[22] This was not an entirely misplaced approach, since the GWR had been revered, even by those among its staff who were strong socialists or trade unionists, the idea of a *pride in the job* inspired by these traditions had a certain appeal. So the reader is entitled to ask what had happened in the years between 1948 and 1965 for WR engines to have succumbed to this appalling neglect. In general terms, it is not too difficult to provide an answer. In the years after 1948 there was a lack both of political realism and later of political good intent, an impossibility of ameliorating the conflicting demands of road, rail and air and straight forward incompetence at every level, to say nothing of personalities fighting their own corner without any consideration of what it was doing to the overall situation. By 1962, a shortage of express power on the WR meant that 9F 2-10-0 freight engines were rostered to passenger duties in addition to the 47XX and 28XX standbys still being used on such work. Steam was almost regularly piloting failed diesels. In those years of full employment but relatively poor wages at some levels among operating personnel there was increased union militancy which further acerbated that appalling state of affairs. Survival of self became more important than pride in the job. The tragedy is that it could have been completely avoided with a little more forethought at the top.

Enough has been written about the modifications carried out on ex-GWR locomotives; they did not however, go far enough. Why not also fit the four cylinder high power engines with roller bearings and crucially, for the benefit of the fireman, mechanical stokers?[23] Even now, there are some prepared to argue against the introduction of mechanical stokers but they would have allowed the exploitation of the full potential of the boiler beyond what was possible with hand firing and, in this context much more importantly, were the one innovation which might just have stopped the drift of men out of loco operating service into other occupations. The *Kings* and a number of the *Castle Class* rebuilt along similar lines, with streamlined steam passages and modern cylinders with outside valve gear would have provided a nucleus of potentially top flight locomotives allowing, where possible for a speed up in services and obviating any need for untried diesels.

In fact, even greater innovations were discussed, such as the fitting of the *Kings* and some of the *County* class with Caprotti valve-gear. Very little is currently known about these particular proposals and shortage of time has prevented me from delving further into them. However, documentary evidence exists to show that approaches were made in the mid-50s to Swindon by Associated Locomotive Equipment and that they were not repulsed. Meetings took place with Ell and Smeddle and drawings supplied to ALE formed the basis of formal proposals to Swindon. That for the *King* seems to indicate a desire to lighten the weight at the front end. However, it all came to nothing and though we can conjecture the reasons for that we cannot be certain until we have to hand all the relevant documents.[24]

Providing locomotives that were easier to operate was only part of the problem, Norman Harvey made the point that little if anything had been done to modernise steam sheds and track layouts which often did not permit the quick turn-rounds that were possible with modern steam power.[25] There is plenty of evidence in chapter one to suggest that cleanliness was rapidly becoming a consideration among young men who regarded employment on car assembly lines as a much more attractive alternative to engine cleaning and firing. Yet no attempt was made to update cleaning facilities, for example by providing steam cleaning equipment. In regard to the LMS streamliners, Cecil J.Allen wrote: *It was no longer possible to keep the engines in their condition of pre-war cleanliness externally, or to paint them in the spectacular fashion of the first streamliners and from a publicity point of view a coal begrimed streamline casing is worse than none at all.*[25] Rubbish! Any locomotive fully enclosed in a smooth shroud has got to be easier to clean, particularly with the provision of simply designed and inexpensive rigs fitted with overhead sprinklers delivering flows of water based detergent and hand held steam cleaning jets. This was a time of enormous shortages which are often given as the reason why none of these things were done. But I do not believe it, the real reason was inertia, the sheer unwillingness to see that change was necessary. And I refer readers again to the first chapter where the reasons behind that are discussed.

In another chapter I have deprecated the 'what if' approach to history. Yet in conclusion to these deliberations I think we are entitled to consider what, left to its own devices, Swindon would have done in the 1950s. We can be certain that the rebuilding programme already outlined would have happened and possibly more rapidly than it was. It is also possible to conjecture an uprated 28xx 2-8-0 freight engine, in the form already discussed. Further 47xx engines, suitably updated and modified as indicated in chapter seven would have provided a very high powered mixed traffic engine. However, the most interesting aspect of this question, inevitably enough concerns express passenger needs. The building of new *Castles* and the developments already mentioned were a relatively inexpensive but short term only delay to the real question of whether any new design was necessary to successfully bridge the gap to electrification. For the purposes of this discussion, and ignoring all the caveats that I have, myself, discussed in this chapter, I am going to assume that it was.

I am not alone in believing that actually Hawksworth was right, a pacific did not provide for the Great Western's future needs, a 4-8-0 would have been a much better bet. And I would go further and suggest that the big Standards would also have been better had they been 4-8-0s rather than pacifics. Concentrating the larger powered passenger engines on a pacific chassis was adopted, we are told, to allow the fitting of a wide firebox which is easier to fire by hand and, logically, ought to be a better generator of heat than a narrow one.[12] Nonetheless this logic is not proven by evidence. A great deal of nonsense continues to be written about the wide/ versus narrow firebox question and I have devoted a lot of time to studying it. Though he used wide fireboxes in his later designs Chapelon showed that when allied with good boiler design, the narrow firebox was no bar to good steam generation. This was also shown by work done at Swindon by Ell and is supported by David Wardale with the proposed 5AT engine.

The rear carrying wheel design does have a serious potential down side. On rising gradients the locomotive weight tends to move towards the rear and in engines with poor suspension can be transferred, disproportionately, to the rear carrying axle with detriment to the engine's rail holding capacity. The latest designs with compensating springs and other devices reduced this problem but where 'other devices' are badly designed the result is horrendous. The West Australian PMR pacific is a salutary example for anyone.[27] On the other hand, where the rear wheel set is a coupled driver, this weight transfer can actually assist traction. The success of the GWR's express fleet owed at least something to being 4-6-0 and not 4-6-2. The conclusion will be strongly contested but the foregoing suggests that the higher powered BR Standard classes might have been better had they been 4-8-0 rather than 4-6-2. Similarly I believe that the next high-performance GWR locomotive should have been a four cylinder 4-8-0 incorporating all the modifications proposed in this and the previous chapter.

The computer generated photograph on the previous page gives some idea of what such a locomotive might have looked like, but without the streamlined steam pipes. Remember that is impressionistic and not intended to be an engineering-perfect illustration.

During those last six months of 1965 I spent a lot of time along the line and at stations between Didcot and Banbury where a fair amount of steam still operated, mainly but not exclusively on goods trains. The major exceptions were the south to north expresses recently transferred off the Somerset and Dorset route of which the *Pines Express* was the best known and in the summer of 1965 they were often hauled as far as Banbury by a *Hall* locomotive. At Banbury the *Hall* was replaced by an LMR Class 5. On one occasion 6910 came into Oxford with its train and the clanking from somewhere underneath strongly suggested that it was in dire mechanical condition. The *Hall* was taken off and as far as I know never ran again.

Notes and references

9) O.S.Nock - letter to the author July 1994
10) *A Lifetime with Locomotives* - R.C.Bond
11) *Master Builders of Steam* - H.A.V.Bulleid
12) *The British Railways Standard Steam Locomotives* - E.S.Cox
13) K.J.Cook - correspondence with the author 1980
14) *Swindon Steam* - K.J.Cook
15) *The GWR Stars, Castles and Kings* - O.S.Nock
16) Dennis Howells - conversation with the author 2006.
17) Probably an exaggeration but not always...
18) *SLS Journal* - May 1962
19) *British Locomotives of the 20th Century* - Volume 2 - O.S.Nock
20) Whether the 4½" recommended by Ell was also deficient is another argument entirely.
21) The DB Class 10 pacific of 1957 enshrined all these concepts in a very handsome and successful locomotive.
22) With former Swindon apprentice Reggie Hanks, another GWR enthusiast as his regional Chairman, it must have seemed, for the first few years anyway as though the Great Western had survived a second funeral pyre, this time arising Phoenix-like from nationalization.
23) In fact a report in a magazine reveals that ten sets of roller bearings were delivered for the *Kings* eighteen months before the first was taken out of service.
23) I am indebted to C.P.Atkins in correspondence during May 2006 for the information about these proposals.
25) *Are the Diesels Necessary* - Norman Harvey - *Railway World* - July 1959
26) *British Pacific Locomotives* - Cecil J Allen
27) *A History of WAGR Locomotives* - A Gunzberg

Nine
Railcars, Gas Turbines and Diesel Hydraulics

The American science fiction writer Elizabeth Moon puts into the mind of one of her characters the notion that men are quite capable of inventing facts in order to support contentious beliefs.[9] Thus are we warned against taking innovative observation into the realm of fantasy. On the question of the wisdom of changing from steam to diesel a good deal of nonsense has been written and continues so to be. Among the worst of these is the statement by the late Bob Reid, Chairman of BR that steam engines were always breaking down, an inaccuracy that is a generalisation out of all proportion to the facts. Even commentators who should have known better were not averse to this kind of special pleading. The late Cecil J.Allen, of all people was an arrogant exponent of the diesel, dismissing the reasoned arguments of correspondents with, on some occasions extremely weak rejoinders. Diesalization became the received wisdom of railway operation and anyone who questioned it was regarded with scorn not so very different from that with which scientists regard UFO watchers. It was in the United States, where there were plentiful supplies of cheap oil available, that the diesel locomotive was first built in large numbers. It was claimed that though they cost three times the first cost of an equivalent steam locomotive, they could achieve three times the amount of work, in some cases reaching six days operation out of seven. Inevitably operators from around the world turned to the United States for guidance not realising that the case for the diesel was never as clear cut as its advocates claimed and that American circumstances were not necessarily replicated elsewhere.

One of the more amusing comments on the results of railway modernisation in Britain is contained in a paper read in 1958 by F.L.Hick then Assistant Operating officer of the NER which runs: *An uplift in morale is noticeable wherever diesels have been introduced... The public have responded to this first tangible result of the modernisation plan quickly and permanently ... it is because it is new in every sense - clean, attractive and with a strong psychological appeal...*[10] That not all BR managers including those strongly in favour of changing from steam to diesel would have agreed with that statement is evident from reading what Gerard Fiennes had to say about his experience while he was General Manager at Paddington.[11] After describing his new commuter services deploying diesel multiple units and the protests this evoked from passengers complaining about bad riding he writes: *...I had committed a great stupidity. I had not made certain that the diesel multiple units were fit for outer suburban work. We retreated rapidly .. We scoured British Railways for better multiple units but without success..* I always remember that statement when I read how wonderful they were and how much they were appreciated by the travelling public because certainly so far as I am concerned the change from steam hauled trains to dmu's was one that I remember without the slightest pleasure. One of the last steam auto-train workings on the WR, actually a former SR working, was that between Yeovil Junction, Yeovil Town and Yeovil Pen Mill, operated until 1963 by Drummond M7 0-4-4Ts and thereafter by WR 64XX pannier tanks. Living by an important main line station and not needing to use auto-trains very much, finding myself, in the spring of 1964, on the Yeovil auto-train I was pleasantly surprised at how comfortable the ride was, how solid and reliable the whole ensemble seemed to be. Not something that could be said about the dmu's operating in the more main line areas of the WR. This is not just my prejudice but was endorsed by a report in 1961 that Oxford passengers were avoiding a dmu train and travelling instead by the one immediately following that was steam hauled.[12] I have always refused to share the pleasure of BR managers at the extinction of steam, while there is no doubt that some form of motive power change had become appropriate, the replacement of steam by diesel power was carried out with the fanatical enthusiasm of the crusading zealot and a great deal of unnecessary financial waste and traffic disruption occurred as a result.

It tends to be forgotten that the GWR operated a petrol electric railcar for a few years before 1919; its first diesel mechanical railcars too, are sometimes overlooked. The first, designed by AEC was put into service in 1933 and eventually there were 16 of them, built, for the most part for express services. Reports of good performances appeared in the press and just one will suffice to give the theme. In 1939 it was reported that Swindon to Paddington had been covered in 70 minutes and Oxford to Paddington with two stops in 65. On the latter over 40 miles was run at 68.5 mph.[13] A new version, authorised in 1938 was intended for local and branch services while two were specifically parcels units. Without a doubt they made a contribution to the GWR's operations but they were not wholly successful. The late K.J.Cook told me that the original units suffered from being too light in the frames and gave poor riding over junctions and points, hence the second batch had Swindon designed frames and bodies.[14] Another factor was that the express units did not work in multiple, any increase in traffic meant that steam trains had to be restored to the services covered. Whether something more along these lines would have been done had someone other than Collett been in charge at Swindon is a moot point.

In fact all the four big railways had built diesels and/or electrics before nationalisation, though (except for the Southern) in no way which altered the conception of them as 'steam railways'. The LMS had a relatively large number of diesel shunters and had operated a multiple unit passenger set. This is often held up as a successful prototype for what came after though there are doubts as to the truth of that contention. And this is one of the problems of establishing a reasonable position on the effectiveness of the changeover, the published facts can be taken to support almost any viewpoint. The one factor that can be stated with certainty is that horsepower for horsepower there could be no difference between steam and other forms of motive power though there are those who will argue that a 2000 hp diesel will haul better than a 2000 hp steam locomotive. And certainly one of the most serious failings of early BR diesels is that they did no more than replace like for like. What really was the point of building diesel hydraulics that could only haul at best one coach more than a *King* or a *Castle*? Trevor Gourvish makes clear that Richard Beeching, had he been able so to do, would have cancelled the LMR electrification and provided in its place diesel locomotives rated at no more than 2000 hp.[15] On that ridiculous proposition, no comment is necessary.

Of course, the GWR, as ever, attempted to go one better than the other railways by ordering a gas turbine locomotive from the Swiss Brown Boveri company. Hawksworth, together with General manager Milne attended the 1947 International Railway Conference at Lucerne where the original 1941 Brown Boveri built gas-turbine was exhibited. The company suggested that it would be suitable for work on the gradients in Devon and Cornwall and as a direct result a 2,500 hp version of this locomotive was ordered for the GWR. The tradition of glorious individuality with which Paddington surrounded itself in those years was clearly the underlying impetus behind this project and there is no doubt that it earned its kudos among the public enthused by the concept of a 'jet powered' locomotive. Perhaps not surprisingly, given the fact that it was one of the first gas turbine locomotive to be built, it was not wholly successful and after initially working expresses it settled down to a daily roster which usually involved taking the early morning newspaper train down to Bristol, returning with a passenger train ex-Exeter and then making another out and back passenger run to Swindon. A British built version, ordered for purposes of comparison was actually even less successful. Three further attempts were made in Britain to make something of the gas-turbine concept of which the ill-fated GT3 and the experimental version of the Advanced Passenger Train are well known. The other was a very interesting attempt to develop a pulverised coal powered version which was initiated by the Ministry of Transport. A lot of work was done on it before the project was abandoned.[16] Interestingly, such machines were built in the USA and very nearly achieved commercial viability but the problem of fly-ash damaging the turbine blades was never successfully overcome.[17] This can only be regarded as most unfortunate because such a locomotive powered by indigenous fuel would have had an immediate advantage over one of the diesel's fundamental drawbacks.

As far as costs are concerned, the following, culled from various sources are representational only in that they convey the same confusion that has always surrounded the arguments for wide-scale adoption of the diesel locomotive. In 1950 the RE produced a table which showed that the dbhr cost of steam was £13 compared with £17.60 for electric power and the amazing sum of £65 for a 1,600 hp diesel which even the present writer must view with scepticism. In a paper read by S.B.Warder, BR Electrical Engineer, in 1961 to the Institution of Civil, Mechanical and Electrical Engineers demonstrated that at every level the cost of diesel power was less than that for steam.[18] This kind of comparison is, of course open to question. Comparisons were often carried out between 30-year old steam locomotives and newly turned-out diesels and in the case quoted was with a BR Standard Class 5 4-6-0, not the best representative in terms of cost for its power range. Again, going back to 1946 the New York Central Railroad demonstrated that modern steam power could achieve 90% of the monthly mileage of diesels and that the operating costs between the different forms of motive power were actually very small. $1.22 for a 6,000hp 4-8-4. $1.15 for 5,000hp electric. $1.11 for a twin unit 4,000hp diesel but $1.48 for a triple unit of 6.000 hp. The figure of availability for the diesel was less than 6% better than that for steam. In 1948 the success of the diesel locomotive was relatively recent: only with the production in 1939 of the Electro-Motive FT class 4 unit type was it demonstrated that diesels could handle both passenger and long-distance heavy freight trains. Other figures suggested that at 1955 prices the difference between steam and diesel railcar operation was an amazing 61d to the latter's favour. Another contributor to the technical press, writing in 1969 reckoned that the annual mileages achieved by diesel locomotives could actually be less per unit than were being regularly achieved by steam in the 1930s. Roland Bond wrote that: *notwithstanding rises in wages and material costs... loco repair costs came down (1948-1953) in shops and sheds together from 12½d to just over 11d.*[19] Bond's comments about these matters display a degree of honesty sometimes lacking from the material left by other commentators; though he was in favour of the change to diesel traction in appropriate circumstances, he is clear that steam operation was expected to continue for many years, paving the way for eventual electrification of the most important main lines.

It was the kind of confusion detailed in the previous paragraph that led to the establishment of an RE committee under Leslie Harrington to consider the form that the new motive power should take. The Committee's Report came out strongly in favour of pilot main line electrification and a large-scale test of main line diesel locomotives and rail cars. Cox claimed that one of the advantages of this committee was that none of its members were professional engineers.[16] Yet, as Bond acknowledges this can only have been a terrible weakness, the true facts of steam operation were not and could not possibly have been properly considered by a committee which did not include a locomotive engineer. Significant questions were soon being asked. In 1961 H. F. Brown told the Institution of Mechanical Engineers that US railroads had been alarmed to discover that the repair costs for steam were less than for diesel electrics as each type aged.[20] This was only three years after the BTC had decided to speed-up the replacement of steam by diesel and the placing of large scale orders for untried diesels. So alarmed were people in certain quarters that an attempt was actually made to suppress Brown's paper and when that failed 'friendly' writers in the technical press were supplied with figures to disprove its arguments. One cannot avoid the conclusion that certain of the advocates of the diesel were displaying a degree of - let us be polite and call it 'spin' - about the change they were advocating. One of the most appalling decisions made at this time was to speed up the scrapping of steam locomotives and to include in that programme even the newly built Standard classes. It cannot possibly be argued that this was a rational policy. But it was so argued in a memo drawn up by F.C.Margetts and Philip Shirley which showed to the satisfaction of the converted that their replacement by diesels would be beneficial to the turnover.[21] Shirley, brought onto BR from Bachelors Foods where he was supposed to be a financial wizard, had no experience of any kind of transport undertaking and is known to have been virulently opposed to steam. It has been claimed that he was behind the ban on the running of steam specials after 1968 and when he returned to his native Australia was behind a similar but short lived ban in New South Wales.

The greatest drawback to the large scale use of oil as fuel for traction was the fact that it was a commodity that had to be imported from strategically difficult areas of the world. This has been put into clear perspective several times, in the Gulf Wars of 1990 and 2003, by the 1956 Suez crisis and again in 1974 when the oil price escalated by 400% in a matter of months. After both latter incidents the price fell back but I am convinced that the money expended on main line diesels after 1956 would have been better employed in making an earlier start on electrification. The long term result would certainly be that more main lines would now be electrified and the reliance on middle eastern oil imports greatly reduced. Yet there is another point which does not appear to have ever been considered, that of the effect on the national economy generally. A private company has no alternative but to consider the position from a appropriate commercial viewpoint. I am not certain that a publicly owned group should always do this. What is the point of reducing costs by say, £10x million if that adds £12.5x million to fiscal difficulty through added balance of payments deficit and increased dole payments. It is not a popular point of view but it cannot be dismissed out of hand.

Gerard Fiennes, in another of his comments says that the WR adopted modernisation with alacrity.[22] I think what he means is that Paddington was keen on diesels, for Swindon was clearly more cautious in its approach. When the BTC design team were looking to give the diesel hydraulic an extended trial, separate from other forms of traction, H.H.Smith, Assistant-General manager suggested that the Western should be the region on which they be deployed. We have already noted WR General manager Keith Grand's policy of continuity, extending the traditions of the GWR into the WR cast of mind and it is clear that this proposal fitted fully into the concept of splendid singularity.[23] It has been suggested that Grand's general approach was a major cause of the WR's hefty operating deficit. That it was serious there is no doubt; operational efficiency may not have been as good as it might and the continued use of non-automatic latching doors on coaching stock contributed to what was probably an over-manning situation. However, it seems clear that, in general this allegation cannot be substantiated. An analysis made in a paper read to the Institute of Transport in 1962 stated unequivocally that the main component of the deficit was a major fall off in coal traffic which had previously formed some 70% of its freight business.[24] Among other problems quoted was the fact that new light industries set up in the former coal mining areas were using road transport rather than rail.

Grand was succeeded by Roy Hammond as General manager, then in January 1962 Stanley Raymond was appointed and, to repeat once again Gerard Fiennes terrible words: *He* (went) *like a destroying wind through the traditional practices of the Great Western. He ... symbolically stripped the works of Brunel and Pole and Milne from the Board Room and the corridors down to the basement and cast the attitudes to the four winds.*[11] This, Fiennes claimed was the major cause of the reduction of the deficit from more than 27% to less than 15% in a year. However, if one considers the implications of the analysis just referred to and the fact that the deficit was already coming down when Raymond took over, a degree of scepticism is permissible. Raymond was clearly following Chairman Beeching's instructions but his approach and any success that he achieved was at terrible cost in staff relations. He forgot, if he was capable of realising, that a first imperative of good management, particularly for a new broom is to take the staff with you. According to Fiennes, Raymond was very proud of his achievements at Paddington though a correspondent to *The Guardian*, a former WR staffer, at Raymond's death described his period of office as *a reign of terror*. His tenure as Chairman of BR was also not a happy one and he quickly fell out with Transport Minister, Barbara Castle.

I do not intend to go into the design of the hydraulics in any detail, for those interested there are many articles in various technical magazines published down the years. It was claimed on the evidence of the units operated by the Deutsche Bundesbahn that the hydraulic provided a unit with lower weight for a higher power output, and that the higher continuous tractive effort at low speed made it suitable for easily graded track with short sections of severe banks. There was and remains a great deal of controversy about the performance of these diesels in service. Despite reports of running at or around 100 mph the performance, certainly of the *Warship* type was little better than that of the steam locomotives that they replaced. The evidence for this is clear. In 1966 I did a study comparing the 1937 GWR public timetable with the contemporary WR edition. This showed that as far as secondary main line stations were concerned diesalization had brought no significant improvement in services. O.S.Nock demonstrated that their performance on high speed services, though at times, very good, was overall disappointing.[25] He was also very scathing about the calculated horse power rating of these units, describing it as a *travesty of what was actually available*. A full study published by J.F.Clay and J.N.C.Law states unequivocally that the Warships *were capable of slightly faster running than the steam locomotives that they replaced* and produced performance figures which imply that as far as normal running was concerned there was nothing in it.[26] The authors concluded that: *the Westerns are of course, far above steam capacity ... on account of greater installed horse power well beyond the limit of hand firing and higher power to weight ratio*. This is offset by the suggestion that they were some 30% less reliable than their diesel electric counterparts, figures confirmed in the official history where it is stated that: *savings obtained from the switch to diesel traction were reduced by higher running and maintenance costs caused by the poor performance of... the WR's Maybach engined Warship and Western diesel and the Beyer Peacock Hymek*.[15] That mention of the *Hymek* class is interesting because they were first employed on express work, albeit at contemporary less than best possible steam timings and were well received by the operators. On the other hand there are plenty of reports in the motive power sections of the old magazines recounting the frequent occasions on which trains were triple headed, by two Type 2 diesel hydraulics and a steam locomotive; an editorial comment says: *some triple heading is unpremeditated of course*.[27] Quite so! In the early 60s the diesel hydraulics were three times as likely to fail in service as the steam power they were supposed to be replacing.[23]

If the performance of the *Warship* and Type 2 diesel hydraulic locomotives was so much poorer than expected, why was the last, the *Western* class built? The most basic failing was a lack of cohesive management on BR, for this kind of problem was not limited to the WR. It seems to me that by 1957 senior commercial management, thoroughly antagonised by several years experience of what they might have termed Riddles arrogance, having got rid of him regarded the rest of the locomotive design team as being of a similarly uncooperative turn of mind and just stopped listening to them. Bond indicates that there was indeed such a breakdown in communications and that it was a serious matter.⁽¹⁹⁾ Here then is part of the explanation for the acceleration of the Modernisation Plan, a shocking mistake, involving the waste of countless millions of what tabloid newspapers delight in reminding us is 'tax payers money'. Expediency triumphed over reality as it has in national transport policy time and time again.

As early as 1961 it was acknowledged that the original power specifications for the *Warships* had been inadequate hence, presumably the much greater installed horse power of the later type.⁽²⁸⁾ But it is a fair question to ask whether the multiplication of units with hydraulic transmission should have ceased there and then. The original Modernisation Plan diesel order, so far as the WR was concerned was for 14 units of three types, the intention being to give them extended trials before ordering any more. It is well known that the protagonists of a speedier change to diesels, mostly financial managers not engineers, now got their way and large orders were made for locomotives that had the earlier policy been followed would never have been built. I believe that the *Warships* and certainly the *Westerns* fall into this category. There is an interesting and revealing account of these deliberations in regard to the WR which shows this to be true and brings into focus the disparate views that were advanced.⁽¹⁶⁾ Grand wanted large orders for diesel hydraulics even before the first had begun to run. Headquarters staff engineers, Bond, Cox etc could, it is claimed advance no solid reason why not. The view of others to continue to 'bridge the gap' with steam was violently opposed by the usual suspects.⁽²³⁾ There was also political influence brought to bear by private manufacturers determined to have a share of construction that had always been done in the railways own workshops. In the end headquarters gave in and allowed the order to be made. By the time the drawbacks of the design had manifested themselves it was too late to halt further construction.

Much later, in December 1972 I was writing an article about Swindon Works and was given a personally conducted tour by the then Chief Publicity Officer of BREL.⁽²⁹⁾ At his request I sent my article through him to the Works Manager for what was called, 'checking the facts'. It came back annotated to indicate that the design and building of the *Warships* and *Westerns* had been done at Swindon. It was quickly pointed out that this was not actually correct and now, I cannot help but think that Swindon would have been better to have avoided making a claim like that.⁽³⁰⁾ I cringe when I read that the Brunel main line is to be made a world heritage site. This line, like the ex-GWR main lines to Exeter, via Badminton and Gloucester to South Wales and via Oxford to the Midlands should be electrified even if that means making material alterations to Brunel's structures. Progress demands that it should be so. But for the dalliance with the diesel hydraulics it might have been done before, a fact with which, paradoxically, Robert Riddles might well have agreed. Had Riddles given the old pre-nationalization design teams freedom, within certain parameters to develop their own designs while devoting his attention to careful research into new forms of traction, much of this nonsense, certainly on the WR would not have happened.

Notes and references

9) *Vatta's War* - Elizabeth Moon
10) *Trains Illustrated* - January 1959
11) *I Tried to Run a Railway* - G.F.Fiennes
12) *Trains Illustrated* - May 1961
13) *Railway Magazine* July 1939
14) K.J.Cook - correspondence with the author 1980
15) *British Railways 1948 - 1973: A Business History* - T.R.Gourvish
16) *Locomotive Panorama* - Volume 2 - E.S.Cox - A diagram of the locomotive with a caption indicating that construction had started will be found in the January 1957 *Trains Illustrated*.
17) *Turbines: King Coal's Battle Against the Diesel* - Eric Hirsimaki *Classic Trains* - Fall 2004
18) *Report on BR dieselisation - Trains Illustrated* - May 1961
19) *A Lifetime with Locomotives* - Roland Bond
20) *Economic Results of Diesel Electric Motive Power on the Railways of the USA* H.F.Brown - I.Mech E 1961. Bond (ref.19) makes clear the attempt to silence this paper.
21) Memo to BRB - Steam Locomotive Stock 11.12.63
22) *GWR into BR* - G.F.Fiennes - *Trains & Railways* Vol 2 Nos. 6 & 7 (1975)
23) *The Western Region Since 1948*. - G. Freeman Allen
24) L.W.Ibbotson: paper read to Institute of Transport reported in *Trains Illustrated* - May 1962
25) *British Locomotives of the 20th Century* Vol.3 - O.S.Nock
26) *How Great Was the Great Western?* - J.F.Clay & J.N.C.Law *Railway World* - August 1974
27) *Trains Illustrated* - September 1960
28) G.A.V.Philips: paper read to Railway Students Association reported in *Trains Illustrated* - September 1961.
29) *Metamorphosis at Swindon Works* - L.A.Summers *Railway Magazine* May 1972.
30) Upon reflection I think that this was due to Harry Roberts, Swindon's penultimate Works Manager who was not actually a Swindon man but who it was clear from our conversation had come under the influence of its traditions.